GUS DIZEREGA

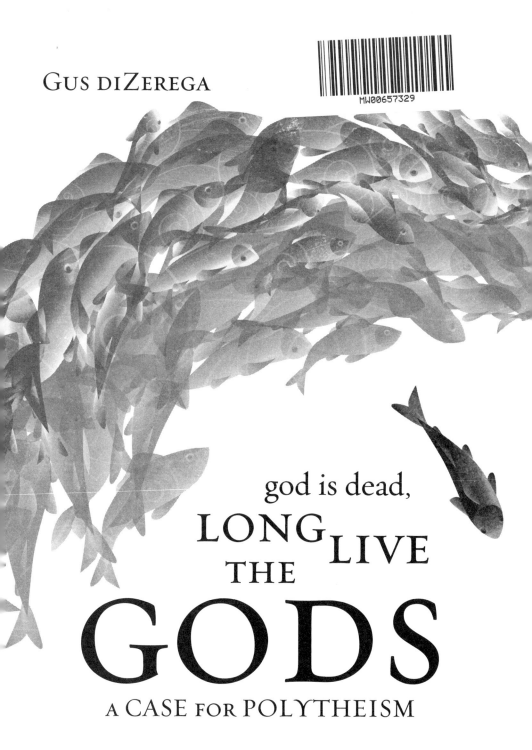

god is dead,
LONG LIVE
THE
GODS

A CASE FOR POLYTHEISM

Llewellyn Publications
Woodbury, Minnesota

FIRST EDITION
First Printing, 2020

Book design by Samantha Penn
Cover design by Shannon McKuhen

Llewellyn Publications is a registered trademark of Llewellyn Worldwide Ltd.

Library of Congress Cataloging-in-Publication Data (Pending)
ISBN: 978-0-7387-6272-2

Llewellyn Worldwide Ltd. does not participate in, endorse, or have any authority or responsibility concerning private business transactions between our authors and the public.

All mail addressed to the author is forwarded but the publisher cannot, unless specifically instructed by the author, give out an address or phone number.

Any internet references contained in this work are current at publication time, but the publisher cannot guarantee that a specific location will continue to be maintained. Please refer to the publisher's website for links to authors' websites and other sources.

Llewellyn Publications
A Division of Llewellyn Worldwide Ltd.
2143 Wooddale Drive
Woodbury, MN 55125-2989
www.llewellyn.com

Printed in the United States of America

god is dead,
LONG LIVE
THE
GODS

© Marla McClymond

About the Author

Gus diZerega, PhD, has extensive teaching and publishing experience both in mainstream social science and on Pagan and shamanic subjects. Gus is a Third Degree Elder in Gardnerian Wicca; has studied closely with Timothy White, founder of *Shaman's Drum* magazine; and has intensively practiced Brazilian Umbanda for six years under Antonio Costa e Silva, later integrating it into his own healing work. He has given workshops and talks on Pagan spirituality and healing in the United States and Canada.

Gus' more secular research has focused on democratic theory, complex adaptive systems in the social and biological world, and environmental theory and policy. His extensive academic publication record includes papers in many refereed journals, chapters, and books, and he has organized international conferences and taught internationally in the social sciences.

God Is Dead, Long Live the Gods brings these two strands of his life together in a way he believes does justice to both.

Much of Gus' work can be accessed on his website: www.dizerega.com.

Other Books by Gus diZerega

*Faultlines: The Sixties, the Culture War and
the Return of the Divine Feminine*

Beyond the Burning Times: A Pagan and Christian in Dialogue

Pagans and Christians: The Personal Spiritual Experience

Persuasion, Power and Polity: A Theory of Democratic Self-Organization

I dedicate this book to
Don Frew
Teacher, colleague, and friend

ACKNOWLEDGMENTS

A book such as this seeks to integrate more fields than anyone can personally master, and so I am deeply beholden to the philosophers, historians, theologians, and social scientists on whose work I have depended to add depth and context to my own. Hopefully I got their insights right! In addition, over thirty-five years of active involvement in the NeoPagan community and related practices as well as interfaith have deepened my understanding of these matters, not least through conversations with many fellow Pagans too numerous to name individually. Finally, I am deeply grateful to my editor, Elysia Gallo of Llewellyn, who worked hard, and I think successfully, to make sure all my manuscript's *I*s were dotted, *T*s crossed, and ambiguous phrasing clarified. This is a far better book due to her hard work.

CONTENTS

INTRODUCTION

THE MOON IS FULL above California's soaring redwoods as the coven meets beneath them to honor the goddess and do magick. The circle has been cast, the directions called, and the High Priest approaches the High Priestess to invoke the goddess, calling out "I call upon Thee o mighty mother of us all …" At the invocation's conclusion, she enters into the woman, to teach and bless those gathered in her name. One of the coven members has a request for the group to help her find an affordable place to live. Aided by her presence, a chant is created and, at its height, the High Priestess sends the energy raised off to help achieve the member's request.

At a signal from the Mae de Santo, the batá drummers begin pounding out a complex rhythm. Within the temple, men and women dressed in white begin singing and clapping to honor and call upon an orisha, an African deity, one of many. Soon one of the participants, a woman, shudders and begins to shake, and then dance, and whirl, as Ochossi arrives to join the celebration. As she better integrates with the divine arrival, her movements shift into the stylized dance associated with that particular orisha. As the ritual progresses, other orishas may arrive as well, each choosing a member with whom to join, dance, and heal.

Within a tent from which all light has been blocked, the Medicine person has been bound tightly. As he lies on the ground, the rest of the space tightly packed with guests and the main person to be healed, drums begin beating a steady rhythm, like the beating of a heart. Soon tiny lights begin to flash overhead in the otherwise total darkness, and people feel feather fans brushing against their heads as they receive healings along with the person for which the Yu Wipi Ceremony has been called. In time the drums cease, the lights and fans vanish, and when the space is illuminated again, the Medicine person is sitting quietly, his bindings neatly placed at his feet.

These examples come from very different cultures: Western Europe, East Africa, and North America. These particular ceremonies occurred in Northern California, but they could have occurred anywhere. What they share is a common experience of participants directly encountering the world of Spirit. Those participating are a varied lot, from construction workers to scientists; from doctors to students; and indeed, just about any other way of life. They usually leave feeling much better than when they arrived, and often personally enriched with new insights for living their lives.

This is polytheism in action as a part of people's reality, American style.

But American culture is usually described as a combination of Christianity and secularism, a society deeply divided by the spiritual and scientific tensions between them. If polytheism is considered at all, it is treated as a way station most have long since passed in humanity's journey toward worshiping one god, or alternatively, none at all.

I will argue here that both perspectives are mistaken, and that what we loosely call polytheism is the natural experience human beings have *always* had of the world of Spirit, and that it is a much more accurate understanding of the world within which we live than the secularism usually considered the alternative to monotheism.

To make my case I will demonstrate that, in practice, monotheism is polytheism, although a very confused one; that modern science's criticisms of monotheism target its incoherence and lack of evidence, but do not touch polytheism; and that polytheism itself is a natural outgrowth of exploring the primordial human insight that our world is alive "all the way down." Thus, the enormous variety of polytheistic experiences is as natural as the enormous variety of life forms that enrich this world. This variety enriches the spiritual world as much as nature's diversity enriches our physical one.

Polytheism resolves the internal problems of monotheistic arguments, is compatible with modern science, and is continually reflected in people's spiritual experiences, even today. In Friedrich Nietzsche's words, the modern world killed God, but in doing so we wiped away the fog of theology that obscured a deeper spiritual reality. Hence the last part of this book's main title: "Long Live the Gods."

The problem with monotheism

Monotheists claim that all existence was created by a single deity. This creation was to further his divine plans, and these plans include demands people must obey, on pain of divine punishment. This deity claims it is omnipotent, omniscient, and good, and demands precedence over all other entities.

Any such image of a divine singularity suffers from many fatal flaws, and I will explore them in the first chapters of this volume. Basically, as soon as these broad generalities are applied to illuminate specific issues, a seemingly coherent concept breaks down. It is this incoherence that prevents any particular deity from winning support among all monotheists.

Given the reality of religious experiences and the incoherence in all attempts to make sense of them in monotheistic terms, it is important to dispose of monotheism's monopolistic claims while recognizing the *sacred also existing within the various Abrahamic traditions*. A polytheistic perspective preserves what is best in the different monotheisms, explains what is worst in them, and harmonizes what is best with other religious traditions.

Modern science is an unexpected ally in this needed transformation.

Science illuminates these issues

Science began its intellectual journey with solid Protestant assumptions rooted in scriptural monotheism. But what sets science off from other ways of seeking knowledge is that it emphasizes not what truth is, but how errors can be discovered and abandoned. As science advanced by eliminating error after error, it abandoned nearly all claims rooted in its initial assumptions.

This book argues one major assumption remains, but only because of intellectual inertia, not evidence. When we set it aside as unjustified, and look at reality without its filters, a living world opens up to us, ranging from the smallest entity to the most divine.

That assumption is that a deep divide separates objective reality from subjective experience. Many scientists describe understanding consciousness as the "hard problem," because there seems no way to derive it from nonconscious matter. Scientists' initial assumption was that the world was a construct into which God inserted souls, as in the Adam and Eve story. As that view failed to fit what scientists were discovering, alternative views developed, but still separated subjectivity from objectivity. Either consciousness somehow emerged from nonconscious physical processes, or it was in some sense an illusion or "epiphenomenon," giving the impression it mattered in a world that, in fact, could be entirely explained in nonconscious deterministic terms.

These attitudes support the common secular belief that early peoples were animists who gradually developed enough understanding to limit awareness to the gods, and ultimately to one god, who was the fundamental cause for the world around them. Modern secularists agreed with this development, but took the progressive squeezing of life from the world a step further. They eliminated any reference to consciousness as part of an ultimate cause, arguing it was in fact a deterministic law of nature. Thus, so this story goes, scientists are pursuing the holy grail of a unified "theory of everything" that, ironically, is devoid of life.

Reductionist secular views were never universal among scientists, and many of the greatest of them suspected that consciousness in some sense penetrated all of reality. Post-Newtonian physics powerfully strengthened the case that more mystical and meditative religious traditions were compatible with modern science. Quantum physics provides powerful evidence that some kind of consciousness is needed for reality to exist, but in practice, the rest of science generally argues these discoveries are irrelevant for their own work. Quantum mechanics' implications are only for the very small, compared to which an atom is huge.

This book argues this avoidance is unjustified.

Even so, another dimension arises regarding the question of consciousness. If it is a fundamental property of the world, how does individuality and the sense of separateness arise? Physics alone can support the reality of experiencing mystical Oneness, but it cannot explain the seemingly discrete individuality of people when they are not having such experiences. It is here that discoveries in biology are shedding a provocative light.

Individuality is quite real, but not in the way we traditionally think of it, a way ultimately rooted in scriptural assumptions. Biological individuality first arose in eukaryotic cells—that is, cells with a nucleus, mitochondria, and (in plants) chloroplasts. These cells made even more complex individuals possible. Recent research demonstrates that this arising of individuality from fusions of simpler individuals seems to continue all the way up to ourselves. Today we are often referred to as ecosystems or superorganisms by biologists, but our sense of psychological individuality is very real.

At the same time, if consciousness is a fundamental property of reality, then as biological complexity increases, the same might well hold true for psychological complexity. From this perspective, taken-for-granted terms such as culture, organization, and society take on a new depth of meaning. This outlook is also in harmony with much of the world's shamanic and occult traditions. In particular, the secular idea of a meme is remarkably close to the occult concept of a thought form. Exploring this connection opens us to an outlook that makes sense of the extraordinary variety of divine and other spirit beings reported in the world's societies, as well as in the experience of many of us.

In particular, the same process by which biological individuality emerges from simpler form of individuality seems to apply within the world of consciousness as well. Exploring these connections helps make the case for individuated more-than-human consciousnesses that many of us have encountered. In other words, polytheism is in harmony with what modern biologists are discovering about biological individuality.

Polytheism not only is compatible with scientific modernity, but it also solves the worst problems plaguing monotheistic practice and theology. It is the only way in which people have engaged with the sacred, other than in traditions emphasizing nonduality or other forms of mystical encounter. However, these latter traditions are themselves compatible with polytheism.

In making these arguments I am benefitting from an increasing number of excellent books on polytheism emerging from within the broader Pagan community.

Viewing from the shoulders of others

Back when I first encountered the Wiccan Goddess, pioneering Neopagan authors did plenty of heavy intellectual lifting, exploring the implications of a Pagan world view and shedding light on our common heritage in classical pagan thought. I am indebted to a great many of them, particularly Margot

Adler, Stewart and Janet Farrar, Gerald Gardner, and Starhawk. Their deeply insightful passages on the nature of polytheism got me started on my own intellectual journey to try and make sense of the divine world I was now experiencing.

Since that exciting time, many scholars within the broad Pagan tradition have built upon their work, and they have built well. They have made powerful contributions exploring the realities underlying our experiences with the more-than-human, and I have learned much from them. While this list of talented and insightful Pagan writers is not exhaustive, I unreservedly recommend the following people as having contributed greatly to my own understanding of the issues discussed in this volume. Although whether or not they agree with how I use their insights is their call, I am grateful to Edward Butler, John Michael Greer, Emma Restall Orr, Jordan Paper, and Christopher Scott Thompson. Not all of these have written from an explicitly Neopagan perspective. Jordan Paper's analysis of polytheism is rooted in his experiences with Native American and Chinese traditions. That Paper came to his conclusions while involved with a different set of traditions supports the universal connectedness within what is loosely called Pagan or polytheistic spirituality.

In addition, the contemporary Western Pagan tradition is developing an important philosophical case for polytheism rooted in classical thought. Edward Butler, in particular, but others as well, are reviving a case for polytheism rooted in classical Neoplatonism, freeing it of the distortions imposed by later Christian writers. The full richness of this, perhaps the most sophisticated pagan philosophy of all time, is coming into ever clearer view.

So why *another* book? It is not as if any of us has time to read every current book and blog on Pagan religion and practice. Why then, another one?

There are three reasons. First, in a world characterized by divine immanence, in principle *any* starting point, rightly pursued, will lead us to a fuller appreciation of that sacredness. The more paths we can take to a similar insight on the nature of spirituality and the sacred, the better. The more different arguments converge on a common conclusion, the greater the case for accepting that conclusion. That writers like Butler and those using more contemporary approaches, such as Paper, come to what seem to me broadly compatible conclusions supports their case for their basic validity. Rooting the case for polytheism in modern science, especially biology, adds another brick supporting this important task.

Second, the most developed philosophical case for polytheism today, inherited from classical civilization, is also a difficult one to master. Even in classical times there was no firm consensus about many important issues, for it was a world of extraordinary richness in thought and subtlety in debate. Today, Neoplatonism's specialized vocabulary makes it a daunting endeavor for modern readers, particularly as the same or similar terms have changed their meanings over thousands of years.

Finally, over and above a common acceptance of polytheism, the ancients' view of the world, and of our place in it, was in some ways very different from ours. Without in any sense denigrating classical insights, our understanding of the greater reality they sought to illuminate will be enriched, and I think modified, by insights from our own dominant ways of obtaining knowledge. One such way is science.

In its own sphere, science is unequaled as a means for eliminating error, and thus advancing knowledge we can depend on. Science does not tell us what is true, but science is wonderful in exposing what we believe to be true, but is not. This point even holds for its own basic assumptions about the world, which is why science proved such an unreliable handmaiden to the church.

I encountered the Wiccan Goddess for the first time a few months after receiving my PhD in political science. In the years and decades that followed, I explored the implications of a Pagan and polytheistic world while continuing to do research in my academic field. I always hoped that at some point I might be able to link the two in a way that did justice to both the reality of Pagan experience and the insights of modern science, political or otherwise. With this volume I think I have succeeded.

Summing up

I am not claiming to have solved the mystery of who and what the gods are. We experience them as super-human because they are super-human.

What I do claim to present is a view, in keeping with modern science, in which the gods as more-than-human individuals play an important role. Our experiences of such divine encounters are not illusory and our attempts to enter into relationship with them are not a waste of time. Far from being a holdover from a more primitive understanding of the world, polytheism remains as relevant and as true today as when it graced the practices of our ancestors. To say "the gods exist" is no more primitive than to say that people exist.

Today, at a time when this country is riven by a cultural schism between a backward-looking, and increasingly brutal, monotheism, and a secular scientific outlook denying any deep meaning to spiritual experience, a revival of a polytheistic spiritual sensibility and all that it touches may contribute to the healing our society needs.

And that is the ultimate purpose of this book.

Chapter 1
POLYTHEISTIC "MONOTHEISM"

Until sufficient Chinese had lived in Christian cultures and gained a better understanding of Christianity, it was commonly understood in China that Catholicism and Protestantism were two unrelated Western religions: the former polytheistic, the primary deity being the Virgin Mary, and only the latter monotheistic.
—Jordan Paper, *The Deities Are Many*

BY THEIR OWN ACCOUNTS, taken as a whole, Christianity is a poly-theistic religion. According to Pentecostal Christian Pat Robertson, "You say you're supposed to be nice to the Episcopalians and the Presbyterians and the Methodists and this, that, and the other thing. Nonsense, I don't have to be nice to the spirit of the Antichrist" (Palast, "I don't have to be nice…"). For Robertson, these Christians do not worship the same deity he does. Many Pentecostals agree with him.

In return, many non-Pentecostal Christians say Pentecostals channel demons from hell. Baptist Pastor Levi Jones describes Pentecostal speaking in tongues as "satanic gibberish," and warns that once you "summon demons to make people give you money, you have blasphemed the Holy Ghost and you will be damned no matter what" (Jones, "Pentacostals"). The one issue both sides agree on is that they do not worship the same god.

Many Baptists agree with Robertson about Episcopalians, Presbyterians, and Methodists, and often argued Catholics are serving the Devil, and their church is the Whore of Babylon described in the Book of Revelation. The minister who leads the first Bible study group for US cabinet members in one hundred years has said that Catholicism "is one of the primary false religions of the world" (Gander, "White House Bible Study"). More than one Catholic has replied Baptists, Pentecostals, and others are going to hell because they have rejected God's true church. Beyond a claim to universal domination, the Catholic god shares little in common with the Southern Baptist or the Pentecostal god.

Bill Keller leads the largest interactive Christian website, with over 2.4 million subscribers. He has a dim view of Glenn Beck's Mormon faith: "Beck likes to call out people for their lies and deceptions, yet he portrays himself daily as a Christian… He uses the words 'god' and 'jesus,' yet the god and jesus of the Mormon cult are NOT the God and Jesus of the Bible…" (Keller, "Liveprayer"). Mormons claim otherwise, arguing they have a revelation through Joseph Smith that clarifies biblical teachings. In Smith's words, "I told the brethren that the Book of Mormon was the most correct of any book on earth, and the keystone of our religion, and a man would get nearer to God by abiding by its precepts, than by any other book" (Nyman, "Most

Correct Book"). Smith overrode the New Testament as it had overridden the Old, supplanting one infallible, divinely inspired authority with another, each describing a different deity or deities.

The god worshiped by some Missouri Synod Lutherans does not want his devotees praying with non-Christians, not even in Jesus' name. In fact, this deity does not want their pastors worshiping with other Christians (Hertz, "Benke"). Many such Lutherans filed charges against Dr. David Benke, a Lutheran pastor who prayed at an interfaith event held in Yankee Stadium following 9-11 (Associated Press, "Lutheran Panel"). Wallace Schulz, the national second vice president of the Missouri Synod argued that "to participate with pagans in an interfaith service and, additionally, to give the impression that there might be more than one god, is an extremely serious offense against the god of the Bible" (*Religious Tolerance*, "Liberal-Conservative Conflict"). More recently another Missouri Synod Lutheran pastor, Rob Morris, apologized to his denomination for participating in an interfaith prayer service for people killed in the Sandy Hook massacre. One of his parishioners had been a victim, but his deity supposedly still found his actions deeply offensive (Otterman, "Pastor Apologizes"). The gods of other Christian denominations were not so bothered. What constitutes a serious offense for one of them is no problem for the others. The Lutheran god is very different from the gods other denominations acknowledge.

Indeed, the language Robertson, Missouri Synod Lutherans, Keller, and others apply to differing self-described Christian monotheists is the same judgment many Christians generally apply to Muslims. General William G. "Jerry" Boykin said of his Islamic opponent's deity "my God was bigger than his. I knew that my God was a real God and his was an idol" (Cooper, "General").

The messages get even more varied when we consider how the various deities Christians worship expect their adherents to act in the world. The "prosperity gospel" movement was closely associated with prominent 1980s televangelists Jimmy Swaggart and Jim and Tammy Bakker, and remains prominent in many of today's charismatic movements. It claims God wants his followers to be wealthy, and immense wealth is a sign of God's favor (Hinn, "Benny Hinn"). *Time* reported in 2006 that three of the four biggest megachurches in America devoted their pulpits to some form of the prosperity gospel. *Time* also emphasized that many other Christian leaders and theologians, from across a wide spectrum, disagree. For example, mega-church pastor Rick Warren argued, "This idea that God wants everybody to be wealthy…[is] creating a false idol. You don't measure your self-worth by your net worth. I can show you millions of faithful followers of Christ who live in poverty. Why isn't everyone in the church a millionaire?" (Van Biema and Chu, "Does God Want You to Be Rich?") There are many traditional biblical passages suggesting a very different attitude toward wealth. Some Christians take seriously Jesus' teachings "Do not lay up for yourselves treasures on earth…but lay up for yourselves treasures in heaven"; and "It is easier for a camel to go through the eye of a needle than for a rich man to enter the kingdom of God." Perhaps the most well-known among these are the Franciscans, who even take a vow of poverty (Paul, "Franciscans"). But they are hardly alone. For these Christians, Jesus taught his followers to give without the expectation of receiving, the opposite of prosperity gospel teachings. Valuing wealth as a sign of divine favor and looking upon wealth as likely to be an impediment to salvation lead to worshiping very different deities.

Christian monotheism is fundamentally polytheistic, with very different deities all called by the same name.

This is nothing new in America

In America, this variety of different deities, all called by a common name, is nothing new. From the beginning, a common Christian "icing" has long covered many flavors of "monotheistic" cake, concealing incompatible views as to what God is. Today, the language of toleration forbids them from looking too closely at what cakes exist under the same icing, from angel food to devil's food. It was not always so.

Central to Quaker theology is the belief that there is "that of God in every man." Consequently, Quakers believe God dwells in every soul. Called the "Inner Light," this principle affirms that in every human soul an element of God's own Spirit and divine energy is implanted. For Quakers there was the historical Christ who had died, and the voice of the inner Christ within each person. Because direct access to God is available, Quaker meetings are intended to give people time to slow down and listen (*Religious Tolerance*, "Friends"). They do not depend on specific beliefs from outside authorities but upon each person's direct experience of God. For Quakers, the Holy

Spirit speaking through people today can trump a supposedly literal interpretation of Scripture written long ago.

The Puritans worshiped a very different god, one memorably described by Jonathan Edwards (1703–58), once America's leading Calvinist theologian. Edwards' god is "the God that holds you over the pit of hell, much as one holds a spider, or some loathsome insect over the fire, abhors you, and is dreadfully provoked: his wrath towards you burns like fire; he looks upon you as worthy of nothing else, but to be cast into the fire; he is of purer eyes than to bear to have you in his sight; you are ten thousand times more abominable in his eyes, than the most hateful venomous serpent is in ours" (Edwards, "Sinners").

In 1641 the Puritan Massachusetts Bay Colony's list of laws specified worshiping any god but the "Lord God" as worthy of death. Quakers did not qualify. In 1656 two Quakers were hanged for not worshiping the Puritans' god.

Nor was the Calvinist god the only Christian deity unlike the Quakers'. Other Christians attacked their anti-slavery views as heretical. Slavery's Christian defenders argued that the Bible never criticized slavery and demanded that enslaved Christians obey their masters. The founding father of all Abrahamic religions, Abraham, had slaves. The Ten Commandments demanded "Thou shalt not covet thy neighbor's house … nor his manservant, nor his maidservant." As one statement by a Southern Christian of the time put it, "if one, or more decisions by the written word of God, sanction the rectitude of any human acquisitions, for instance the acquisition of a servant by inheritance or purchase, whoever believes that the written word of God is *verity itself,* must consequently believe in the absolute rectitude of slave holding" (Morrison, "Religious Defense"). According to another pro-slavery Southern minister, James Thornwell, "The parties in this conflict are not merely Abolitionists and slaveholders, they are Atheists, Socialists, Communists, Red Republicans, Jacobins on the one side and the friends of order and regulated freedom on the other" (ushistory.org, "Southern Argument"). (This was in 1860. Some mindsets never change although Republicans and Democrats have switched sides.) The Quakers clearly worshiped a different deity than those holding slavery to be the will of *their* god.

Radically different theologies

Like the Quakers, Orthodox Christians also believe God is everywhere. Orthodox Bishop Kallistos Ware writes, "The whole universe is a cosmic Burning Bush, filled with divine fire, yet not consumed" (Ware, *The Orthodox Way*, 118). Consequently, they have developed practices of meditation and contemplation by which they might come into greater harmony with him. These Christians claim the Apostle Paul endorsed their view when he referred to God as the One "in whom we live and move and have our being" (Acts 17:28). So for both Quakers and the Orthodox there is no deep gap between God and the world.

But unlike Quakers, Orthodox Christians insist Scripture is never to be set aside in favor of community illumination. For Orthodoxy, absolute truth exists only in holy Scripture whereas the Quakers' god frequently speaks to people within the context of their lives. The Orthodox god requires us to subordinate any insights we receive in mystical communion to what he reportedly told other people thousands of years ago. Nonconforming insights do not come from God. The Quaker deity is not so reticent. These are very different gods.

Whereas Quakers and the Orthodox believe God is in the world as well as transcendent to it, other monotheists disagree. Unlike the Orthodox, most Western Christians reject panentheism, the view God is both immanent and transcendent, and, with Edwards, say their god is purely "transcendent." Many Western Christians consider the world as intrinsically fallen, with all of us fatally tainted by Original Sin, though few today would go so far as Jonathan Edwards. Even though their deities are usually kinder than his, we still cannot find God except through his grace. He reaches out to us, but he is not in us. The gulf here is cosmic, requiring Jesus' willing sacrifice to bridge it. These Christians' gods are quite distinct from the god of the Quakers and the god of the Orthodox who exist in the world as well as transcendent to it (Ware, *The Orthodox Way*). Original sin is a key element in most Western Christianity, accepted by Catholics and Protestants alike. We are radically separated from God because of sins committed earlier by other people in Eden. However, the Eastern Orthodox churches do not believe in Original Sin, arguing it is a fabrication of the Western church (Orthodox Church in America, "Original Sin"). In one case we are guilty of sin at birth, and if not baptized, deserve damnation. In the other, we are born innocent. Our relationship with God could not get much more different, while still focusing on the need for salvation.

Divine despots

Some years ago, a young evangelical sought to save my soul in a California coffeehouse. In the course of our conversation he argued that, were it not for the promise of divine rewards and punishments, people would behave badly. I told him I knew many atheists, and none had run amok. Some generously gave of their time to charitable causes, such as helping Habitat for Humanity. By comparison, my evangelical acquaintance was admitting he would run wild through the world, raping and killing and stealing when he thought he could get away with it, if his god did not compel better behavior from him with the threat of hell and promise of heaven. I reminded him of Friedrich Nietzsche's words: "Principle of 'Christian love': it insists upon being well paid in the end" (Nietzsche, *The AntiChrist*, chap. 24). He had no answer. And his dilemma points to a deep split in the morality between competing "monotheistic" claims. This evangelical, and many others, worshiped their god as an Orwellian Big Brother on steroids, who rules through fear of everlasting hell and the bribery of eternal heavenly bliss. In the presence of such a deity it was in everyone's self-interest to take the bribe and avoid an eternity of torture.

A long Christian tradition describes this kind of divine tyranny, and the kinds of people it appeals to. Many early church fathers, such as Augustine and Irenaeus, argued some would *be damned forever*. Tertullian (155–240), among the most venerated among them, wrote

> Which sight gives me joy? Which rouses me to exultation?—as I see so many illustrious monarchs, whose reception into the heavens was so publicly announced, groaning now in the lowest darkness with great Jove himself, and those, too, who bore witness of their exultation … What world's wise men besides, the very philosophers, in fact, who taught their followers that God had no concern in ought that is sublunary, and were wont to assure them that either they had no souls, or that they would never return to the bodies which at death they had

left, now covered with shame before the poor deluded ones, as one fire consumes them! Poets also, trembling not before the judgement seat of ... Minos, but of the unexpected Christ! I shall have a better opportunity then of hearing the tragedians, louder-voiced in their own calamity; of viewing the play-actors, much more "dissolute" in the dissolving flames; of looking upon the charioteer, all glowing in his chariot of fire; of beholding the wrestlers, not in their gymnasia, but tossing in the fiery billows (Tertullian, *De Spectaculis*).

Centuries later, Saint Thomas Aquinas (1225–74), the "Angelic Doctor," anticipated others' eternal sufferings with as much satisfaction:

Nothing should be denied the blessed that belongs to the perfection of their beatitude. Now everything is known the more for being compared with its contrary, because when contraries are placed beside one another they become more conspicuous. Wherefore in order that the happiness of the saints may be more delightful to them and that they may render more copious thanks to God for it, they are allowed to see perfectly the sufferings of the damned" (Aquinas, *Summa Theologica*).

Moving to the Protestant tradition does not make the matter any different. Jonathan Edwards (1703–58), whom we encountered earlier, wrote

the saints will be made the more sensible how great their salvation is. When they shall see how great the misery is from which God has saved them, and how great a difference he has made between their state and the state of others, who were by nature (and perhaps for a time by practice) no more sinful and ill-deserving than any, it will give them a greater sense of the wonderfulness of God's grace to them. Every time they look upon the damned, it will excite in them a lively and admiring sense of the grace of God, in making them so to differ (J. Edwards, "Eternity").

Calvinists such as Edwards *looked forward* to watching others suffer for eternity even though their own Calvinist theology of predestination held there was *no difference in desert* between themselves and those suffering for eternity. All were justly condemned and only God's mysterious grace saved some and not others. But the saved would enjoy observing the suffering of those who were no more deserving of hell than were they themselves.

Today other Christians actively hope for the "second coming" where most people will be subjected to hideous suffering while they will be "raptured" up to heaven. Some contemporary Christians even believe their god sends aborted babies to hell (D. Edwards, "Alabama Lawmaker"). However, worshiping divine sadism is not universal among Christians. These all appear to be competing deities worshiped under the same name.

Divine love

There is a long tradition of Christians who worship a loving deity that would ultimately save everyone. These Christians find it difficult to accept a deity worthy of worship would eternally damn their friends, loved ones, and neighbors who practice different forms of Christianity, or maybe were not Christians at all. They most certainly would not enjoy watching the eternal suffering of friends and family members. Today these Christians are called "universalists," but universalism's roots are ancient, going back to Christianity's earliest years.

A majority of early Christians in the East apparently did not have a sadistic view of heavenly bliss. In his lengthy study of universalism in Christianity, J. W. Hanson quoted the early church Father Gregory of Nyssa (335–95), who wrote that

> the nature of evil shall one day be wholly exterminated, and divine, immortal goodness embrace within itself all intelligent natures; so that of all who were made by God, not one shall be exiled from his kingdom; when all the alloy of evil that like a corrupt matter is mingled in things, shall be dissolved, and consumed in the furnace of purifying fire, and everything that had its origin from God shall be restored to its pristine state of purity" (J. W. Hanson, *Universalism*, 237).

Gregory was hardly alone. Hanson also cites Clement of Alexandria (115–215): "We can set no limits to the agency of the Redeemer to redeem, to rescue, to discipline in his work, and so will he continue to operate after this life" (J. W. Hanson, *Universalism*, 55). For Clement, "God does not punish, for punishment is retaliation for evil. He chastises, however, for good to those who are chastised, collectively and individually" (Clement, *Stromata*, 7.16). Nestorian Christians also believed ultimately everyone would be saved, as befits a loving deity. Timotheus II, a twelfth-century patriarch, wrote that "by the prayers of the saints the souls of sinners may pass from Gehenna to Paradise" (J. W. Hanson, *Universalism*, 30). Rather than enjoying the eternal sufferings of sinners in hell, the saved would use their prayers to rescue them. No greater contrast is imaginable between these Christians and Catholic and Protestant Christians who anticipated the pleasure of watching others' eternal suffering.

In the early power struggles within the church the universalists lost out to men like Augustine and Irenaeus. Enforced by the sword, and later the gun, those who looked forward to seeing the damned suffer for eternity imposed what became the dominant view. The Nestorians were persecuted wherever the politically supported churches dominated. Today fewer than two hundred thousand Nestorian Christians survive in Syria, Iraq, and Iran.

However, where religious freedom exists, people have the opportunity of worshiping much more attractive alternatives to the Divine Despot. Many Christian laity now believe in everyone's ultimate salvation. Universalism in various forms has long existed in the United States, and in some cases gradually transformed into contemporary Unitarianism. Surely a god who saves everyone is different *in kind* from a god who sends many, perhaps most, to hell for eternity. To say these people worship the same deity is absurd, unless their god is the god of multiple personality disorder.

Truth and lies

The Bible is full of passages such as "No one who practices deceit shall dwell in my house; no one who speaks falsely will stand in my presence" (Psalm 101:7). For many Christians these passages undergird John's admonition to "know the truth and the truth will set you free" (John 8:32). According to this view, lying has its origins in Satan. In John 8:44 Satan is described as "a murderer from the beginning, not holding to the truth, for there is no truth in him. When he lies, he speaks his native language, for he is a liar and the father of lies." (All biblical passages are from the New International Version [NIV] translation.)

This emphasis on the central importance of truth is rejected by a majority of White evangelicals. As of October 14, 2019, Donald Trump had told 13,435 verifiable lies, dwarfing the record of previous presidents (Fact Checker, *Washington Post*). The number continues to increase. In sharp contrast to those who associate lies with Satan, a majority of White evangelicals support Trump as a divinely chosen modern-day Cyrus. According to the prophet Isaiah, the Persian emperor Cyrus served God's purposes as no one else could at the time. For these evangelicals, the biblical account of Cyrus enabled them to develop what they call a "vessel theology," allowing them to reconcile Trump's personal history of womanizing, alleged sexual assault, fraud, and endless lies with his divinely ordained purpose to restore a Christian America (Burton, "Biblical Story"). When responding to Donald Trump's many infidelities, one of his religious advisors, Southern Baptist pastor Robert Jeffress, said what he had done "doesn't matter." God forgives his chosen, apparently, even when they do not ask for forgiveness (Rupar, "Trump religious adviser"). Other Christians see continual dishonesty as a fatal flaw in any leader. In early 2018, twenty-three prominent American Christian leaders including Bishop Michael Curry, leader of the Episcopal church; the Catholic Richard Rohr; and evangelical Jim Wallis, founder of *Sojourners* magazine, stated that many policies supported by Trump and his Christian advocates are deeply anti-Christian (Eagan, "Trump Christians"). Some evangelical leaders reject "vessel theology" and are explicit in condemning Trump's amorality (J. Jenkins, "Group of nearly 80 evangelical leaders"). I think it no exaggeration to say that they worship very different gods than do evangelicals supporting Trump.

This dispute between Christians who revere truth as best they can, and those who endorse lies when useful, is not a new division. The Mormons are sometimes singled out for endorsing lying for God (Clark, "Lying for the Lord"). But long before Joseph Smith, John Chrysostom, the fifth-century Bishop of Constantinople, argued, "Great is the power of deceit, provided it is not applied with a mischievous intention. In fact, action of this kind should not be called deceit, but rather good management, cleverness and skill, leading to ways where resources fail, and correcting defects of the mind" (Chrysostom, *Treatise*).

Centuries later, Ignatius Loyola wrote, "We should always be disposed to believe that which appears to us to be white is really black, if the hierarchy of the church so decides" (Reyes, *In His Name*, 236). Nor were these views confined to Catholicism. While he worshiped a different deity, Martin Luther also supported lying when useful: "What harm would it do, if a man told a good strong lie for the sake of the good and for the Christian church..." (Brecht, *Martin Luther*, 211–212).

Another moral chasm

The United Churches of Christ makes a point of welcoming practicing gays and lesbians, people whom some other denominations declare are abominations in the eyes of *their* god. Lauren Ashley, who calls herself Miss Beverly Hills, argues her god commands that practicing gays and lesbians be put to death. She explains the biblical passages in Leviticus are very clear on the matter (Thornton, "Some lady"). Citing Leviticus 20:13 to justify the slaughter, in 2014 Pastor Steven Anderson advocated killing all gays before Christmas to ensure an AIDS-free country (Mai, "Pastor calls for killing gays"). Pastor Kevin Swanson agreed that all gays should be killed (Swanson, "Death to Gays"). The same reasoning was used by predominantly American Christian leaders to get Uganda to pass anti-gay legislation that initially had death as the penalty for homosexuality (Rwakakamba, "Uganda"). Ashley is not alone. Donnie Romero, a Baptist pastor, supported the gunman who murdered forty-nine people at the gay Pulse Nightclub in Orlando. He even wished for the wounded to die and for God to finish what the murderer had begun (Allen, "I have been a terrible husband").

Some Christians go further, and suggest that God enforces collective punishment for everyone when a society does not do as their god commands. As hurricane Irma approached Florida, prominent conservative Christian pastor Kevin Swanson announced "God is in control of what is going on..." He added, "The wrath of God against this nation is intense... The Supreme Court of the United States needs to reverse Roe v. Wade and Obergefell now, this afternoon, before Irma does her damage... God is a personality and God is offended by the sins of this nation" (Mehta, "Kevin Swanson").

It's not just gays

In 2004 many Americans were surprised that the group in American society most likely to endorse torture was White American evangelicals, by a large majority. Many evangelicals found no conflict between supporting torture and being a Christian (MacAllister, "Yes, Christians Can Support Torture"). On the other hand, *Christianity Today* denounced such actions in the strongest terms, as "human evil," and compared it to actions by the Nazis (*Christianity Today*, "Editorial"). Some Christians argue that torture is *always* wrong even as others approve it (Gushee, "5 reasons").

"The Family" is a powerful Christian organization active in the highest halls of American political power. It originated Washington's annual "Prayer Breakfast," and among its public members are a sizable minority of current and former Republican senators. The best known currently in office is Lindsey Graham. Through its network of public and secret members the Family extends throughout the government.

In *Salon,* Jeff Sharlet reports advice its spiritual leader, Doug Coe, gave to a younger follower. Coe asked the follower, "Let's say I hear you raped three little girls. What would I think of you?" Sharlet reported that the young man thought Coe would "think that he was a monster." "No," answered Coe. "Because, as a member of the Family, [you are among] the 'new chosen.' If you're chosen, the normal rules don't apply" (Sharlet, "Sex and Power").

These views are in harmony with a fifth-century Christian fanatic's claim: "There is no crime for those who have Christ" (Gaddis, *There Is No Crime*; Brummett, "Mark Pryor and theocracy"). Aggressive amorality is what passes for "Christianity" within an important part of the religious right, and, indeed, throughout Christian history.

To pick one Christian leader among a great many who would disagree, George Fox, a founder of the Quaker faith, said of slavery,

> If this should be the condition of you and yours, you would think it…very great Bondage and Cruelty. And therefore consider seriously of this, and do you for and to them, as you would willingly have them or any other to do unto you…were you in the like slavish condition (Quakers, "The Abolition Project").

Diverging roads to salvation

Salvation is the common promise of all traditions calling themselves Christian. Yet when we look closely, there are few commonalities between many of them. For some Christians, *nothing* we choose to do can win salvation. We are predestined for heaven or hell because it was God who chooses who makes it to heaven, and who goes to hell. From a purely human standpoint all are equally unworthy. Technically this is called "double predestination" because God chooses whom to save and also whom to damn. We *all* deserve damnation, and there is no injustice in his choosing a few for salvation just because he can. It is difficult to apply the term "loving" or "just" in any human sense to such a being, because in human terms it appears demonic. This is just the point, say some Calvinists, who argue we *cannot* grasp God's goodness because we are so fallen.

For many other Christians there is no pre-destination, either double or single. God has given us the freedom to choose. These are not only radically different conceptions of our relationship to God, they are also radically different understandings of what kind of being God is. Think of two human beings. One condemns people for life for actions over which they had no control and gives them no credit for doing anything good. The other recognizes people can act responsibly and credits them for what they do right, as well as holds them responsible for what they do wrong. We would describe them as very different people. The same holds for deities.

But among Christians who emphasize our freedom, the divisions are also very deep. Catholic Christians hold that good works and sincere repentance will ultimately win salvation, through the Holy Mother Church. But many Protestants argue we are saved through acquiring a personal relationship with God or Jesus, unmediated by the Holy Mother Church. Some Christians proclaim that faith alone is all that is necessary. Works do not play a role. Martin Luther even excised a part of the Bible that had been in use for nearly one thousand years because James wrote, "You see that a person is considered righteous by what they do and not by faith alone" (James 2:24), whereas Luther claimed faith alone was needed for salvation. What was an important teaching from the perspective of one god was utterly rejected by another. And universalists say all of us will make it someday.

Looks like polytheism to me

A recent study of American monotheism concluded different monotheists worship four basic types of deity, each quite different from the other: an authoritarian deity who actively punishes those who anger him; a benevolent one, who helps them despite their shortcomings; a critical one who has standards but does not intervene to punish (at least in this life); and one that after creating the world has left it to its own devices (Froese and Bader, *America's Four Gods*). This diversity only scratches the surface, for when we look more closely we find a pantheon of Christian deities who could fit in each category. All these deities' adherents claim they are acting in accord with their wishes. As monotheism, this diversity makes no sense. It makes plenty of sense as polytheism. Christianity is a polytheistic religion where all claim their various gods have the same name, even though they clearly abhor one another.

The same holds for Judaism and Islam.

The many gods of Abraham: Judaism

The Aramaic word we translate as "God" for Assyrian Christians is 'Ĕlāhā, or Alaha. Arabic-speakers of all Abrahamic faiths, including Christians and Jews, use the word "Allah" to mean "God." At this level, to say those who worship Allah do not worship God is like saying those who say "Guten Tag" are not saying "Good day," because they are speaking German. All claim to be worshiping the "God of Abraham," which is why they are called Abrahamic religions, in contrast to other religious traditions around the world.

As a rule, Judaism and Islam emphasize practice over dogma, and so are *relatively* free from the theologically rooted battles that have defined so much Christian history. But this is only a matter of emphasis, and the same kinds of problems appear within their traditions as well. Neither Judaism nor Islam emphasize getting the textual message right as much as Christianity, perhaps because their concept of monotheism is not as complicated nor their thinking about salvation as counterintuitive.

Neither Judaism nor Islam have any conception of a Trinity, and both regard this notion as, at best, a confused understanding of monotheism. No equivalent of Jesus as the son of God had to be incorporated into Jewish or Islamic monotheism. Like Moses, Mohammed was never regarded as more than human. But, even so, these other monotheistic faiths have their own internal divisions. The various gods of Muslims and Jews make different enough demands that some Jews in the past killed each other over their differences on a regular basis, as do some Muslims to this day. The killers are always seeking to please whatever deity they worship.

The bloody history of religious persecution in the Old Testament is well known. Less well known, at least outside Jewish circles, is that such lethal divisions did not stop with Israel's demise as an independent power. For example, there was and remains a deep division between Sephardic and Ashkenazi Jewish traditions that led some Jews to urge Christian persecution of Jews with whom they disagreed.

Sephardic Jews favored Maimonides' interpretation of Jewish texts that permitted Jews to treat tradition more critically. Ashkenazi rabbis rejected this rationalism, favoring a purely subjective Jewish tradition that also elevated rabbinical authority. In 1232, Ashkenazi rabbis gave Maimonides' texts to Dominican friars, to burn. Which they did. The German Jewish historian Heinrich Graetz writes in his *History of the Jews*, "Rabbi Solomon, the upholder of the Talmud and of the literal interpretation of the Holy Writ … and his disciple Jonah said to the Dominicans: 'You burn your heretics, persecute ours also …'" (Shasha, "Killing Off Rational Judaism").

The biblical Samaritans claim common descent from the original twelve tribes of Israel and also claim to worship the one true God. The Bible seems to support this claim. Yet Samaritans are rejected by Jews, apparently for mixed theological and historical reasons (McCloskey, "Jews and Samaritans").

In 1850, riots broke out in Albany, New York, on Rosh Hashanah over the nature of the Messiah, when what became Reform Judaism began to form. Reform Jews deny the reality of a personal or national Messiah. On the other end of the theological spectrum, the dominant view among Hasidic Jews rejects evolution. Orthodox Jews, like Christian Fundamentalists, generally argue their Scriptures are historically accurate and one cannot be Orthodox and accept the findings of modern scholarship. They even argue that doing so is intrinsically anti-Semitic. But other branches of Judaism distinguish between reading Scripture as historically accurate, which they acknowledge it is not, and its theological truths (Batme, "Embracing Academic Torah Study").

In 2017, the Knesset (Israel's parliament) granted the Chief Rabbinate sole monopoly over the conversion process to Judaism. The Chief Rabbinate controls Jewish marriage, divorce, conversion, and burial in the Jewish state, and it is largely run by hard-line conservative leaders. This move excluded Reform, Conservative, and Reconstructionist conversions altogether. As in so many other cases, when mixed with power, monotheism seeks to destroy its doctrinal incoherence by eliminating competing alternatives (Sales, "Israel's Conversion Laws").

To pick a final example, some American Jews worshiped a deity that approved of slavery, others a deity that did not. Some Jews were prominent in the abolitionist movement before the Civil War, others vocally defended slavery. The prominent New York Rabbi Morris Raphall defended slavery on biblical grounds, and received powerful rebuttals from Rabbi David Einhorn and biblical scholar Michael Heilprin (Yellis, "Jews Mostly Supported Slavery"). As with Christianity, these issues demonstrated Jews worshiped different deities under the same name.

The many gods of Abraham: Islam

Often Jews, Christians, and Muslims will argue that, despite their differences, they all worship the "god of Abraham." But this claim is a smokescreen, hiding vast differences behind a thin rhetorical veil. I earlier quoted General William G. "Jerry" Boykin describing a Muslim's deity: "I knew that my God was a real God and his was an idol" (Cooper, "General Casts War"). Boykin, of course, is not a religious leader, but Franklin Graham, the son of Billy Graham, most certainly is. He put the point even more bluntly. In 2001 Graham said, "The God of Islam is not the same God. He's not the son of God of the Christian or Judeo-Christian faith. It's a different God and I believe it is a very evil and wicked religion" (CNN, "Franklin Graham").

Like the Jews, Muslims have a more coherent kind of monotheism than Christians, and so have not had to solve unsolvable questions such as how the Trinity fits into One God. Islam has one god, and unlike Jesus, Mohammed was entirely human. Even so, as in other monotheisms, that One God turns out to be many. The best-known division is between Sunni and Shiite Muslims. The initial issues that divided them were both doctrinal and political, I think because almost from the beginning Islam united religion with political power.

Because religion and politics are united in Islam, political differences can easily become religious differences, and vice versa. Sunnis, the largest group of Muslims, believe Mohammed did not appoint a successor, whereas Shiites, centered in Iran, believe members of his family inherited spiritual authority after the Prophet's death. Many wars and other violence have arisen from these differing approaches to understanding their sacred Scripture. As with the Christians, there has been plenty of sincerity on all sides.

For at least two hundred years Sunni Wahhabi Muslims have held that Shi'a Muslims are evil and worthy of being killed. This Sunni sect is powerful because it is united with the ruling families of Saudi Arabia, and so influences the Muslim world as a whole (Commins, *The Wahhabi Mission*). It is no accident that Saudi Arabia has contributed disproportionately to the most extreme Sunni groups, such as ISIL and Al Qaeda. Nor should it surprise us that, like Christian extremists of the past, most of their victims claim to follow the same religion they do. Today Sunni Saudi Arabia and Shiite Iran contend for dominance in the Arab Muslim world and have no compunctions about laying waste to countries and people caught in the middle, as in Yemen.

Sufism is also a well-known current in Muslim cultures, and perhaps the one some of whose major figures are best known in the West, such as the poet Rumi. Initially arising within Sunni traditions, Sufism is now also present in Shiite Islam as well, and is particularly powerful outside the Arab world, such as in the Balkans and the world's most populous Muslim nation, Indonesia.

Sufis distinguish between exoteric and esoteric Islam—that is, between a religion as it is practiced by people who focus legalistically on its surface, and those who seek direct experience of the sacred. Dan Alexe writes: "Dervishes, who often drink openly, do not go to the mosque and do not say their regular prayers, are actually shunned by the official government-supported Islam…dervishes are a guarantee against the outside pressure of militant Islam of the Wahhabi type" (Alexe, "Influence of Sufi Islam"). Sufism remains the main form of Islam in many parts of the Balkans, especially in Kosovo and Macedonia. Baba Mondi, the leader of the Bektashi Order, an old Sufi tradition now headquartered in Albania and representing perhaps 20 percent of Albanian Muslims, says religion's role in the rescue of Albanian and refugee Jews from the Nazis was both central and indirect. He explained, "In Albania there is a tradition of religious tolerance…I wouldn't mind my children marrying a Jew, a Christian, whoever" (Liphshiz, "Muslim Albanians"). Other, more conservative, Muslim traditions have long been hostile to Sufi Islam.

In addition, smaller groups identifying either as other kinds of Muslim or arising out of Islam have long existed in the Middle East, including the Druze and the Alawites. They have also been frequently persecuted by more absolutist schools of Sunnis and Shiites. If religious freedom were secure in Islamic countries, such groups would multiply still more.

Since each contending Islamic approach believes it is the correct way to worship Allah, and since for many the differences are often great enough to kill over, it is no stretch to say that everywhere under the rhetoric on monotheism, we again find a variety of different deities honored by their respective followers. The Allah as worshiped by Wahhabis is very different from Allah as worshiped by Sufis.

A weak response

Upon hearing early versions of my argument that Christianity is polytheistic in practice, some Christians told me this apparent diversity of frequently feuding deities within Christianity is not polytheism. Their god is simply too complex for a single human description. For example, their god is a god of justice as well as a god of love. Because he is perfect, God harmonizes what we cannot. His justice is in harmony with his love, and vice versa. If we knew him we would recognize this.

But what constitutes justice and what is its relation to love? There is no agreement among universalist Christians who believe all will ultimately be saved through a perfect balancing of love and justice, and those believing that even unbaptized aborted babies will spend eternity in hell, again through perfectly balancing love and justice. This claim about God's complexities simply shifts the conflicting terms from different conceptions of God to different conceptions of love and justice, which are supposedly basic traits of their deities.

In addition, if this Christian argument is true, why have there been so many religious wars and killings and general intolerance among Christians? I would guess that nearly all on all sides would say it is *their* god who perfectly balances justice and love. But each balances these perfect traits differently. The disputes go back nearly two thousand years, and the fratricidal violence nearly as long, lasting well into the twentieth century even in Europe.

Many people have shifted from one Christian perspective to another, but only after great personal introspection and prayer. However, believers have shifted back and forth, in a kind of "serial monotheism." Personal sincerity and fervent prayer have not led seekers to a common understanding, nor has God made it clear who has gotten it right, yet the traditional doctrines of Christian (or any other) monotheism continue to say there is ONE way that is right. Serial monotheism is no more monotheism than serial monogamy is monogamy. In both cases a partner makes a vow for life, and then changes it to make a similar vow to a different partner for life.

One would think a single god, supreme above all others, interested in human history, demanding we worship him alone, and concerned with people's salvation, would intervene to bring his sincere followers into greater clarity about these matters. Yet such intervention has never happened. He remains silent. Or worse, Christians with different perspectives assure us he has told *them* they are correct.

This "explanation" of a superhuman balancing of perfect love and justice waves words in the air, while ignoring their meaning. This is not a question to be solved by verbal sleights of hand.

A polytheistic view of Christianity

Two thousand years of history testify the biblical tradition has no solution to this dilemma. Both Socrates and the Aztecs were pagans. But modern-day Pagans would say that Socrates and the Aztecs were attuned to *different* gods. From a polytheist point of view, what today calls itself monotheism is a diverse polytheism, one where the devotees of each deity claim their deity has sole dominion over everything and everybody. As with nations making conflicting claims to dominion over peoples and territory, the result is often war and killing because there is *no other way* to determine who is right. There is always plenty of sincerity on all sides.

Because they worship *different* gods under the *same* name, Christians worship a god who loathes us, and a god who loves us; a god who wants all to be saved and a god who sends aborted babies to hell; a god who welcomes gays and lesbians, and another who wants them killed; a god who surrounds us with intricate rules that we violate at the cost of eternal damnation and a god who only requires us to take Jesus as savior; a god who holds us guilty of Original Sin, and a god who holds us guilty only of sins we personally commit; a god who predestined us to salvation or damnation long before we existed and a god who gives us freedom; a god who will save us all because he loves us, a god who will save most, and yet another god who will save only a few because his anger toward those who reject him is eternal.

The variety of sincere interpretations arising from a single text is almost endless, and to the degree unity in understanding has *ever* existed, it has *always* come from political force. Monotheistic unity has *always* proceeded from the edge of a sword and the barrel of a gun, not from the persuasive power of argument and faith. When freedom of belief is established, the swords sheathed, the guns stilled, diversity *always* emerges.

One might even guess that this is what God wants since, as soon as people stop killing one another, it happens. But such a god is not a monotheistic god.

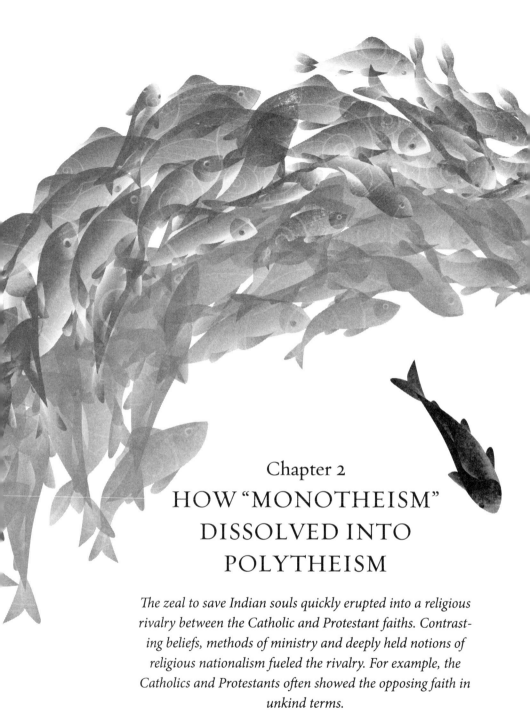

Chapter 2
HOW "MONOTHEISM"
DISSOLVED INTO
POLYTHEISM

The zeal to save Indian souls quickly erupted into a religious rivalry between the Catholic and Protestant faiths. Contrasting beliefs, methods of ministry and deeply held notions of religious nationalism fueled the rivalry. For example, the Catholics and Protestants often showed the opposing faith in unkind terms.

It did not take long for our people to become disenchanted by the missionary enterprise.
—TAMÁSTSLIKT CULTURAL INSTITUTE,
UMATILLA RESERVATION, OREGON

MONOTHEISM'S CURRENT DOMINANCE AS a way of thinking about religion is not because it is spiritually superior to other religious traditions. It is due to the success with which it has been forcibly imposed for millennia. When monotheism triumphed, nearly everywhere it did so at the point of a sword or the barrel of a gun. Nor is this simply a trait of the Abrahamic traditions. Earlier ones did so as well.

The Egyptian Pharaoh Akhenaten was perhaps the best-known early monotheist. He ruled for seventeen years, dying in 1336 or 1334 BCE. During his reign he sought to replace Egyptian polytheism with a sole focus on Aten, depicted with a sun symbol. Aten was not a new deity. Before Akhenaten sought to make him the only deity, he was considered an aspect of the composite deity Ra-Amun-Horus, where Ra represented the daytime sun, Amun the sun in the underworld, and Horus the sunrise.

Aten was now declared to be the only true deity, and the sun's disc simply a symbol, for Aten could never be fully understood or represented. Conveniently for the Pharaoh, however, his will could be reliably interpreted by Akhenaten himself. Idols were banned, the traditional priesthood was disbanded, and funds diverted from traditional Egyptian religion to support the new one he attempted to establish. There is evidence of serious oppression of those who did not conform to the new order (Reeves, *Akhenaten*, 154–5). However, his effort failed. Upon Akhenaten's death, the old gods were restored, and the Pharaoh's name erased from history as best his successors could manage. Nor was Akhenaten's attempt the only one to impose a monotheism from outside the Abrahamic traditions.

Zoroastrianism was the dominant religion of the Persian Empire from around 500 BCE, until Alexander's conquest in the third century BCE, and subsequent Hellenistic domination. This religion honored one ultimate creator god, Ahura Mazda, who was in perpetual struggle with an evil deity destined for defeat. Like future monotheisms, its message was based on a revelatory text. All adherents were required to state publicly "I believe in whatever this religion says or thinks" (McEvilley, *The Shape of Ancient Thought*, 122). Zoroaster also taught each person "should show kindness to the follower of the truth but should show evil to the follower of the Lie." He emphasized "he who is most good to the follower of the Lie is himself a follower of the Lie" (Lent, *The Patterning Instinct*, 140). During the Sassanid dynasty (205–651 CE), the last before the Muslim conquest, emperor Ardashir sought to restore the earlier Persian Empire. In his effort, Ahura Mazda was declared sovereign and polytheistic deities were labeled demons and their devotees suppressed, as in time were Christians, Jews, Buddhists, Hindus, and followers of other religions. Heresy was made a political crime and Zoroastrians fought a war of conquest and forcible conversion against Christians in what is now Armenia (Brown, "Between Two Empires"). Zoroastrianism still survives today, numbering perhaps two hundred thousand followers, many in polytheistic India, where they fled after the Muslim conquest. A polytheistic culture provided a haven for one monotheism that lost power to another.

Scholars frequently debate just how monotheistic Zoroastrianism really was (Boyd and Donald, "Zoroastrianism"). However, as we shall see in chapter 3, this problem is inherent in the idea of monotheism. What is clear is Zoroastrianism triumphed for as long as it did through support from imperial power that often attacked competing faiths. When that support ceased, its numbers shrank dramatically.

The Christian example

Abrahamic monotheism was also established and long maintained by the same top-down violent means. As importantly, when recourse to violence was absent, it fragmented. I will use the Christian example to make my point.

Different groups of Christians initially interpreted their Scriptures and the story of Jesus in different ways. This diversity presented a problem for a religious movement claiming an absolute monopoly on spiritual truth. For example, Arianism was an early "heresy" that those later to become identified as Orthodox long combated. Arius argued the Son of God was made by God, as God's very first creation. Therefore, the Son had a beginning. Only the Father had no beginning. Therefore, the Father's divinity was greater than the Son's. Plenty of Scripture supported this interpretation. Long years of struggle for imperial favor occurred between Arians and those arguing for the view that finally won out.

Ultimately the Roman state enforced what is now regarded as canonical, and imposed the decision by law and sword. Alternative accounts were suppressed because, as Augustine argued, "Why … should not the church use force in compelling her lost sons to return, if the lost sons compelled others to their destruction?"(Augustine, *Letter 185*). Right actions alone were insufficient for salvation, right beliefs were required as well. Consequently, what people thought was as important to control as what people did.

In his argument for punishing "heresy," Augustine displayed a core problem with monotheistic Scriptures: sincere people inevitably interpreted Scripture differently but, given the stakes, agreement was all important, and impossible to obtain peacefully. Erring people would always be spreading devilish errors threatening other people's ultimate salvation. In a way, this was worse than murder, which killed only the body whereas these errors led the deceived into an eternity of suffering. Better by far to stamp them out, if for no other reason than to save others' souls.

While Augustine personally opposed executing fellow Christians, his argument made that conclusion seem reasonable, and the Roman state began killing "heretics." The same point of view was held by the "heretics," who viewed themselves as truth's custodians. Sadly, for them, they lacked access to the Roman state to enforce their own views.

Because doctrinal unity grew from the threat of violence, such unity as existed did little to make monotheism a coherent view. Some heretics, such as the Nestorians, fled the Empire to survive. In Egypt, the Coptic Christians remained secure there because they were too powerful locally to suppress. But for the most part, early Christian Orthodoxy prevailed because it was backed by Roman arms. But had the Arian Goths maintained control of Rome, Arianism would have been the Christian Orthodoxy.

The price of state support to suppress endless conflict was high. The Roman church was under the authority of the emperor. Emperors appointed, or at least ratified, their church's pope, or later, Patriarch, subjecting religious authority to their own political priorities. The emperor's religious opponents could never attain the ultimate church office.

After Constantine moved the imperial capital to Constantinople, Christianity's primary institutional center remained in Rome. This geographical division of secular and religious power set the stage for the later division between Catholicism and Orthodoxy, a division with both political and theological roots. The final split arose over banning the veneration of icons. The pope opposed banning icons and the emperor supported those who sought to do so. Ultimately the pope excommunicated the iconoclasts, and in turn the Byzantine emperor Leo III confiscated papal properties and sought to limit its power in 732/3 CE.

By this time the empire was not strong enough to enforce the emperor's decisions, and it finally lost control of Italy, with the church remaining the only universal presence over regions now controlled by different political entities. Ecclesiastical power now claimed superiority over political power, perhaps best symbolized on Christmas, 800 CE, when Pope Leo crowned Charlemagne Holy Roman Emperor. Political power, Rome argued, should be subordinate to the church. In the East the old relation of the church's subordination to political power remained. Institutionalized Christianity's first big split had occurred.

By 1054 the divisions between Byzantine and Catholic Christianity had become so great no reconciliation was possible, nor has it emerged in the nearly one thousand years since. This split reflected both doctrinal disagreement and different bases of political power. There was no way for different scriptural interpretations to be settled except through force, and by this time there was no longer a force strong enough to compel unity.

In the Orthodox East, the emperor's authority over appointing Patriarchs remained even after the Byzantine Empire had been reduced to a tiny fragment of its former self. Despite his increasingly tiny domain, the emperor still claimed to be the emperor of all Christianity, even as far away as Russia. The Turks soon solved this theological problem by eliminating the "empire" and the emperor when they conquered Constantinople in 1453. Since then, Russian Patriarchs have answered to a home-grown despot.

In the West, the Catholic Church maintained religious domination until the fifteenth century. Until then, whenever challenged by dissidents, it usually could compel political authorities to do its bidding. While seemingly endless struggles occurred between political and ecclesiastical power during the Middle Ages, on the whole the Catholic Church preserved its dominance within Western Europe. Powerful ecclesiastical challenges, such as by the Albigensians, were crushed by ruthless crusades.

Victorious monotheisms have always succeeded when and only when they could crush opposition through political means. As importantly, when successful, monotheists used political power in new ways.

Totalitarianism and the integral world

Writing from a spiritual perspective, some scholars describe the medieval Christian West as a society where no sharp distinction existed between the religious and the secular dimensions of life. All of life, even the most mundane elements, took place in and drew its meaning from a spiritual context enveloping and permeating it. Certainly, this view describes a great many pre-Christian and pre-Islamic societies in Europe and elsewhere. However, the integral outlook of pre-Abrahamic societies usually emerged and developed without deliberate direction, shaping and being shaped by people's day-to-day spiritual, economic, and social networks. They were not top-down affairs. If we must use the term "integral" to describe Christian Europe, it was integral in a very different way than in the non-monotheistic world. Its unity was imposed, not organic.

The integral worlds of classical Greece and Rome, of Native American and African tribes, and of traditional India and China, among others, had apparently existed as long as had these societies themselves. Few people doubted the existence of the gods, spirits, and powers of the world, of Earth and sky, beliefs which fit comfortably with life as most experienced it. For most people, the sacred thoroughly penetrated the mundane. Change happened in these cultures, of course, but it was mostly evolutionary and gradual.

The "integral" society of the Christian Middle Ages was different. As conquering powers, Abrahamic monotheisms considered themselves in "holy" conflict with the societies, and especially the religions, that preceded them. From Moses' attempt to replace Hebrew society's worship of at least a male and female divinity with a single one (Patai, *Hebrew Goddess*), to later Christian and Muslim efforts to do the same for the entire world, monotheism was always a top-down project, seeking to transform everyone's way of life from following "error" to serving "truth."

As a concept, totalitarianism was developed to describe states such as Communist Russia and Nazi Germany, which sought to transform not just people's behavior, but also their beliefs. There was nothing new about autocracies demanding obedience, but for totalitarian regimes, obedience was not enough. People had to actively believe the official ideologies. Scholars described totalitarianism as something new (for example, Friedrich and Brzezinski, *Totalitarian Dictatorship*). But all that was new about twentieth century totalitarianism was that it was secular. In the West, totalitarianism was a Christian invention.

The twentieth century's secular totalitarian states did not last long, and the transformations they attempted did not deeply change their societies. The longest lived, the Soviet Union, rose and fell within the space of a single lifetime. Germany's Third Reich lasted only twelve years. By contrast, Christian totalitarianism had over a millennium to work its will.

For centuries powerful central churches largely succeeded in suppressing "heresy" where they dominated (P. Jenkins, *Jesus Wars*). Knowledge of alternative religious and spiritual perspectives vanished from most people's memory, or survived as context-free hints in custom and folklore. Some people today recognize the polytheistic names of our weekdays, but most know nothing of the deities named. The same applies to the "Christmas tree," and the Maypole. Many of my Hispanic neighbors in northern New Mexico descended from Jewish *conversos* who fled here to escape the Inquisition many hundred years ago (Perry and Nathan, "Mistaken Identity?"). For most, only vestiges of Jewish practice survived, such as avoiding pork and spinning a top at Christmas. They came to think of themselves as Catholics, not Jews. This happened within a few hundred years whereas pagan Europe became Christian over a thousand years ago. Today, when they think of God, virtually all modern Westerners think in monotheistic terms, whether they accept or reject it.

Cultures change all the time, but the pagan world's becoming Christian was something new, directed from above to serve a single goal: making a culture completely monotheistic in every way. Once they had the power, monotheists tried to shape not just what people did, but also how they thought. This was new. Religious totalitarianism emerged within the Christian Roman Empire, and spread throughout Europe as it was increasingly Christianized.

Long before George Orwell wrote *1984,* an Orwellian "Newspeak" was created, making it difficult to even think about religion and the sacred in any other way than as the church decreed. Classical literature was suppressed or twisted to serve monotheistic ends (Nixey, *The Darkening Age*, 152–4).

Complex cultural and spiritual ecologies thousands of years in the making were reduced to cultural and spiritual monocultures of the mind. To achieve this, the past had to be destroyed, and what could not be destroyed had to be reshaped. Pagan writings were burnt, replacing classical philosophy and myth with biblical Scriptures and commentaries on those Scriptures. As classical scholar Catherine Nixey noted, the triumph of Christianity led to "the largest destruction of art that human history had ever seen" (Nixey, *The Darkening Age*, xxxvii). Words began to change their meaning, and as they did, long-established ways of thinking were lost, replaced by others in harmony with the new Orthodoxy. For example, the classical *daimones*—benevolent or benign nature spirits, lesser deities, and perhaps the souls of exceptional men—were redefined as demons. In its original Greek, "heresy" referred simply to choice, as when young men examined different schools of philosophy to determine how to live. Now it meant making a bad or evil choice against the doctrines of the church.

The much talked about Roman persecution of Christians was for the most part greatly exaggerated (Moss, *The Myth of Persecution*). When it was enforced, Roman pagans only asked Christians to pour a libation to the emperor's *genius*. What they really believed was their business (Nixey, *The Darkening Age*, 73–9). Traditional religions emphasized practice, not correct belief.

Monotheists took a different view. With monotheism, for the first time a distinction was made between "true" and "false" religion (Assmann, *The Price of Monotheism*). And it was vital to get it right. In 356 CE, fewer than fifty years after Emperor Constantine had instituted complete toleration throughout the empire, regardless of belief, the death penalty was instituted for making sacrifices to the gods. Spying on others, even within private homes, became official policy. For those who refused to spy on their neighbors, John Chrysostom (349–407), archbishop of Constantinople, threatened "the most grievous penalties" not only from God, but from worldly power (Nixey, *The Darkening Age*, 209). As in Stalin's Russia, where in time the Bolsheviks themselves became the victims of the state, the terror unleashed on pagans was ultimately also applied to the "wrong" kinds of Christians. Priests with the wrong views about the Bible's message were attacked at their altars, their eyes were gouged out, their tongues were cut out, and they were often murdered. If they were not at their churches, their homes could be invaded.

This was a small price to pay for people's salvation. "Where there is terror," Augustine wrote, "there is salvation" (Shaw, *Sacred Violence*, 227). So long as the church had the power to act, this totalitarian enforcement of right beliefs never ended. In the sixteenth century, Spanish Jews who had become Christian to avoid being expelled from the land they long called home, and dutifully went to church, could still be tortured, because the torturers wanted to verify what was in their hearts (Schwartz, "Lost diary"). Were they *really* Christians? Did they eat pork, or not? Did they cook food on Fridays to be eaten on Saturdays? (*Forward*, "In Spain") Who did they associate with?

In all, more than thirteen thousand conversos were put on trial in the first twelve years of the Spanish Inquisition. More than seven hundred were ultimately burned to death in Seville alone (Jewish Virtual Library, "Christian-Jewish relations"). Some conversos who actually were Jewish wisely emigrated to the most remote parts of the Spanish Empire, where the power of the church was weaker. Today their descendants are among my neighbors here in northern New Mexico.

Given enough time, and applied ruthlessly enough, religious totalitarianism can succeed in shaping how people interpret what they perceive. In time, monotheism became the only way most people in the West could think about religion and spirituality. For centuries, those who had what they considered spiritual experiences interpreted them in a monotheistic vein. God, or perhaps one of his angels or saints, was communicating with them. However, if the experience did not fit that person's understanding of Scripture, it must have come from a deceiving spirit, and had to be rejected.

In the process, perennial dimensions of human experience, of encountering the sacred, or the more than human, became linked to a religious concept unable to bear the weight put upon it. But it took time and the gradual increase of religious freedom for this incoherence to bring forth its full implications. To see how it happened, let us start in late medieval Europe, after Christianity's triumph, when Christian monotheism was at its most unified. If ever there was a time when monotheism would make sense, it would be when our civilization's greatest minds sought to better understand the One True God's divine nature.

Chapter 2

It all starts coming apart

Beginning in the fifteenth century, this faux integral world started to dissolve from within. Totalitarian control depends on both force and belief. As the demise of the Soviet Union demonstrated, when belief decays enough, even a mighty army is not enough to prevent collapse. The same collapse of belief happened in the fifteenth century, though more slowly and from different causes.

During the mid-1400s Johannes Gutenberg and his partners combined movable type with the technology of a wine press, creating the first printing press in Europe. From Gutenberg's small shop in Germany, printing presses rapidly proliferated throughout Europe, so that by the end of the century, presses existed in at least 270 cities. Like the internet and World Wide Web of our time, the result was transformative beyond anyone's expectations. Ideas could be spread much more cheaply through printing than by copying texts by hand.

In Western Europe the printing press dissolved the Vatican's monopoly of control over what monotheism meant, and in so doing began its internal dissolution. Martin Luther's (1483–1546) efforts to reform the Vatican were similar to John Huss' (1369–1415) earlier attempt. Huss, a Czech, advocated reforms sharing much in common with those promoted in the future Protestant Reformation, but after being promised safe passage to the Vatican to argue his position, he was burned at the stake.

Martin Luther succeeded where Huss failed, in no small part because he had access to printing presses, and so could rapidly disseminate his ideas and translations throughout Germany, and then Europe at large. Luther translated the New Testament, published it in 1522, and within two months had sold five thousand copies. The complete Bible, with both New and Old Testaments, came out in 1534, and sold perhaps as many as one hundred thousand copies in forty years. As Luther built support, he was better able to forge alliances with the German nobility, already resentful of the Vatican and its allies. They protected him from the church's forces. Excommunication lost its sting when the church doing the excommunicating was regarded as illegitimate. The politically enforced unity of Christian doctrine in the West dissolved, never to be regained.

In making the Bible available to all, Luther unintentionally exposed Christian monotheism's fundamental incoherence, an incoherence long hidden by prohibiting most people from reading the Bible while enforcing the "correct" interpretation with the threat of sword and stake on those few who could read it. Luther believed that when sincere people read Scripture, they would see the truth of his interpretation, for it seemed obvious to him. He was to be disappointed. Not much later another important religious reformer, John Calvin (1509–64) read it differently, disagreeing with Luther about the Bible's true meaning. This disagreement also divides Christianity to this day.

With the best will in the world, Catholics, Lutherans, Calvinists, and many others could not harmonize their different interpretations of the Bible. Sincerity alone could not settle their differences because all sides were sincere, and all could quote Scripture to support their position. Over time, tensions rose to the point where wars broke out. The Thirty Years War (1618–48) was the final and bloodiest in this series of violent encounters. In terms of the percentage of casualties, it was perhaps the bloodiest conflict in Europe's history. Percentages that died vary, but a sense of the scale can be grasped in Stephen Toulmin's observation that about 35 percent of what is now Germany's population at the time died (Toulmin, *Cosmopolis*, 101). Ultimately, Protestants and Catholics alike realized they could never kill enough of the others to prevail. Bad as allowing other faiths to exist seemed to be, perpetual war was worse. Peace was the lesser evil.

The resulting Peace of Westphalia created a series of treaties that mandated a degree of mutual toleration between the major warring sides. Smaller sects, such as the Anabaptists, were still suppressed, since toleration depended on having enough troops rather than the intensity of their faith. But in countries dominated by one of the big three, Catholics, Calvinists, and Lutherans achieved a degree of legal security.

England went through somewhat similar processes, again arriving at toleration through mutual exhaustion. John Locke (1632–1704), the most important voice for religious toleration in England, had spent time in exile in the Netherlands, then the most tolerant land in Europe. The Netherlands' domestic peace and prosperity deeply influenced him, resulting in his *Letter on Toleration* (1689) (Locke, *Toleration*). Its influence helped establish a degree of toleration in England.

Institutionalizing heresy

However grudgingly and partially initiated, toleration transformed Western Europe's religious landscape. When "heresy" became legal, it transformed *everyone's* relations to their religion, even the most conservative. For centuries, a person's religion had simply been the way things were, like the language one spoke. But now it became a personal choice (Berger, *The Heretical Imperative*). What had long been condemned as religious heresy now became a part of many Europeans' daily lives, enabling them to choose between competing churches. Even if that choice meant remaining with their previous tradition, it was a choice, not a fate. They also increasingly lived among others who had chosen differently. While initially limited to Catholic, Lutheran, and Calvinist denominations, religious choice expanded over time to embrace ever widening groups with competing visions of what it was to be a Christian. *Heresy was institutionalized*, although its implications were masked by the more neutral word, "toleration."

In the "new world," even before our own revolution, the colonies of Pennsylvania and New York had established universal religious toleration. Encouraged by their example, Thomas Jefferson argued that "their [Pennsylvania and New York's] harmony is unparalleled, and can be ascribed to nothing but their unbounded tolerance, because there is no other circumstance in which they differ from every nation on Earth. They have made the happy discovery, that the way to silence religious disputes, is to take no notice of them. Let us too give this experiment fair play, and get rid, while we may, of those tyrannical laws" (Jefferson, *Notes*). Based on their examples, after its founding, one of the United States' most unique achievements was to universalize religious toleration within its constitution. The first sentence of the Constitution's First Amendment reads "Congress shall make no law respecting an establishment of religion, or prohibiting the free exercise thereof." Any honest doubts as to its meaning would be laid aside by a 1796 treaty with Tripoli that proclaimed "the Government of the United States of America is not, in any sense, founded on the Christian religion; as it has in itself no character of enmity against the laws, religion, or tranquility, of Mussulmen [Muslims]." This treaty was initiated by George Washington, adopted during John Adams' presidency, and unanimously approved by a Senate filled with Founders. The United States institutionalized universal heresy in its founding document.

Even before the full implications of toleration were grasped, people had a choice of churches and freedom to read and interpret their Scriptures as they thought best. In every society people's understanding of God diversified, but not most people's certainty he existed. What is called Christianity has continued to fragment into a growing number of churches and sects. In the United States today, by one measure, there are twenty-five denominations all using the same texts, and frequently drawing radically different conclusions when doing so (Hartford Institute for Religion Research, "Fast Facts"). Whether theologically liberal or conservative, these churches and sects all depended on a monotheistic framework of belief and meaning, but as chapter 1 demonstrated, many different deities were concealed under a common name.

Transforming Scripture

One unexpected result of printing the Bible in popular languages was a transformation in how Christians, particularly Protestants, interpreted Scripture. Peter Harrison describes three major changes. First, interpreting Scripture shifted to emphasize literalism over allegory. Second, people were encouraged to read Scripture for themselves and not simply rely on ecclesiastical authority for answers. Third, which chapter 4 will explore further, these new approaches ultimately proved supportive of science (Harrison, "The Bible: A Rejoinder"). These changes were profound.

Long before monotheism arose, people in different cultures understood events and beings in the world in various levels, from the purely objective, to patterns, coincidences, and symbols pointing to a greater meaning. Allegory could illuminate these multiple levels of meaning, and served as an important means through which human beings made sense of their world. There was a literal meaning, but there were often other levels, and these levels were often the most important (Butler, "Theological Interpretation"). This way of interpreting sacred stories had long characterized how pagan myths were understood, and some of the early church fathers had studied with pagan philosophers. This approach probably seemed natural to them (diZerega, *Faultlines*, 34–43). In keeping with this primordial tradition, the early churches had often interpreted Scripture allegorically from the very beginning. The author of the earliest Latin translation of the New Testament yet unearthed explicitly used allegorical rather than literal reasoning (Moss, "Interpreting the Bible"). For Origen

(185–254) the world was filled with symbols that could teach deeper levels of understanding, and these symbols sometimes could not be grasped by treating the Bible literally, As Origen wrote respecting the creation story described in Genesis 1–3: "For who that has understanding will suppose that the first day, and second and third day, and the evening and the morning existed without a sun, and moon, and stars? And that the first day was, as it were, also without a sky?… And if God is said to walk in paradise in the evening, and Adam is to hide himself under a tree, I do not suppose that anyone doubts that these things figuratively indicate certain mysteries, the history having taken place in appearance and not literally" (Origen, *On First Principles*, 39).

Origen was not alone (Ku, "Interpreting Genesis"). More than one hundred years later, the greatest figure in early Western Christianity, St. Augustine (354–430), took a similarly cautious view toward scriptural literalism. Augustine argued everything in the universe was created simultaneously by God, and not in seven days, as Genesis seemed to demand: "It not infrequently happens that something about the earth, about the sky … may be known with the greatest certainty by reasoning or by experience, even by one who is not a Christian. It is too disgraceful and ruinous, though, and greatly to be avoided, that he should hear a Christian speaking so idiotically on these matters, and as if in accord with Christian writings, that he might say that he could scarcely keep from laughing when he saw how totally in error they are" (Augustine, "On Genesis"). From a Christian perspective, good allegorical interpretation of nature illuminated meanings that reinforced Scripture. When correctly grasped, the world embodied meanings that supported and strengthened the core of Christian teachings. Augustine wrote the "book of nature" could deepen our understanding of Scripture, but not contradict it when both were wisely understood.

What really mattered for these Christians was Jesus' nature and the meaning of his death and resurrection, not the details of biblical stories on other matters. By illuminating divine information within the world, allegory could cope with where Scripture might be literally mistaken, as in Origen's comments about Genesis.

The Reformation era arguments, and those that followed, did not focus much on Jesus' nature, which had been forcibly settled, but on the meaning of Scripture as a whole. This took two forms. First, whereas the church had claimed sole authority over the meaning of Scripture, Luther argued Scripture took precedence over the church. In making their case. He and other reformers relied on techniques of textual criticisms developed by Renaissance humanists (Harrison, *The Bible*, 101). Their techniques enabled the Bible to be translated into many languages while rigorous scholarship rooted out errors of translation in the old Vulgate Bible. This unintentionally set the stage for habits of textual criticism that in the future would seriously undermine claims to divine inerrancy.

Second, Luther and Calvin rejected allegorical interpretations. As Luther put it, Scripture was best understood "in their simplest meaning as far as possible." He also argued for the "priesthood of all believers," which meant all who were literate were competent to understand Scripture. All anyone needed to know for salvation was written in Scripture, and Scripture was infallible.

For the reformers, Origen was perhaps the first major offender against this principle, for "ignoring the grammatical sense, he turned trees and everything else into allegories" (Harrison, *The Bible*, 108). The reformers' arguments separated the world from being used to illustrate biblical truths, and in the process perhaps modifying them. The world became a state on which the drama of salvation took place. In the long run, this desacralization of the world helped provide the groundwork for modern science, to which I will return in chapter 4.

But even for Luther this principle had a problem, for Scripture was ambiguous. Luther argued salvation came from faith alone, and not from works. He also rejected the Catholic doctrine of purgatory. But, in the New Testament, James 2:24 taught: "You see that a person is considered righteous by what they do and not by faith alone," supporting the Catholic doctrine on the importance of merit. Luther preferred Ephesians 2:8,9: *"For by grace are ye saved through faith… not by works."* He also believed 2 Maccabees 12:43–46 supported the doctrine of purgatory, which he opposed, and Hebrews 7 was used by the Catholic Church to support its priesthood. Luther ultimately removed the last seven Old Testament texts from the Bible, and sought to relegate offending New Testament passages to an appendix. Literalism sometimes had to eliminate literal meanings that contradicted other literal passages. However, most of the traditional text remained, but even it sparked vigorous debates between the competing parties over what those books actually taught.

Luther claimed everything important for salvation was in the text. For Luther and those influenced by him, nothing important had been added to Scripture since it was adopted during the time of the Roman Empire. Luther claimed everything important for salvation was in the text, *his* text. The Bible was instruction, history, and some prophecies.

The central role played by biblical literalism by conservative Christians today has its roots here. For Protestants, Christianity became a historical religion based on the unfolding of God's plan. The "magic" so central to Catholic worship was rejected. For example, the Eucharist no longer involved partaking of Christ's body and blood, as in the Mass, but was historical remembrance of the last supper, and celebration of its meaning. The sermon replaced the Mass.

The Catholic Church continued to teach that two sources of revelation existed: Scripture and tradition. Importantly, both could be better understood in light of scholarship or possibly mystical experience, with the church having the ultimate authority to judge. According to Catholic position, new revelations were still possible, but had to be in harmony with the church's basic teachings. God was far more active in the world and could teach through it.

In a competitive context, claiming your views were explicitly supported in God's communications with us, whereas your opponents' represented sinful people's efforts to read into them what they wanted to find, was a powerful, mostly Protestant, move. Further, what they imagined to be literal readings came naturally to people inexperienced in studying complex texts written long ago. Alternative interpretations were elitist, or supposedly imported the reader's own bias into the text.

One point of particular tension was the dual claims that the Bible was literally true, and that the physical world was without intrinsic meaning beyond being a demonstration of God's creative power. Physical facts were facts, not allegories, and so could not contradict Scripture. This tension brought natural philosophy, as it was called then, into conflict with the church in ways that would not have been the case over a century earlier.

Before the Reformation, Christianity was little concerned with doctrines that interfered with the doing of the natural sciences. In the mid-1440s, scholars safely considered ideas that about 150 years later led to Giordano Bruno's execution in 1660. After the Reformation, Catholic and Protestant authorities were under pressure to fit everything into their interpretation of the Bible. Such issues had not much bothered the early church fathers, nor medieval theological discussion, because they were interpreted allegorically. However, as the monolith of Catholic Orthodoxy shattered, their nature became matters of partisan debate, and the Catholic Church became more committed to literalism over allegory when it did not contradict their earlier dogmas.

Stephen Toulmin emphasized "... in the attacks on such men as Servetus, Bruno, and Galileo did not involve long-standing matters in medieval theology ... Far from perpetuating 'medieval' intolerance, the condemnation of Galileo, Bruno, or Servetus represented cruelty of a specifically 'modern' kind" (Toulmin, *Cosmopolis*, 144). In earlier, less contentious, times these men would have fared better. Intense theological debates, all claiming validity in identical infallible texts, exposed Scripture's incoherence as an objective document, and its inability to be matched with human experience. Allegorical approaches would have had less difficulty handling scientists' challenges.

As religious conflict grew in Europe, contesting sides used supposedly literal readings to attack allegorical elements in the views of those they opposed. Catholics were hindered here by their previous development of dogmatic theology, especially Aristotle's influence via Aquinas, which the church continued to support, but where possible, they also placed increasing emphasis on literal interpretations (Harrison, *The Bible*, 111–12). The ground work was laid here for the inability of certain kinds of Christians to cope with modern science even as its desacralization of the world facilitated it.

There were no pagans around to point out what Augustine had described as Christians "speaking idiotically."

It has never stopped

Christianity has continued to fragment since those times. While there are many ways to count these different ways of being Christian, a conservative interpretation would list at least seven growing out of the establishment of religious freedom in the West: Catholicism, Eastern Catholicism, Lutheranism, Anglicanism, Calvinism, Anabaptism, and the Restoration Movement. A smaller number exist in the East, with its far more limited experience of religious freedom: the Eastern Orthodox Church, Oriental Orthodoxy, the Assyrian Church of the East, and the Ancient Church of the East. Every other figure I have seen is bigger. For example, this list does not distinguish between Baptists and Southern Baptists, who split based on different biblical interpretations of slavery and today are splitting over the role of women in the church (Meyer, "Congregation"). These are not minor issues. As chapter 1 demonstrated, these divergences have grown so vast that even though all claim to revere the same texts, for all reasonable purposes they worship different and often diametrically opposed deities.

Once a complex text that contradicts itself is taken literally, the subjectivism its advocates try and reject reappears in their different interpretations, all claiming to be the objective truth. Those scholars who took claims to literal inerrancy seriously and have sought to prove it have often become agnostics as a result of their studies. Perhaps the best-known contemporary example is Bart Ehrman, who began disciplined biblical study as a convinced evangelical. However, once he learned the languages the texts had been written in, and read them as objectively as he could, Ehrman entered onto a spiritual path that ultimately led him to agnosticism (Ehrman, "An Interview"). In his view, the internal contradictions and evidence of later textual insertions had become too great to support any reasonable claims of divine authority.

Another method to solve the problem of disagreement as to what the Bible means is to try an end run around it. Christian neo-Orthodoxy arose after WWI in reaction to both liberal and literal branches of Christianity. Its adherents argued the Bible is a *medium* of revelation, in contrast to the more Orthodox claim that it *is* revelation. Consequently, biblical interpretation was subordinate to Jesus' life, death, and resurrection. What mattered was having a life-changing encounter with Jesus. Christ is the revelation of God, and the Bible is a witness to that revelation but not itself revelation.

Truth became experiencing an encounter with Christ rather than being definitively stated in the Bible. As W. W. Bartley observed: "Many doors are opened; one door is closed. Christian identity is defined in terms of commitment to the messenger, not to some interpretation of his message. Claims to knowledge about God are exchanged for faith in Christ" (Bartley, *The Retreat to Commitment*, 39). Today's more liberal Protestant Christian traditions have been powerfully influenced by this view.

Modern fundamentalism has its origins in a rejection of this approach, and return to emphasizing literalism as it understands the word. Scripture possesses divine authority and all of modern science and historical research that conflicts with the doctrine of biblical inerrancy is false. Biblical truth became an act of faith and commitment that insulated the entranced person from any challenge to their understanding.

And so, fragmentation continues. There is no reason to believe it will ever stop, as long as men and women are free.

The stage is set

Using Christianity as my example, I have argued monotheism's dominance in how we think about religion is a result of its usually violent imposition on other traditions through alliance with the state. When the power exists, this imposition is always followed by the suppression of any diversity of interpretations, even in its own name. Over millennia, people's awareness of alternatives withered, so that religious debate generally assumed a monotheistic framework, to be either embraced or rejected, and in that rejection, a rejection of religion. I could have made the same claim with Judaism or Islam.

Once the union of church and state weakened, resulting in a degree of toleration, the spiritual and intellectual glue that gave monotheism a veneer of coherence began to dissolve. The result is today's hundreds, if not thousands, of Christian sects and churches, many with mutually contradictory ideas about the god they worship. Religious freedom leads to this outcome because the entire idea of monotheism is incoherent, as I shall argue in the next chapter.

.

Chapter 3

THE INCOHERENCE
OF MONOTHEISM

*No one has ever seen God, but the one
and only Son, who is himself God.*
—John 1:18

I saw God face to face, and yet my life was spared.
—Genesis 32:30

IN A SENTENCE, MONOTHEISM is the doctrine that there is one all-powerful deity who demands a monopoly on religious worship and has communicated how we should behave through sacred Scriptures. As a distinct personality, with wishes and preferences, God cares that those wishes and preferences are realized. Consequently, this deity can be pleased or displeased, satisfied or impatient, merciful or just, loving or vengeful. If people do not obey these commands, those deemed rebellious will suffer severe punishment. On the other hand, good things are promised to those who obey.

Central to monotheism is the claim that all other alleged deities are false, or even evil. All forms of religion that do not recognize this one deity's teachings and demands are also false or evil, and those who follow them will suffer for doing so. The stakes of getting the true religion right could not be higher.

But as we have seen, under monotheism's apparent unity, an incredible and contradictory variety of views emerges. When we look at the details of the gods they worship, we discover that those calling themselves monotheists worship many mutually exclusive deities. Hidden under the mask of monotheism is an almost explicit polytheism, with each deity claiming to be the only one.

But monotheism shares an uneasy space with an older tradition that also holds there is ultimately one source to all that is: monism.

Monism

As Maijastina Kahlos explains, important early Christians, such as Augustine, were willing to grant the pagans' argument that angels were the same as gods for them *if* the gods were blessed *only* because of their devotion to the one God. Pagans had no problem acknowledging a supreme source existed; their problem was in treating it as a personality desiring to be worshiped alone (Kahlos, "Refuting and Reclaiming," 175). The belief there is one ultimate source from which all reality in some sense emanates is an ancient insight. The classical pagan philosopher Olympiodorus wrote, "The philosophers believe that the principle of all there is is one, and that the

<50></50>
52
</50>

cause which is the first of all causes and supracelestial is one. From it derives everything. But they did not even call it by a name" (Athanassadi and Frede, *Pagan Monotheism*, 11). This insight appears to be the natural outgrowth of early polytheism, as cultures came into ever closer contact, such that some dominated others. Thomas McEvilley writes that this is the common origin of monism and its more violent counterpart, monotheism (McEvilley, *The Shape of Ancient Thought*, 24). This process took two forms. The pantheon that led to monotheism, as in Mesopotamia, imitated a state: their deity was the deity of other gods. By contrast, McEvilley tells us, "the more metaphysically inclined Egyptians were apt to declare that the newly dominant deity had absorbed the other gods into himself or become them" (McEvilley, *The Shape of Ancient Thought*, 25).

While patriarchal cultures, or their modern translators, often used the masculine form to refer to the monistic One, in reality its origins appear to have been from within a feminine context. Greek and Indian philosophers were apparently aware from the Paleolithic, Neolithic, and Bronze Ages to their time, the goddess religions iconography foreshadowed the monistic view of the universe (McEvilley, *The Shape of Ancient Thought*, 58). By contrast, monotheism's dependence on the state as a model of relationship is patriarchal "all the way down."

From a monist perspective, as Celsus, a Roman Platonist, explained, "it makes no difference... whether we call Zeus the Most High or Zeus or Adonai or Sabaoth or Amoun like the Egyptians, or Papaeus like the Scythians." Describing classical Platonism and Neoplatonism, Michael Frede observed: "the vast majority of philosophers in antiquity believed in one god who providentially governs the universe, [and] this is what they were also perceived to believe by the ancients themselves." Aristotle wrote similarly, calling the "unmoved mover" God, and only then describing the existence of other gods (Frede, "Monotheism and Pagan Philosophy," 56). Maximum of Madaura spoke for many when he wrote, "Who is so insane, so deluded, as to deny the utter certainty that there is one highest God... We invoke under many names his powers that are diffused throughout the created world, because, obviously, none of us knows his name: God is the name common to all religions. So it is that while we honour his parts (so to speak) separately, with various supplications, we are clearly worshiping him in his entirety" (Clark, "Augustine's Varro," 190). If we turn to the very different West African traditions that made it into the West when their adherents came as slaves, we find the same insight. Olodumare is the ultimate source of all that is, but in terms of daily life, followers of Santeria and Candomblé, among others, focus on lesser deities concerned with human affairs. Olodumare is not a focus of worship.

This monism apparently was already present even in hunting and gathering cultures. John-Paul, a traditional Ojibwe shaman in Canada, was interviewed regarding his shamanic journeys. He reported three kinds of flight: to inspect the people under his care, to seek advice from the Spirit world about a person or event, and a third, which requires a quote: "The spirit upon arrival meets the Spirit which appears in the form of a brilliant ball of light... Then a harmonizing union of the Spirit and the spiritual essence of the shaman takes place."

The shaman experiences a fulfilled nothingness state; he is not aware of anything—there exists a fulfilled void or holistic emptiness" (Paper, *The Spirits Are Drunk*, 146–7). In most cases, within classical polytheism, Native American shamanism, African Diasporic religions, and the world's other non-monotheistic spiritual traditions, everything existed within or emerged from an all embracing One. The subtle world of Spirit was filled with deities, daemons, and other more-than-human spiritual beings and forces, with many of whom people could interact. Some monotheists call this common view polytheistic because people's attention is on other beings than the One. And I accept this label. But let us remember, for Catholic and Orthodox Christians alike, there are angels and saints who influence life, and who are often requested to aid believers. Even many Protestants have no problem saying angels exist. Given these remarkable similarities, why did Christians, and other monotheists, insist that other religions were not only wrong, but also evil?

As Edward Butler puts it, Hellenistic philosophy was appropriated into Christian thought by "a particularly bold transformation in the relationship between the first principle in Platonic thought...[the One] is treated as identical to the monotheists' god, the 'supreme being.' The... Platonic first principle [is] the *principle of individuation* and not itself an *individual*." This distortion made the One "no longer 'unity,' but a single supreme being" (Butler, "Bhakti and Henadology"). The monist One of classical paganism was not a personality, nor was it monopolistic or jealous. It did not have a divine plan in the pursuit of which the universe was created. Consequently, this One did not interfere in human affairs to pursue this plan. In the views of most polytheists, it did not seek worship, for it was entirely self-sufficient.

The Roman pagan Plutarch described this ultimate source as Isis, who said "I am all that has been, that is, and that shall be." Yahweh on Sinai says "I am who I am." As Pierre Hadot observes, "Isis says she is all that exists whereas Yahweh, by contrast, entrenches himself in his selfhood, or his ego" (Hadot, *The Veil of Isis*, 267). Isis is the world, Yahweh is separate from it. With this move, a single personality was added to what was coherently understood as the ultimate source of *all* personalities.

Monotheism seeks to combine the experience of an ultimate One, probably occurring in some sense in all cultures, with the limiting qualities of an individual personality. Because there is no rational, objective, or agreed-upon faith-based way to determine which combination of personality traits among others is most compatible with universality, monotheism's theological history demonstrates endless attempts to combine the truly universal with what is unavoidably partial. It was a problem thousands of years ago, and it is no less a problem today.

Connected to this problem is that of how mystical experiences were understood. In most cases monotheists distinguished God as radically distinct from the world. Personalities, after all, have boundaries. If God was a distinct personality, it followed that mystical experiences, once regarded as so important, became suspect because they dissolved apparent boundaries. In Western Christianity, the doctrine of Original Sin erected a chasm between human beings and God that only Christ's sacrifice could bridge. The Catholic Church looks on mystical experiences with suspicion because if the gulf between us and God could be bridged, the church's authority as an intermediary would be undermined. Even so, some saints had mystical experiences, but were generally treated with caution as a potential threat to dominant dogma.

Protestants are even more suspicious. The written text is what counts, and nothing else. The Quakers are relatively free of this attitude, but they are also free of the usual Protestant belief that an unbridgeable gulf separates God from humans, necessitating reliance on Scripture alone.

Orthodox Christianity does not recognize Original Sin, and sees God as existing within the world as well as transcendent to it. It follows that Orthodoxy endorses the spiritual value of mystical experiences (Ware, *The Orthodox Way*). While within Orthodoxy some having such experiences can become saints, interpreting such experiences depends on Scripture. However, Paper observed, Orthodoxy's saints "would often be deemed heretics" in Catholicism (Paper, *The Mystic Experience*, 118–23). Islam has been more receptive to this classical insight about the One, particularly among Sufis (Paper, *The Mystic Experience*, 124–9). However, such experiences are threatening to institutional hierarchies and systems of dogmatic authority. When enforcing a Scripture is institutionalized and linked to power, its interpretation will ultimately be subordinated to the needs of the institution to maintain and exercise its power. Much of Islamic history is an excellent example of this distortion. Today Muslim Sufis are major victims of terrorism and murder, especially by the "Islamic State."

The incoherence of monotheism

For monotheists, the Creator is a personality with likes and dislikes, who possesses a plan for the world, and who has standards that human beings must meet to be acceptable in its eyes. In that sense, God is a person, like us, but unlike us, he is perfect and omnipotent. At first glance, this view seems coherent. After all, we are personalities, and God is simply the ultimate personality. But this seeming coherence falls apart when carefully examined.

Early in the church's history, when polytheism remained a viable option for people, Augustine argued that while in pagan cities the laws provided sure means for determining disputes over land or things financial, no such certainty applied to the big questions of life. Pagans could never agree and Christians considered their diversity of views and practices to be a flaw. Christianity, they argued, could provide the same certainty in religious matters as the law already supplied for property and finance (G. Clark, *Monotheism*, 200–1). Muslims make the same argument.

While Augustine did not intend it, his argument opened the door to totalitarianism and endless violence because any particular claim to certainty could never be agreed on by all monotheists. However, any such claim automatically discredited conflicting claims, even those by other monotheists. There was and is no clear way of determining which view is correct solely from monotheistic sources. There is plenty of sincerity on all sides, but with no argument compelling to all.

I will focus here primarily on Christianity, because religious freedom and large numbers of adherents have given Christianity more time to reveal its underlying incoherence than have other monotheisms. *But all brands of monotheism suffer the same problem.* The issue is not who is "right." There is no good reason to believe anyone is "right."

The first problem

In the early years of Christian history, the church could never agree on the nature of Jesus. The New Testament provided no clear guidance and, as reported in Scripture, his statements were often ambiguous. How could a *man* also be the sinless son of God, and still preserve a monotheistic point of view? The interpretations were many, and no scriptural grounds existed to clearly determine which was correct. Some attempts were pretty clearly sophistic. Marius Victorinus wrote "The … pagans, talk of many gods, the Jews or Hebrews of one, but we, as truth and grace have come later, against the pagans talk of one God, against the Jews of the father and Son" (Frede, "Monotheism and Pagan Philosophy," 41). Among the earliest serious attempts to solve this problem was the claim Jesus was the first being created by God. The Christian priest Arius held that when God made the world, he also created his son out of nothing. Consequently, the son preceded anything else in Creation but did not always exist as God had always existed. Knowing what would eventually happen, God created the son to bring salvation to the world. He was ultimately born into a human body to achieve that goal.

Scripture could easily be cited to support this view, as when John wrote "Now this is eternal life: that they may know you, the only true God, and Jesus Christ, whom you have sent" (John 17:3). Thus, Christ was not God, but was superior to all else that God had created. This view, called Arianism, was important in the early church and has never entirely disappeared (Got Questions? "What is Arianism?").

For different reasons, many Unitarians also reject the doctrine of the Trinity, arguing Jesus was a man who never sinned, but he was not God (*Biblicalunitarian*, "Trinitarian or Unitarian"). In this respect they are similar to Islam, which also denies a Trinity while recognizing Jesus as a great prophet.

Mormons, by contrast, argue that the Bible suggests all human beings can acquire a divine nature and be called "gods" (John 10:33, 34; Matt 5:48, Ps. 82:6, Deut. 10:17). This event is called "deification" or "theosis." People could, as Peter put it, "participate in the divine nature" (2 Peter 1:4). They could become one with Jesus just as he is one with his Father. So, there can be many "dimensions" of one god, but only the one god is worshiped.

Jehovah's Witnesses argue that the Bible indicates there can be other gods, but only one "big G" god. The other gods do God's bidding, and are always subordinate to him. However, they and the Mormons will be the first to say they disagree theologically on central questions.

For some Christians, the biblical Jesus Christ existed as two persons sharing one body, his divine and human natures being completely separate. They argued that Christ entered into a very human Jesus, and departed afterwards. This divine departure explained why the dying human Jesus asked why he had been forsaken (Matthew 27:46–7, 15:34–5). The divine part had in fact departed.

Christian Eutychianism by contrast, argued Jesus' humanity was dissolved by his divine nature, "like a drop of honey in the sea." Christ's human nature was absorbed into his divine nature in a way that changed both natures, forming a third nature. This view was a version of monophysitism, the claim that Jesus had only one nature, and it was not human. Some Christians argue that the Coptic church maintains a view similar to this down to the present. Christ has one nature, but that one nature consists of two natures, united in one "without mingling, without confusion, and without alteration" (from the Coptic liturgy) (Got Questions? "What is Monophysitism"). Other Christians argued Jesus had two natures, one human, one divine, united in one being, as in the statement "I and the Father are one" (John 10:30). They argued that both the human and the divine were necessary if the logic of his sacrifice opening the way to salvation for all made any sense. But even here there were divisions. Nestorius emphasized Jesus' human dimension to explain why he could be tempted by Satan. Others emphasized his divinity. Much ink was spilled over whether, as Nestorians put it, Mary was "the Mother of Christ our God and Savior" or, as the Catholics put it, Mary is "the Mother of God" and also "the Mother of Christ." The view that Jesus was both man and God ultimately triumphed in Rome. Had Jesus not been a man, his death could not have been a true substitute for us all; had he not been truly God, his death could not have atoned for our sins. This is the dominant Christian view today. But it became so through politics rather than persuasion, and another side could have won.

The patriarchs of Alexandria and Rome led the Western branch of the church, and viewed Jesus as having two natures in one. The patriarchs of Constantinople and Antioch led the Eastern branch, and were more attracted to Nestorius' teaching emphasizing Jesus' humanity. Due to some nasty politics, as well as the issue's fundamental incoherence, a council called in 431 to straighten the situation out just made matters worse.

Cyril of Alexandria opened the proceedings before any of Nestorius' supporters arrived, would not let Nestorius speak, and quickly condemned and deposed him. When John of Antioch arrived, angered by what had transpired, he called another council and deposed Cyril. Then the Emperor, Theodosius III, imprisoned Cyril, Nestorius, and John. Ultimately Cyril convinced Theodosius to bring together a council in 451, where his position won imperial favor.

Nestorius was forced to leave Constantinople but continued to actively promote his views. In time his followers became the dominant Christian group in Persia, from where their missionaries spread their message to central Asia, India, and China. Today Nestorian churches still exist in Iraq, Iran, India, and in the United States. After centuries of antagonism, in 1994 the Nestorian church—today known as the Assyrian Church of the East—and the Catholic Church jointly declared that the truth of Christ's mission was continued in both of their traditions. It took them only fifteen hundred years to recognize that this was the case.

Like many "heretical" Christians, other monotheistic faiths have found this solution about Jesus' nature unconvincing. Needless to say, Jews and Muslims are no more satisfied with Christian attempts to justify a Trinity than they are with Christian attempts to make sense of Jesus as in some way more than human, and perhaps even God himself. By making a prophet divine, they argue that Christianity has abandoned monotheism. There is no need for us to go there because we have seen that even the first step along that path—integrating Jesus' humanity and divinity—had no persuasive answer without the outside force of Roman arms. Instead, I want to criticize the idea of monotheism in *all* its forms.

Personality: limiting the unlimited

God's supposed personality is most clearly expressed in the Old Testament, which all Abrahamic traditions accept as divinely authoritative. He can be pleased, patient, annoyed, angered, and jealous. He even regrets or repents earlier acts (depending on the translation), as in Genesis 6:6–7 and 1 Samuel 15:11. Oddly for an omniscient being, God is even described as anticipating his regretting future acts. Exodus 32:12–14 is an example, and it is not alone.

This view is encountered less explicitly in Islam, but it still exists. In the Koran, God is all merciful, but also gets angry, and can be happy, but his anger and happiness are supposedly not human attributes. Yet supposedly God becomes angry if he is not worshiped by those who should be his followers, and will send them to hell, a very human attitude (*Islamweb*, "Allah gets angry"). And most Muslims generally regard the other Abrahamic faiths as also serving God, if not so well.

God is supposed to be perfect. When he is pleased, he is perfectly pleased. When he is jealous, he is perfectly jealous. The list of perfectly expressed traits possessed imperfectly by every other personality goes on and on. God is a perfect personality. I suppose he is also perfectly regretful.

A response could be that when God is pleased, he is perfectly pleased; when he is jealous, he is perfectly jealous, but need not be both at the same time. But this just moves words around. Monotheists have never agreed as to what constitutes perfect jealousy or being perfectly pleased, as distinct from imperfect kinds of both. And if the most basic terms are unclear, so is the argument.

Any personality is partial and *any* personality trait exists on a continuum of more or less with no agreement as to what is perfect. When I am patient, I am not ready to subject wrongdoers to vengeance. When I resort to vengeance, my patience has ended. I cannot be both simultaneously, as when I say "You have exhausted my patience." Consequently, every personality is limited in the traits it expresses at any particular time. When I am annoyed, I am not filled with equanimity. When I enjoy equanimity, I am not annoyed. If I am jealous, I am not simultaneously happy. If I seek vengeance on the children of those who displeased me, I am not simultaneously just or loving. When I demand complete obedience, I do not value others' freedom except if they subordinate it to my will. In such a case I do not value freedom, I value subordination, "freely given" (when threatened by eternal punishment). This describes the "freedom" enjoyed by a hold-up victim handing over his wallet at gunpoint. He is free not to hand over the wallet if he is willing to pay the price.

Saying whatever version of God is perfect in these qualities is only reasonable if it is clear what is perfectly merciful and perfectly just, and so on. But the fact is there is no agreement among monotheists here.

Some monotheists claim that these traits for God are unlike their human equivalents, but this does violence to language. If God's mercy is so different from ours that an "all-merciful" deity can send someone to hell for eternity, it is sloppy to use the same word. Certainly, no human would be regarded as merciful who came anywhere close to such an act. The same is true for other terms describing a personality. And as we have seen, monotheistic universalists regard sending people to hell for eternity as an imperfection unworthy of their deity.

Personality traits only carry meaning in the context of other personalities, distinct from them. How, for example, can anything be jealous without there being at least one other entity to provoke it? And if someone is jealous, we often know other people who, in similar contexts, will not be jealous. From the standpoint of a limited personality, in some situations, jealousy can be appropriate, and in others, inappropriate. But different personalities will draw that line in different places.

And in what way is it evidence of perfection, or even sanity, for me to be jealous of nonexistent beings that others honor? It is difficult to seek a human comparison, but perhaps this will do: Imagine if I discovered that my goldfish somehow decided that the pump that supplied their tank with air bubbles was their creator. Would I be jealous? Only if I were pathologically insecure. And yet, many monotheists insist their god is jealous of nonexistent gods.

Any given person's personality is identifiable only because other people have at least to some degree different personalities. I think it is impossible to imagine what constitutes a "perfect personality," especially one that can be jealous and vengeful. That is why monotheists never agree. One could of course say "God is a being who always reacts perfectly." But this argument says nothing about perfection's qualities other than that omnipotence determines what is perfect. How do we recognize perfection from imperfection among competing interpretations, because monotheists endlessly argue over that issue?

This ideal personality always has some desires when he could theoretically have other desires. He makes plans when he could have made other plans. He even admits he made mistakes for which he has regrets. But, as chapter 1 demonstrated, monotheists who claim their god has a personality describe gods with different personalities. How can anyone determine which of these competing personalities is perfect compared to the others? The claim of an ultimate divine personality is incoherent, and its incoherence has led to the deaths of millions over disagreements as to its character. For monotheists to argue that my criticism is wrong, why have they continued to fight and even kill one another over this issue?

One Christian theologian took exception to an earlier, less developed, criticism of mine concerning God's supposed personality. In *Connecting Christ*, Paul Louis Metzger wrote, "God is supremely personal, not other than personal … For the universe to be a Thou … there must be an I in creation, and an I-and-Thou implicit in relationality." Metzger argues the I-Thou implicit in the Trinity is the core reality which makes I-Thou relations possible between people as well as between people and God (Metzger, *Connecting Christ*, 167). This interesting argument fails in ways important to my later argument for polytheism. First, it claims personality is necessary to relate to a personality. But consider the purest love we have for another. Of course, the word "love" covers a wide range of states of mind, from lust to chocolate to romance to our favorite activities, as well as love's deepest meaning of valuing and cherishing a person's inner beauty. In human terms anyway, what they have in common is a focus on the moment, and to satisfy us so we are not otherwise distracted.

From chocolate to devotion, what these states share in common reaches its most complete expression in love embracing the other entirely for his or her own sake. We focus on the value we see and experience in the other, and forget ourselves. It is perhaps the most fulfilling fully human experience.

Our personality is irrelevant when loving in this most fulfilling way. *It is the other's personality that matters.* What we love about the other is not their relationship with ourselves (much as we might also value that). We love them for who they are. More than a few descriptions of God as love capture this dimension of reality. The apostle John famously writes "Anyone who does not love does not know God, because God is love" (1 John 4:8). Many mystics from a variety of traditions describe their encounter with what is Ultimate as experiencing unconditional love, care, and compassion. In a way I will develop further later, all-embracing love does not require a personality or any other distinction on the giving end, only on the receiving one.

The second problem with Metzger's argument is that he is forced to speak of the Trinity as an I-Thou relation, but such a relation implies division. When I, a human, love a Thou in relationship, I do not lose track of my I being separate from a Thou. I forget myself but do not confuse myself with the beloved. I am filled with love for the other. By loving another, I am the fulfilled one. Metzger has gone beyond monotheism and unintentionally given an argument I will use later with respect to polytheism, and its relation to a loving Ultimate that is not a personality.

But this argument must wait.

Gender

God is almost always characterized as masculine. But is masculinity more perfect than femininity? If God is perfect and masculine, that is what is being implied. But what does that even *mean* since, according to Scripture, except for Adam, all men come only from women? Even Christ. The Creation was not "very good" nor God "very pleased" until both genders were created.

In addition, "male" makes sense only when we can also think of "female." An amoeba is sexless, and reproduces from division. It is neither "male" nor "female." An organism either is self-contained, like an amoeba, or in almost every other case its sex implies the existence of at least one other sex. Some organisms have more than two: some crustaceans have three sexes and paramecia from four to eight (Sonneborn, "Paramecium"). Among other organisms, including some fish and amphibians, an individual will switch to the missing sex if only one is present. Sex is fluid in the world God created, but is almost universally multiple. When only one sex exists, as in some lizards, it is female, reproducing without need of males, although both sexes were initially needed for that evolutionary step to take place. Why, then, is God usually considered only male?

The problem of a monotheistic god's sex does not go away if we argue that "male" refers only to those psychological characteristics that we associate with maleness, rather than to those we associate with femaleness. We are back to the problem we encountered with personality, because one set of characteristics implies the existence of complementary characteristics, and so *is not sufficient in itself*, and in isolation is imperfect. Alternatively, it creates a necessary duality in which only one side of two traits is "perfect" with the "perfect" male characteristics implying the equally necessary existence of other "imperfect" female characteristics. Most of us can easily see that such a being is neither perfect nor omnipotent.

According to the Bible. the original creation was both perfect and of two sexes. How can a perfect and complete being who lacks the feminine trait of mothering depend on imperfect others with that trait for his perfect creation to exist? Is "mothering" a sign of imperfection such that a perfect being does not ever "mother"? If this is so, God's creation was initially and necessarily imperfect and depends on continued imperfections for it to exist at all.

What then are we to make of God's perfection if he cannot create unless he deliberately creates imperfect beings to sustain it, or alternatively, if there are perfect qualities that God does not have? How can a being who does not possess some perfect attributes claim to be both omnipotent and perfect?

Such fundamentally incoherent thinking may explain why there is considerable feminine imagery of God in the Bible without most Christians even noticing it exists (Mollenkott, *The Divine Feminine*). Without feminine attributes, the idea of monotheism becomes still more muddled, but paying attention to them creates problems for most Christians, and other monotheists, who worship what they consider fully male deities.

But if both traits are necessary, as some modern Christians increasingly recognize, what is the balance between them? What does it mean to say one perfect trait is superior to another perfect trait when each implies the other? How can we settle different points of view here?

There is another problem with considering monotheism as both male and female. Within the monotheistic world, this insight is new, responding to the rise of religious feminism (Borg, *The God We Never Knew*, 69). If it is true, millennia of monotheistic worshipers, men and women alike, have failed to appreciate a *fundamental* dimension of their god. For thousands of years they have been wrong. And their god never set them straight about the matter.

Alternatively, how a monotheistic deity is conceived reflects the social conditions surrounding its devotees. I have no problem with this interpretation, but monotheists should.

Love and power

A particularly intractable problem is rooted in the idea that God is both perfectly good and omnipotent. The problem is easily stated: goodness and omnipotence cannot both be *ultimate* traits of God, because each limits the other. One must come first. Probably the best-known example of the view that God is good are John's words, "God is love" (1 John 4:8). If God is always good, and so cannot do evil, his omnipotence is *limited* by his goodness. If he did something to hurt another, he would not be a god of love, and so he cannot do it. But then, God is not really omnipotent because goodness is more fundamental to God's nature than power. He can do anything compatible with perfect goodness, but not do what is not good. Omnipotence is subordinated to and limited by goodness.

On the other hand, there are also many biblical verses suggesting God is omnipotent, and *nothing* limits him. To refer again to John, "Through him all things were made; without him nothing was made that has been made" (John 1:3, see also Isaiah 44:24, Colossians 1:7, Nehemiah 9:6, Jeremiah 32:27, Hebrews 1:3, Job 42:2). But, if God's primary characteristic is omnipotence, then *by definition*, "good" is whatever God does, *because he does it.*

Power is the ultimate criterion for goodness. No ultimate standard exists to determine the meaning of terms like love, mercy, justice, and evil, other than God's will backed by infinite power. None of these moral terms have any intrinsic meaning. If an omnipotent God destroys the world, and says he did so because of his love, that ends the debate. Power is fundamental, and everything else is subject to it, including what words like love mean to the rest of us.

This issue has long been a topic of Christian theological discussion (*Stanford Encyclopedia of Philosophy*, "Perfect Goodness"). Arguing against Thomas Aquinas' view that God did what was good because God was good, the medieval scholastic Duns Scotus claimed that because God was completely free and omnipotent, he could not be limited by reason or by human conceptions of what was good. Therefore, God's *will* was the distinguishing mark of his divinity rather than any sense of divine reason. God was not good because he did good things judged independently of God; anything God did was good because it was God who did it. Reasons and love as we understand the word were unacceptable limitations, if God's power is total (Latourette, *A History of Christianity*, 515–17).

The rise of mechanism in early science both reflected and reinforced the idea that God was omnipotent. Mechanists argued, as Carolyn Merchant put it, "that *things* rather than relations are the ultimate reality, relations being externally imposed by God in the form of natural laws" (Merchant, *The Death of Nature*, 282). And God could impose them any way he wished. Descartes wrote that even mathematical truths were established by God so to say they are independent of him "is to speak of him as a Jupiter or a Saturn, and to subject him to the Styx and the Fates" (Hadot, *The Veil of Isis*, 133). Because God was omnipotent, Descartes argued, we could never hope to discover truth. All we could do is discover reliable ways to reproduce an effect, but what *really* causes that effect is only for God to know.

This view is subtly different from science as we think of it today. To be sure, science as a system at any time gives us the most reliable knowledge we have access to, knowledge that might later be replaced by more reliable knowledge. But individual scientists are motivated to get as close to truth as they can, a motivation that is pointless if God is omnipotent.

This tension exists in all monotheistic religions.

For example, Ma'taz-zilite Muslims predominated when Islamic civilization was culturally and scientifically the leader of the world. They argued that the Koran commanded men to seek knowledge and read the natural world for signs of the Creator, very much as early Western Christian scientists would interpret Scripture during the Enlightenment. Far more than medieval Europe at the time, the Muslim world had integrated its way of life with Greek philosophy and thought, and leading thinkers argued the Koran must be interpreted through reason. This meant the world could also potentially be understood through reason.

In time they were swept aside by a rival school of monotheists, the Ash'ari Muslims, who considered the Koran as coeval with God. Reason and philosophy were suspect, and because God's will was completely free, causality was an illusion. Things happened only because God willed them, and God's will was entirely free. The world consisted of discrete events whose only unity was the will of God.

Scientific laws do not exist in this view because such laws limit God. Order arises from the will of God, and should he ever will differently, those apparent laws will vanish as quickly as drops of water hitting a hot pan. Fire burns not because of any causal relationship between rapid oxidation releasing energy from chemical bonds, nor do rocks fall because of the power of gravity on their mass and the mass of the earth, but because in both cases God wills it, and should he decide differently, fire could freeze us and released rocks rise in the air. As one Muslim philosopher argued at the time, "Were it God's will, we would even have to practice idolatry" (Ofek, "Why the Arabic World turned away from Science," 10). Asking "why" of such a God was obviously a waste of time. It was all a matter of divine will. As this point of view triumphed, science in the Islamic world withered and rigid dogma replaced reason. People were not to think, but to obey.

Today, to a greater or lesser degree, this general perspective dominates the Sunnis, Islam's most numerous group. For example, Pakistan's Institute for Policy Studies recommends that physical effects not be related to causes. According to Pakistani physicist Pervez Hoodbhoy, "You were supposed to say that when you bring hydrogen and oxygen together then by the will of Allah water was created" (Overby, "How Islam Won"). Islamic leaders influenced by the Ash'ari view attribute natural disasters to God's vengeance, not to natural causes. Such a culture can never develop scientific knowledge very far. Today, Hoodbhoy says, Muslims make up 1 percent of the world's scientists, far smaller than their share of 20 percent of its population.

A similar split occurred in Judaism. Maimonides incorporated Greek respect for reasoned thought into Judaism, criticizing the view that natural things that seem to be permanent are simply matters of habit. His approach was violently opposed by Ashkenazi Jewish literalists who viewed reason as a limitation on omnipotent power (Shasha, "Rational Judaism"). In a Christian version of the Ash'ari and Ashkenazi, many Christian fundamentalists exhibit the same outlook, rejecting science whether it be of global warming or the behavior of hurricanes. God controls the climate and the science of global warming is a mirage. He targets hurricanes due to his anger. For some, the evidence of the earth's age is utterly misleading, as is evolution. God determines everything and scientific knowledge is a mirage.

If Christian fundamentalists do not go so far as Sunni ideologues (who are actually more consistent here), it is because the discoveries made possible by science provide them with power. So long as science avoids ever addressing anything they feel was described in Scripture, they are OK with it, just as they are usually OK today with immoral actions if the result is power, as we saw in chapter 1.

What is good is subordinated to, and defined by, power, a view going against every normal human being's understanding of what "good" means. Pierre Hadot refers to Leibniz's argument against the doctrine of divine omnipotence, that will without guidance by reason is the same as pure chance (Hadot, *The Veil of Isis*, 135). In terms of traditional morality, this is nihilism.

Terms like "good," "mercy," and "just" are often used to *criticize* the abuse of power by an external standard. The Bible has many passages with this message, as does the Koran. Power is abused not because it is limited but because it violates what is good and just. In evaluating the worth of these terms, power is subordinated to them. Even the most hard headed of political commentators, Machiavelli, said that while a ruler need not be good, he must at least appear to be so (Machiavelli, *The Prince*, chapter 18). Despite this long record of debate among theologians, these issues have never been resolved to people's satisfaction. Different people prefer different solutions. The difficulty here does not arise from ambiguous texts, it is inherent in the idea of there being one omnipotent *and* perfectly good God. Either what is good is defined by power, which is nihilism, or power is limited by what is good, and so true omnipotence does not exist.

The challenge of proving God exists

Christian theologians have long attempted to prove God exists. Over many centuries many of the best minds in Christian thought have devoted enormous intellect and passion to this task, and yet, today the question remains very much alive. For someone such as myself, who comes at this question from a polytheistic perspective involving direct encounters with deities, the strangest dimension of this question is that it exists at all.

Worldwide, and for as long as we have written records, polytheistic religions not only take it for granted that the gods exist, but also that many people within them have powerful personal encounters with those deities. Socrates, from whom Western philosophy is usually said to derive, is one example. In the *Phaedrus* he is sitting outside the walls of Athens when a Nymph, a minor deity or tree spirit, inspires him to make a speech about love. He breaks off contact with her when he is afraid the inspiration will become so strong it might possess him. He asks his friend, Phaedrus, "Do you not perceive that I am already overtaken by the Nymphs to whom you have mischievously exposed me?"

Most interestingly, *no one present is surprised*. Athenians were used to at least some people going into trance and having spirits speak through them. Equally importantly, a wiser entity instructs Socrates to correct the errors in his Nymph-inspired speech. Socrates then says:

> There is also a madness which is a divine gift, and the source of the chiefest blessings granted to men. For prophecy is a madness, and the prophetess at Delphi and the priestesses at Dodona when out of their senses have conferred great benefits on Hellas, both in public and private life, but when in their senses few or none. And I might also tell you how the

Sibl and other inspired persons have given to many an inti-
mation of the future which has saved them from falling. *But
it would be tedious to speak of what everyone knows* (Plato,
"Phaedrus").

Around seven hundred years later Plotinus, perhaps the most important
single philosopher of late classical civilization, referred to divine possession
as something quite widely experienced within Roman society (Spanu, "The
Magic of Plotinus' Gnostic Disciples"). Iamblichus, one of the last classical
Platonists before pagans were suppressed by Christian Rome, wrote "There
are many kinds of divine possession, and divine inspiration is awakened
in several ways" (G. Shaw, *Theurgy and the Soul*, 89). This phenomenon is
nearly universal among polytheistic religions, which is why there is so little
interest among them in proving the gods exist.

Classical thinkers often speculated about the nature of the gods, but rarely
about their existence. There were atheists in classical antiquity, but given the
reports of people like Socrates, Plotinus, and Iamblichus, these must have
been people to whom such experiences did not happen. We can sympa-
thize with their skepticism while still noting that the question apparently did
not much interest those to whom it did happen. It was a taken-for-granted
dimension of commonly encountered experiences.

John Michael Greer observed that most attempted proofs that God exists
are also compatible with there being many gods, and so, following his example, I will not examine them (Greer, *A World Full of Gods*, 44). However, one,
the ontological argument, is an explicit argument for monotheism. It was
first made by the eleventh-century Catholic theologian Anselm (1033–1109),
who argued that God is the greatest thing that can be conceived, and argued
that this being must exist, even in the mind of the person who denies God's
existence. "Greater" is anything it is better to be than not be, and "greatest" is
the best possible form of "greater."

If the greatest possible being exists in the mind, it must also exist in reality, because if it only exists in the mind, an even greater being must be possible—one which exists both in the mind and in reality. If something perfect is
imagined, it is even more perfect for it to actually exist. Therefore, on logical

grounds it is impossible to imagine the greatest conceivable being without that being actually existing. Anselm's argument has been repeated or slightly modified by many major thinkers since, while other major thinkers have found it fatally flawed.

Clearly an in-depth discussion of this attempt at a proof is beyond the scope of this volume. On the other hand, I think it is not necessary. All the definitions of "greatest possible" or "supremely perfect" leave the content of that quality unstated. This opens it up to three different objections which seem to me fatal. *And* a way in which it might be correct, but at the cost of refuting monotheism.

At the time Anselm wrote, the perfect was considered unchanging, because change supposedly implied that what preceded it was not perfect. Yet the Bible itself indicates otherwise. God supposedly created a world of finite beings subject to constant change. If perfection cannot be added to, he created an imperfect world. How could a perfect being create an imperfect world? So, the monotheism supposedly demonstrated by Anselm did not fit his own conception of God.

Then there is the problem of *what counts as perfection*? That Anselm viewed perfection as unchanging and Hartshorne viewed it as creative suggests that, like so many other issues in monotheistic theology, this word conceals more than it illuminates. Greer probes still more deeply, arguing Anselm's account of perfection disagrees with that of a medieval Hindu saint or a Theravadan Buddhist of the same time (Greer, *A World Full of Gods*, 41). The notion of one god is incompatible with coherent ideas of "perfection" because there is no general agreement about what is perfect.

Finally, the ontological argument assumes God is omnipotent, omniscient, and morally perfect. But if God is omnipotent, then he should be able to create a being with free will; if he is omniscient, then he should know exactly what such a being will do, which denies any strong concept of free will. The same holds for omnipotence and moral perfection, as I explained previously. This ontological argument becomes incoherent because the concept of monotheism itself is incoherent. Therefore, such a being could not exist any more than could a round square.

Charles Hartshorne, who is sympathetic to Anselm's project, if not his exact conclusion, argued if, in creating the world, God increased perfection, then his previous perfection was not infinite. The issue is the nature of change. Hartshorne's answer to this problem is that change is not destruction of the perfect but creation of novelty (Hartshorne, *Omnipotence*, 8). *Change* becomes a necessary part of perfection. Think of a beautiful sunset, the beauty of waves rolling into a rocky coast, or the Wheel of the Year.

Change is always of actual particulars, whereas any all-inclusive definition of perfection is necessarily abstract. Therefore, using Anselm's logic, concrete changes are necessary aspects of divine perfection. But change is always a change in concrete relationships, either of the existing relationship or of gaining a new one or leaving behind an old one. And God would manifest perfection in perfect relationships of male and female, and in any number of other perfect relationships.

We now return to Paul Metzger's discussion of I-Thou relationships (Metzger, *Connecting Christ*, 167). If such relationships, characterized by love, care, and appreciation of a Thou, are part of a perfect world, then it would appear the more such relationships exist, the more perfect it becomes. This observation holds not just among people, but for all beings capable of such relationships. From this perspective, there might be a nonpersonal monist source of everything, but no reason to believe a single god-as-personality exists.

John Michael Greer argues, insightfully, that monotheisms have been drawn to eschatology, the view that God will eventually overthrow and destroy this fallen world and its sinful inhabitants, in order to account for the obvious imperfections and injustices we see around us. Jews, and especially Christians, and Muslims all share this view. Once this divine event happens, a new world will be created, one that is perfect, and within which people will live lives of eternal blessedness. As Greer observes, the need for a cosmic setting of things right "points up the awkward fact that the world we actually experience is one in which classical monotheism is not obviously justified— indeed where its claims don't actually make much sense" (Greer, *A World Full of Gods*, 185). Finally, if Anselm's argument is accurate, it is a description of the One, the ultimate source of all things. This One is not a personality, and is not the monotheistic god. Interestingly, it has also long been and continues to be actually experienced by people, who subsequently become very disinterested in questions like "does God exist?"

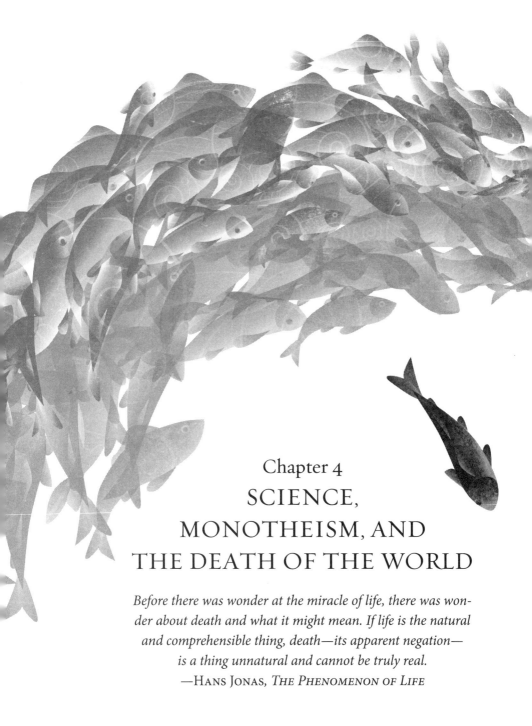

Chapter 4
SCIENCE, MONOTHEISM, AND THE DEATH OF THE WORLD

Before there was wonder at the miracle of life, there was wonder about death and what it might mean. If life is the natural and comprehensible thing, death—its apparent negation— is a thing unnatural and cannot be truly real.
—HANS JONAS, THE PHENOMENON OF LIFE

FROM PRE-CHRISTIAN TIMES, UP through the Middle Ages, the world was widely experienced as alive. Life permeated everywhere, and the great mystery was death. This outlook had prevailed in an unbroken chain extending to a time probably predating the existence of our own species. More than four thousand years ago, humanity's earliest surviving literature, *Epic of Gilgamesh*, is concerned with it.

In this respect, the major difference between pre-Christian times and the Christian era that followed was, for Christianity, God created the world and continued controlling it. With the coming of monotheistic domination, the world was subordinated to God's absolute control, but the world itself remained alive, and able to teach divine lessons of its own. Nature was considered permeated by life, and even depicted as a goddess, although one subservient to God (Merchant, *The Death of Nature*, 1–42). The mystery of death lay in punishment for human disobedience to his commands.

The Renaissance strengthened this ancient view, through the growing influence of the pagan heritage of Hermeticism, Gnosticism, Neoplatonism, Aristotelianism, and Stoicism. As Pierre Hadot put it, the old pagan gods became "names or metaphors of the incorporeal forces animating the universe," resulting in "a paganism that could cohabit fairly well with Christianity" (Hadot, *The Veil of Isis*, 79). This "pagan" view was compatible with the church fathers' long use of a Christianized Neoplatonism to understand the world.

However, it was also during the Renaissance that the view of the world as a lifeless mechanical place grew stronger, eventually displacing this ancient animism. In such a world, life became the mystery and its absence the normal condition of things. Science is often blamed (or credited) with animism's demise, but the story is more interesting than this. Science played and continues to play a more complex and ambiguous role. The "death of the world" had several intertwining causes.

In the next part of this chapter I will cover this transition from an animistic to a mechanical view of the world. First, the death of allegory in much

Christian thought, particularly Protestantism, severed the natural world from providing insight on Scripture. In addition, printing made modern science possible by enabling early scientists to easily communicate, sharing their discoveries and theories. At the same time, while major church institutions supported the desacralization of the world, they also channeled early science in directions that would not contradict Scripture. They unintentionally linked their theology with early understandings of the physical world, guaranteeing science's future discoveries would abolish rational cases for Christianity. Within this larger context, early scientists gradually fused the medieval traditions of natural philosophy and magic, thereby elevating the status of experiments and other empirical investigations. This fusion supported arguments the world was best understood mechanically, even though Newton's theory of gravity could not be understood mechanically.

The death of allegory

Chapter 2 described in part how the Protestant Reformation led to the death of allegory as an important tool in explaining the ways of God. As allegory's role in Christianity shrank, Protestants in particular emphasized what they regarded as Scripture's literal meanings, buttressed by claims of divinely supported inerrancy. The Bible became a book of sacred history and Christianity a historical religion, and Scripture a record of sacred facts (Harrison, "The Bible and the Emergence of Modern Science," 124). Biblical literalism transformed not only how people thought about Christianity, it also transformed how the physical world was conceived. The physical world went from being a place filled with sacred meanings illuminating Christian theology to a mechanical system designed by a divine engineer (Harrison, "The Bible"). Augustine's "Book of Nature" could no longer illuminate Scripture, for it contained no teachings beyond demonstrating God's power and ability to design the world. Contemplating this world led to no more spiritual insight than contemplating a clock. The world became the stage on which a divine drama of salvation unfolded, strengthening what appeared to be its mechanistic elements at the expense of its living ones.

This theologically shaped perspective strengthened the case for what became the modern scientific view of the world. Especially in the Protestant world, knowledge of the nature was increasingly freed from subordination to theology. People were freer to explore this world, seeking its laws, so long as they avoided theological concerns.

Printing and science

As I explained in chapter 2, printing made the Reformation possible. But printing did much more than this. It also made it possible for early scientists to create the networks of communication that ultimately grew into modern science.

Around 1439 Johannes Gutenberg invented the printing press in Mainz, Germany. By 1481, the tiny Netherlands already had presses in twenty-one cities and towns, and Italy and Germany each had them in at least forty. Growth continued exponentially. Within another twenty years, one thousand printing presses throughout Western Europe had produced eight million books (Eisenstein, *The Printing Revolution*, 13–17). By 1550 there were at least three hundred printers and booksellers in Geneva alone (Eisenstein, *The Printing Press*, 410). Printing was at least as transformative of medieval society as the advent of the internet has been for ours, and for similar reasons: it transformed and simplified communication. Printing rapidly expanded the potential audience for new ideas, which could now rapidly spread far beyond personal connections. The Reformation was one result and the rise of modern science another.

Individuals fascinated with the challenge of discovering more about the world's underlying principles have always been among us. They have also always been a minority, and therefore largely isolated from one another. Brilliant ancients had discovered the Pythagorean theorem; that solstices and equinoxes were natural events caused by the earth's relation to the sun and moon; the distance of the moon from the earth; that the earth was round; and had even gotten within about forty miles from current calculations as to its circumference, and much more. But they lacked easy communications with like-minded people.

Nor did many of the most insightful think they were coming to the end of what could be discovered (Edelstein, *The Idea of Progress*). Pierre Hadot quotes the Roman Seneca as saying, "Many things that are completely unknown to us will be known only to the coming generation. Many discoveries are reserved for future centuries, when all memories of us will be extinguished" (Hadot, *The Veil of Isis*, 169). Pliny the Elder observed, "There will come a time when our ignorance of such obvious facts will amaze posterity" (Hadot, *The Veil of Isis*, 173). But the geniuses of those times worked alone, or within small face-to-face communities. Possibilities for the sustained growth of specialized fields of knowledge could not be supported with the limited numbers found in such communities, no matter how brilliant the individuals involved. The *scientific mentality* has always been with us, but *science as a system* for enlarging human knowledge is new, and its roots are in the printing press.

With communicating discoveries made easier by printing, early scientists could more easily inspire and benefit from one another's work. People across Europe could be working on common issues. For example, the discovery of oxygen was made almost simultaneously by three scientists: a Swede, Carl Wilhelm Scheele; an Englishman, Joseph Priestley; and a Frenchman, Antoine Laurent Lavoisier. Scheele was first to recognize the substance, but, using a different method, Priestley published first, and so is usually credited with the discovery. Lavoisier performed the experiments that proved what these men had discovered was in fact an element, and in doing so rebutted an important competing theory that burning was caused by phlogiston.

Until oxygen's discovery, air had always been regarded as a basic indestructible substance, one of the four elements. Now it was known to be made up of multiple substances, which opened the door to investigating what these might be. Based on this discovery, many more scientists were inspired to search, and in short order more elements were discovered. Chemistry began moving from alchemy to science as we understand it.

However, the actual gas had been discovered about one hundred years earlier, by a Polish alchemist, Michael Sendivogius (1566–1636). In 1621, a Dutch engineer, Cornelis Jacobszoon Drebbel (1572–1633), had even used it to sustain life in a submarine (Poole, White, and Whipp, "The Discovery of Oxygen"). But networks of interconnected scientists did not then exist and so these events remain intriguing historical facts rather than building blocks contributing to the growth of knowledge.

Leonardo da Vinci was arguably the most brilliant thinker of the Renaissance, and perhaps in history. Along with his brilliant art, he was an engineer and an inventor, and he made original discoveries in anatomy, geology, optics, hydrodynamics, and more. But da Vinci's role in the rise of science is small. While many of his discoveries could have been world-transforming had they been more widely known, da Vinci described them in a secret script, and never published. When others made these discoveries later, they got (and deserved) the credit for doing so. Only later was his script able to be read (Capra, *The Science of Leonardo*).

Science and the transformations it brought into the world depended on the printing press, and the networks of communication it enabled. But there is more to consider. Christianity's role was more complex than simply turning the world from a place permeated by life to a divine stage set.

Christianity's contradictory influence

The shift in viewing the world from organic to mechanistic did not automatically open the door to science. While seventeenth-century scientists were often encouraged in their research by their Christian faith, they were not encouraged by the ecclesiastical authorities (Hadot, *The Veil of Isis*, 131). The Reformation had strengthened claims of biblical literalism on all sides, and, as Galileo's fate demonstrated, the Bible contained much that, when taken literally, contradicted what people were discovering about the world. This led to conflicts between religion and science that had not characterized the medieval world. The distinction between the living human world and an external world of inert matter given its energy by God removed the material world from theological interest, at least so long as what was discovered did not contradict Scripture (Toulmin, Cosmopolis, 89–137). But when read literally, Scripture was filled with inaccurate accounts of natural phenomena.

Allegory and admitting not everything in Scripture could be understood literally had long provided a means for avoiding clashes between Scripture and what seemed true of the world. Further, arguments contradicting Scripture could be put in hypothetical terms, rather than as claims of fact. As Copernicus wrote regarding his hypothesis of a heliocentric universe with the earth orbiting the sun, "*if* the earth were in motion *then* the observed phenomenon would result" (Leveillee, "Copernicus, Galileo and the Church," Finnochiaro, 16). But he refrained from saying it actually did. Copernicus described his theory as a useful tool enabling astronomers to correct mathematical errors that they discovered in their observations. Copernicus and many early scientists could argue math and mechanics were merely tools for finding the patterns an omnipotent creator had created as he willed. They said nothing about how he had actually done so (Hadot, *The Veil of Isis*, 133–4).

However, as religious disputes led to an increased emphasis on biblical literalism, *anything* undermining its claim to truth *anywhere* potentially undermined Christianity as a whole. Churches are more than places of worship. They are also controlled by ecclesiastical institutions, and these institutions, Catholic and Protestant alike, were now fighting for their existence. What was at stake here were not only interpretations about the world, but the institutions claiming authority in determining which interpretations were correct.

Protestant and Counter-Reformation theologians alike suppressed a relative freedom of inquiry that had characterized medieval Christianity (Toulmin, *Cosmopolis*, 77).

Galileo's arguments contradicted Catholic institutional interests at a time when the church was on the defensive, and worse, Galileo claimed he had discovered a truth and not just a useful tool. But Galileo's claims were not just a Catholic problem. Martin Luther rejected any argument that the earth moved, saying "I believe the Holy Scriptures, for Joshua commanded the sun to stand still, and not the earth" (Luther, *Table Talk*). John Calvin went farther, preaching some "are so deranged ... *that they will say that the sun does not move, and that it is the earth which shifts and turns*. When we see such minds we must indeed confess that the devil posses them ..." (Calvin, "Sermon"). The problem was not so much a particular church as the increasing dependence of all competing churches on biblical literalism.

Desacralizing the world not only encouraged what became scientific ways of thinking, it also increased the future tensions between religion and science because allegorical interpretations could not be applied to heal tensions when science contradicted Scripture. Toulmin explained the issues provoking religious attacks on men like Galileo and Bruno "all turned on the novel assumptions about the order of nature that made up the scaffolding of the modern world picture" (Toulmin, *Cosmopolis*, 144).

These early scientists found that mechanistic interpretations of natural phenomena, such as Galileo argued for the earth and the planets, were both immensely promising and very dangerous when they contradicted Scripture. They had to tread carefully.

Natural philosophers and magic

In a sense, modern science had two "parents": natural philosophy and magic. "Natural philosophy" is sometimes thought of as the platform from which science arose. The story is more paradoxical. Natural philosophy had a long history in medieval Europe, and had become respected as one of two ways of learning about the world, the other being divine revelation.

Traditionally, natural philosophers wanted to describe and understand nature, and relied on philosophy and speculation to do so. In the Middle Ages it was dominated by Aristotle's authority, an authority that began eroding during the Renaissance, when other classical pagan writers' work became better known. Even before Galileo's discoveries, astronomers had come to doubt the Aristotelian doctrine of the world being at the center of crystalline spheres through their studies of comets. So natural philosophy incorporated respect for careful observations. However, experiments were not a traditional part of natural philosophy and, given its frequent focus on astronomy, would have been impossible anyway.

Experiments and empirical investigation were originally more closely associated with medieval and Renaissance magic than with natural philosophy. Traditional authorities were not as important. Carolyn Merchant emphasized that the Renaissance magus sought knowledge in service to personal power (Merchant, *The Death of Nature*, 109). A practitioner of magic wanted to control the world around him, and hoped to achieve it by investigating it and its occult properties (*Stanford Encyclopedia of Philosophy*, "Natural Philosophy"). This may have been a crucial reason for their secrecy, for while science grows through shared knowledge, a quest for power is threatened by others' power.

I previously described how oxygen was actually first discovered by a Polish alchemist, although in a way that did not contribute to science. But when applied within a new context, the techniques alchemists devised did. John Henry writes that leaders of the scientific revolution, "like the magicians, developed and extended the experimental method to make it one of the most fruitful means of investigating nature. The new philosophers recognized the validity of experimentally defined occult qualities" (Henry, "Magic and the origins"). Magical traditions contributed importantly to the rise of modern science (Yates, *The Rosicrucian Enlightenment*). The natural philosophers used investigative techniques rooted in magic, especially investigations to discover connections between phenomena, rather than relying on respected authorities.

A good example of natural philosophy and magic coming together is the influence of Francis Bacon (1561–1626), who played an important role in integrating these two traditions. A pioneering advocate of using empirical investigation in science, Bacon also considered "magic as an operative knowledge of hidden forms and the harmony of things, which displays the wonderful works of nature" (*Stanford Encyclopedia of Philosophy*, "Natural Philosophy"). Bacon's view of the *purpose* for acquiring knowledge as serving humanity helped to shift the magical tradition toward seeking power for the good of all (Merchant, *The Death of Nature*, 169).

The coming together of these two traditions was not without tension. What were thought of as "occult qualities" could not be explained mechanistically. They were two very different models of reality. After the mechanical wheel clock was invented in the late thirteenth century, it had often been used since as a model for mechanical views of nature (Hadot, *The Veil of Isis*, 83). Like today, early scientists and others used the most advanced technologies of their time to shed light on what they were studying. Then it was clocks; today it is computers.

The clockwork model provided an alternative to the dominant animistic one, and over time it gained in persuasive power. For example, astronomer Johannes Kepler (1571–1630) wondered why, if all planets had souls, the ones farthest from the sun were less active than the inner ones. Perhaps, Kepler wondered, only the sun had a soul whose "force" moved the planets, the more strongly the closer they were to it. But this surmise of his was only a way station, and in time Kepler endorsed a fully mechanical model, writing: "My aim is to show that the heavenly machine is not a kind of divine, live being, but a kind of clockwork, insofar as nearly all the manifold motions are caused by a most simple, magnetic, and material force, just as all motions of the clock are caused by a simple weight" (Koestler, *Sleepwalkers*, 345).

Protestantism's reduction of nature to inert matter given energy by God further strengthened the mechanistic model, facilitating early scientists' separation from magical traditions. Methods of experiment, measurement, and prediction came naturally to people who studied mechanical processes, whether clocks or the universe. Francis Bacon, Descartes, Galileo, and Newton's emphasis on analyzing what was measurable and quantifiable in the sensible world broke with magical practices, but not with its aspirations to exercise power over the world (Hadot, *The Veil of Isis*, 123).

But the mechanical model was not without serious problems of its own. Newton's concept of gravity required action at a distance, and was not itself mechanical. The mechanist G. W. Leibniz (1646–1716)—who, along with Newton, discovered calculus—criticized Isaac Newton's (1642–1727) concept of gravity as an example of occult forces acting on things with no physical connection. Newton responded that people should not make up hypothetical explanations of phenomena that clearly existed, but instead rely on the experiment and the mathematics. John Henry observed "Any magician from the preceding 700 years would have agreed with him" (Henry, "Magic and the origins"). One fascinating attempt to link the "occult" dimensions of Newton's thought with mechanism helped inspire the rise of mesmerism. Franz Anton Mesmer (1734–1815) was initially a Newtonian mechanist and physician who had successfully treated a hysteric with magnets. He hoped he had discovered scientific evidence that gravity and magnetism were closely related (Webster, *The History of Theurgy*, 238). In time he shifted away from mechanism to ultimately provide support for vitalism. As I read about his later work, it seems a kind of what, today, we call "energy healing." But that is an avenue we will not explore here.

In science, mechanism's triumph was not because all important phenomena could be explained mechanically, but because it was so incredibly useful where it did work. Newton himself was not a pure mechanist, arguing mechanism did not hold for all natural phenomena (*Stanford Encyclopedia of Philosophy*, "Newton's Philosophy"). Newton was convinced God had created the laws he discovered, but was not bound by them, so that there was no mechanistic account for gravity did not bother him.

Despite the "occult" characteristics of action-at-a-distance implied in his theory of gravity, because the rest of his work incorporated it so spectacularly, Newton vastly strengthened the mechanistic paradigm. That a vast range of phenomena on Earth and in the heavens could be explained on the basis of a few universal principles lent strength to the idea the universe could be thought of as a great machine. Gravity's nature was reserved for future work. Ironically, given his own views, today he is best known for discovering "Newtonian mechanics."

A troubled relationship

Initially those relying on authoritative Scripture and those relying on empirical investigations largely agreed about nature and God. Most natural philosophers were believing Christians, and many were churchmen. Modern Protestant Christianity and the first modern scientists both generally saw the world as a collection of things, created and ordered for our use by God. While agreeing on the big picture, Protestants based this understanding on Scripture; early science explored its implications through empirical investigations.

By relying on his own reasoning rather than authority of the ancients such as Aristotle and Galen, or Scripture, Rene Descartes (1596–1650) is often considered the intellectual father of the Enlightenment. A man of wide-ranging interests, Descartes wrote on physics, cosmology, geometry, and physiology. As a convinced mechanist, he argued all physical phenomena could be explained in terms of contact between moving bodies and the motions and shapes of their parts. But Descartes was also a convinced Catholic.

Descartes is famous for writing "I think, therefore I am," and for the argument he developed from it, which is usually interpreted today as freeing philosophy from the authority of the ancients and elevating the autonomy of the mind. However, Descartes saw the matter somewhat differently. For him, his reasoning demonstrated the necessity for not only God's existence, but also for the case of the soul's immortality. In his thinking, the soul was completely freed from mechanical matter, strengthening the case for materialism. As with so many others of his time, Descartes saw no tension between treating the natural world as divinely designed mechanical objects, and Christian theology (Gottlieb, "Think Again?"). Another of the greatest scientists of this time, the Protestant Robert Boyle (1627–91) was also active in spreading his version of Christianity (MacIntosh and Anstey, "Robert Boyle"). Boyle saw the two as interrelated, supporting mechanistic atomism for explicitly religious reasons: "to keep the glory of the divine author of things from being usurped or entrenched upon by his creatures" (Jacob, 1978, 215, quoted in Myers, 2013, 111). Boyle argued, "If water is endowed with the ability to avoid a vacuum, then in some sense it is possessed by a kind of rationality and this exists on a par with man. In turn, if man is fundamentally no different from the rest of creation, why should he think of God treating him differently… why then should he be concerned to live according to the rules of established religion here on earth" (Myers, *The Earth, the Gods, and the Soul*, 111–2). Matter's passivity was theologically important for Boyle and others because it removed moral considerations from the nonhuman world. And when morality ceases to matter, what matters is power.

Power and spirit

The dominant medieval view of nature as alive had encouraged its contemplation (Harrison, "The Bible: A Rejoinder," 157). Nature, as well as we ourselves, was part of a larger living order ultimately ruled by God. By desacralizing the world all moral weight was removed from the world, and concentrated in God's will and in people insofar as they were obedient to that will. There was nothing really to contemplate in nature beyond its intricate construction as evidence of divine power. Mechanism was the ultimate outcome. Carolyn Merchant put the matter accurately, and bluntly: "The mechanists transformed the body of the world and its female soul… into a mechanism of inert matter in motion, translated the world spirit into a corpuscular other, purged individual spirits from nature, and transformed sympathies and antipathies into efficient causes. The resultant corpse was a mechanical system of dead corpuscles, set into motion by the Creator" (Merchant, *The*

Death of Nature, 195). The magicians' focus on power shifted into science as we understand it when it moved from power regarding occult forces and entities to power over material objects. Experiment as a method required the power to manipulate what was investigated. Prediction required the power to foresee what would happen. Explanation required the power to encompass what was happening within the framework of human understanding. And so scientific knowledge was intimately connected to the ideal of power as the ability to control. As God controlled a mechanistic universe, by discovering the laws of control, human beings could, in principle, do so as well.

This outlook had important implications beyond religion. Morality was removed from the world, and in its place was the power of divine will. This perspective also strengthened views of God as all powerful rather than all good. But hidden within this view, as I explained in chapter 3, was the apotheosis of power as the ultimate value. If an omnipotent god did not create the world, and it was simply a material thing, the dominant value serving human beings was power over all within it.

When God's role shrank to ever more transcendental levels, many Enlightenment thinkers concerned with freedom and individual liberty simultaneously became obsessed with despotic rulers who claimed to rule in the name of enlightened reason rather than religious authority. The *philosophs* agreed with the despots that ordinary people were incompetent to understand reality. Thus the competent needed the power to rule over them as a father ruled his family. Enlightenment values of reason and freedom attempted to meld with absolutist political power under the doctrine of "enlightened despotism."

Absolute monarchs claiming this title, such as Frederick the Great, Catherine the Great, Leopold II, Maria Theresa, and Joseph II, implemented more or less policies of religious toleration and expanded education, public health, support for science, and other social reforms inspired by Enlightenment thinking. But in practice, Enlightenment values were used to replace the old "divine right of kings" argument that had fallen on hard times. The cake of claims to absolute power remained but the icing had changed to rhetoric about Enlightenment—rhetoric quickly abandoned in service to still greater power (Gay, *The Enlightenment*, 483–96). The language of mechanism proved a good servant to the exercise of power, as it remains today.

To be sure, some Enlightenment thinkers such as John Locke argued for the existence of individual rights, but on balance, the immediate effect was to strengthen power over morality and hierarchy over equality. Unlike medieval defenses of domination, however, hierarchy was based on reason and expertise, not God's will. This view was captured in the striking image of a giant man made up of thousands of little men, but with the all-powerful giant head of a king atop it as the frontispiece in Thomas Hobbes' *Leviathan* (see "Hobbes" in the bibliography for a link to the image). Even when limited and constrained by Christian assumptions, science's elevation of power as a guiding principle would gradually undermine the moral foundations of the West (diZerega, *Faultlines*). But its full impact lay in the future. At first science opened new kinds of power up to humanity while proving to be a worthy handmaiden to the church.

Those who thought this would last, scientist and churchmen alike, were wrong.

Something new under the sun

Despite this widely assumed compatibility between science and particularly Protestant monotheism, the seeds for eventual divorce had been planted, and planted deeply. The growing scientific community had developed their own standards for investigating purely physical phenomena, standards unrelated to Scripture (Gaukroger, *The Emergence of a Scientific Culture*). Nature was a different text than Scripture and could be read independently from it. Most scientists believed that scientific discoveries would be compatible with Scripture, and offer independently verified evidence for the truth of its claims, but these beliefs were subordinate to the judgment of the community of scientists based on their evaluation of their research.

Science proved to be an entirely different way for seeking knowledge from what had gone before. Scientists might pursue truth, as had philosophers, theologians, and scientists of the distant past. But the context within which they worked had changed decisively. Whereas Scripture tipped theologians off as to what the truth really was, and philosophers sought to unpack the deepest implications of whatever philosophical tradition they followed, the better to understand truth, science did something different. As individuals, scientists might seek truth, but science as a system only exposed error.

Affirming truths versus exposing errors

The difference between religion and science was that the latter developed procedural standards regarded as fair by all involved for judging claims about the world, whereas religious authorities believed in the infallibility of Scripture, and of their interpretation of it. Even when they differed theologically, Protestants, Catholics, Jews, deists, agnostics, and atheists all could agree measurement, experiment, and prediction were particularly persuasive qualities for testing statements about the physical world. Claims that survived such tests could be at least provisionally accepted. Whereas the church sought to subordinate method and inquiry to serve an already agreed-upon conclusion, natural philosophy, and the science it birthed, subordinated conclusions to what emerged from the process of inquiry.

At its core, what we loosely call the "scientific method" is a way of discovering and rejecting errors about claims regarding reality. This "method" developed out of the natural give and take of people propounding theories and others seeking to test their validity. No truth could be regarded as certain, but the more a scientific explanation could be measured, predicted, and duplicated by others, and do so better than competing alternatives, the greater its persuasiveness became. Science does not so much discover truth as winnow out ever more subtle forms of error. As a system, science sought *reliable* knowledge (Ziman, *Public Knowledge*). Such open-ended methods of study could reveal unexpected outcomes able to dissolve long-accepted conclusions.

I am distinguishing fundamentally between science as a system and scientists as people. Being human, there were always heated arguments among scientists as to what counted for accurate measurement, an accurate prediction, or a fair experiment. What one scientist judged to be merely an anomaly that would be cleared up later, was another's sign something was seriously amiss with the current understanding. Sometimes the one was right and sometimes the other, with no way to tell in advance. Human judgment always played a role, no matter how objective the experiments, measurements, and predictions sought to be (Polanyi, *Personal Knowledge*). However, the goal was always to minimize such grounds for differing, and consequently, the scientific community developed ever more precise methods to measure and predict.

More purely human motives could also intrude on the abstract ideal of disinterested people applying common standards to their own and others' work. Pride, envy, greed, and dishonesty have played roles in all human endeavors, including science. But there have always been such people. What was new was that science had become a community of exploration that devised methods of exposing errors.

Every new generation of scientists was filled with people seeking to explore the margins revealed by what was already known. Sometimes their discoveries appeared to confirm existing frameworks, as discoveries in physics appeared to confirm Newton for two centuries. But at other times discoveries challenged existing Orthodoxy, and could rapidly transform "what everyone knew," as had Albert Einstein's discoveries, even though initially he did not even have a teaching position.

What few, if any, appreciated at the time was that the scientific community had given birth to something truly new: a community of practitioners able to correct even central misunderstandings in their model of the world. Every scientist could be to some degree influenced by bias and ambition, but science as a whole was not. As a system, science had become independent of scientists.

Scientific "truth" is always what has most successfully passed tests applied to it. "Truth" became something we could always pursue but never be certain we attained, because every advance was provisional, open to being replaced by a new, even more reliable, one.

Science's foundational Christian assumptions

Although science's original assumptions about the world were shaped by Christian dogmas, its methods for eliminating errors enabled science to outgrow them. By basing knowledge on freely given persuasion rather than an authoritative text, early scientists laid the foundations for much more than they imagined, and in directions neither they nor anyone else ever suspected.

The mechanistic revolution of the seventeenth century rested on Christian foundations (Hadot, *The Veil of Isis*, 129). Early scientists had to begin with some initial assumptions about the nature of the world in order to ask questions about it. The assumptions that seemed most reasonable were rooted in a Christian perspective, supporting a biblical view of reality. They assumed that, once answered, the questions they explored would validate these views. Science was to be another means for appreciating God's actions on Earth.

Much of science's subsequent history involved discoveries that eliminated foundational Christian assumptions, replacing them with alternative explanations better able to account for what scientists encountered. In the process, science transformed itself. Early scientists thought their discoveries would support Christian dogmas, but over time, space for God's intervention in the world shrank to remaining "gaps" where we did not know something. For example, Newton thought God's occasional need to rewind the universe's "clock" was proof he existed. But later research eliminated any need for such a divine intervention, and so abolished that particular proof God existed.

This gradual filling and narrowing of the gaps in our knowledge, where God had supposedly acted, has never stopped. Much of science's subsequent history involved discoveries undermining and ultimately eliminating ever more of its foundational Christian assumptions, replacing them with different assumptions better able to account for what scientists encountered. In the process, science transformed itself. By the time of America's founding, God still very much existed for most well-educated people, but he no longer intervened in the world. Most of our nation's founders were deists in this sense (Stewart, *Nature's God*, 32–4).

We can get a sense of how deeply early science was immersed within a Christian worldview by looking at Stephen Toulmin's division of these initial assumptions into two groups: one concerning the created world of nature, the other applying to humanity as distinct from and superior to nature. From this perspective, whereas the Bible taught us about the world of people, it did not claim to teach us much about the world of nature and matter (Toulmin, *Cosmopolis*, 109–115; Merchant pointed out a minority of early scientists looked at nature differently, and their perspective was long overshadowed by the judgments of the majority: Merchant, *Death of Nature*, 103–36).

Nature

1. Nature is governed by fixed laws established a few thousand years ago. These laws were originally considered as reflecting God's will.

2. Physical nature is composed of inert matter. Motion and change were the result of conscious entities, especially God.

3. Physical objects and processes do not think. Unlike earlier times, matter could not think because thinking is not mechanical.

4. God created stable systems in which material objects found and maintained their place.

5. Physical reality exists in a hierarchy of higher and lower, with God at the top, providing motion for all through a divine hierarchy.

Humanity

1. What is *most* human about us is our capacity for rational thought and action. Experience provides sensory inputs and the conscious mind handles them rationally.

2. Rationality in humans and mechanical causality in nature follow different rules.

3. Therefore, our actions cannot be explained by any causal science of psychology. Science deals with material objects, physical processes, and causal relations whereas the human mind is not described in terms of causal regularities.

4. Human beings can create stable systems in society like stable physical systems in nature. Social institutions can be designed rationally.

5. Humans are part rational and part causal, with the latter rooted in our physicality. Emotions are rooted in our physicality, and so are causal. By contrast, reason is intellectual and spiritual.

6. Emotion frustrates and distorts reason and so should be distrusted. Rational calculation gets preference over any emotion.

Over time these biblically based assumptions were rejected in favor of very different ones. But the value most deeply underlying these assumptions remained unchallenged. All the methods developed by scientists excelled at studying phenomena insofar as they were *things*. We measure things, we predict things, we experiment on things, but insofar as what we study is not a thing, these traditional methods become less practical. Science was regarded as ill-suited to study human beings because ultimately human beings were not things.

Dissolving boundaries

Mechanism depends on two insights. First, that things are not conscious in any relevant sense; and second, that boundaries can be clearly distinguished. A force applied to one thing will move it in some way, and if it encounters another thing, will influence it. A machine has parts and in a good machine the parts should be as durable as possible. Once energy is applied from the outside, they work together in predictable ways because of their shape in relation to one another. But over time science gradually dissolved the rigid boundaries between nature's "parts," setting the stage for another problem on which we will focus in chapter 6: the nature of consciousness.

When Nicolaus Copernicus (1473–1543) proposed the sun and not Earth as the universe's center, he began the dissolution of this theologically derived idea that we were fundamentally distinct from the rest of the universe. Seen from this perspective, Galileo further weakened the boundary between Earth and the heavens when he discovered the planets and moon were as material as the earth. Newton's discoveries united a wide range of seemingly distinct phenomena, from falling apples to tides, as phenomena all governed by a single set of predictive equations. In all of them, connections between disparate phenomena were discovered that had not been previously imagined. But still the boundary between people and Earth seemed secure.

But these discoveries had merely set the stage for what was to come.

Evolutionary theory was the most fundamental challenge of all to this boundary-centered view. Darwin and his successors demonstrated how all life was interwoven, connected through networks where complex biological orders emerged from simpler systems, be they organisms or the ecologies within which organisms lived. Far from being absolute distinctions between different life forms, species were temporary patterns along a line of descent.

As more was learned about genetics, these patterns could frequently entwine with similar patterns, as with our own sharing of Neanderthal genes. Species were mutable and had blurry boundaries. Along the way, evolution upended Genesis and demonstrated we are connected far more intimately than we had imagined to the rest of Earthly life.

Einstein demonstrated that matter and energy were different states of the same "stuff." Matter is very far from inert. Even more unsettling, the passage of time varies from place to place and people looking at the same place while moving at different speeds will observe different amounts of time passing relative to a third observer. No objective "now" exists in the universe. And recent work on the nature of time suggests it may be still more difficult to comprehend that this (Brooks, "Quantum time"). Whatever the universe might be, it is definitely not a machine.

Boundaries still exist, but their nature is different from what they were once thought to be. Today the scientific community would endorse very different principles:

1. The laws of nature are not mechanical.

2. The world is billions of years old, in a universe even older, probably originating in a Big Bang. Even this universe, vast beyond human comprehension, may itself be but one of innumerable other universes.

3. Far from being inert, matter is a form of energy where its quantum foundations exist in a state of radical indeterminacy.

4. Mental and moral life are subject to scientific investigation.

5. From organisms to complex societies and ecologies, complex "higher" phenomena emerge from "lower" simpler things and relationships.

6. There is no *qualitative* distinction between human beings and other living organisms.

7. Emotion is an essential dimension of rationality.

8. Matter and awareness reciprocally influence one another, although just how this happens is almost universally called the "hard problem."

One traditional theologically rooted assumption remains *relatively* unchallenged because it has played such a fundamental role in science so far. The world is fundamentally objective, devoid of any inner meaning of its own and ultimately devoid of awareness. What is subjective is ultimately not real. I shall return to it.

The death of nature ... and of God

I have described how life was expelled from the world in stages. First, the animacy of the world was reduced to subordination to divine will. Then all life was concentrated in that being or ourselves, with the world being inert matter moving in accordance to laws imposed by divine power. Then the realm of divine power began steadily to shrink, as God became a "god of the gaps." The gaps continued shrinking until many came to think of God as simply a place holder for what was not yet known.

As this discovery process worked its way through our edifice of knowledge, the chief casualty was the plausibility that a creator god was actively involved in ordering the world. His revelations and miracles were necessary in order to achieve a predestined divine plan involving his specially created human beings, and they supposedly existed where things happened that we could not understand. Evidence for God was in the gaps in our knowledge. Those gaps have steadily diminished. Today, many people assume that, in time, the gaps will close completely. The last holdout, among people who believe in a supreme deity and accept science as our most reliable source of knowledge, is the god of deism, a being who set the whole process into motion, and now sits back and observes us, perhaps as we might observe our goldfish.

But the case for secularism is not nearly so strong as its advocates believe. Science has indeed administered the coup de grâce to any reasonable case for the monotheistic god. Nietzsche was right, we have killed that god, and by so doing undermined the stability of a world based on assumptions rooted in that belief.

But if God was not alive, *life now became the mystery.* How could life exist in some things in the universe and all the atoms and molecules that made it up not be alive? Perhaps life is also an illusion rooted in deterministic laws regarding nonliving matter? At present scientists and philosophers making this claim can only offer a promissory note. The physical explanation for consciousness also remains a promissory note.

There are reasons to believe these notes will never be redeemed. Christian de Quincey offers what I believe is a wiser question: "Instead of asking, 'How can I know if any other being is sentient?' The more reasonable question is 'How can I know if there is any other creature *without* consciousness or sentience?'" (de Quincey, *Radical Nature*, 86). Alexander Wendt emphasizes the subject-object dichotomy is itself not objective, but is "*produced* by acts of 'objectification,' since it is only by taking our mind *out* of nature that the world can be constituted as an object" (Wendt, *Quantum Mind*, 66–7; Wendt also cites Erwin Schrödinger, *Mind and Matter*, 36–51). Science did not undermine belief in an inspirited world or in the existence of awareness as a fundamental aspect of reality. These denials remain assumptions ultimately based in Protestant theology. Science's tools for investigating the world assumed this was true, and so sought to replace awareness in any form with objective measurement and prediction.

The original motive was a good one. In a Europe torn by religious war and oppression, all arising from beliefs resisting any rational examination, it seemed truth about the world could be best approached by eliminating as much subjective belief as possible. By eliminating subjective involvement, and becoming spectators rather than participants within the world, we might truly find out the truth about it.

But as we have seen, science by its very nature *cannot* discover truth, or if it does, scientists cannot know it did so. All science can do is eliminate error, and in that way get us closer to whatever truth might be. From this perspective, insofar as it is a source for error, subjectivity is a problem to be minimized as much as possible. And since we do not know the truth, it is best to eliminate subjectivity as far as possible from science. But in fact it is subjective judgment that enables scientists to discover errors in current beliefs and insights into more reliable explanations.

I will argue that there are no good reasons for rejecting views of the world as ultimately nonconscious stuff. But before going there I want to describe how I came to *know* this is so. For my interest in polytheism and a living world where such phenomena exist is *not* based on philosophy or science, but on direct encounter.

This book is inspired by a many-decades-long effort to make sense of these experiences while still honoring science, the modern world's most inspiring and unique way of increasing knowledge on which we can depend.

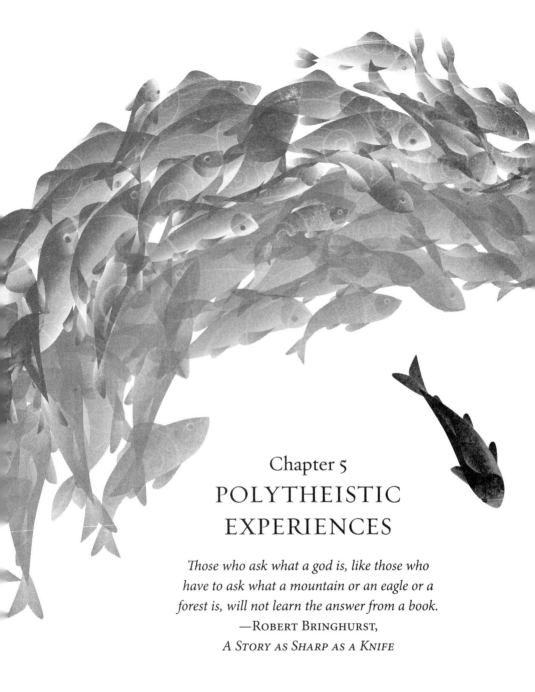

Chapter 5
POLYTHEISTIC
EXPERIENCES

*Those who ask what a god is, like those who
have to ask what a mountain or an eagle or a
forest is, will not learn the answer from a book.*
—Robert Bringhurst,
A Story as Sharp as a Knife

WHEN I BECAME AN adult during the sixties and seventies, social scientists' general view was that religion was a declining force with little future. Anthropologist Anthony Wallace spoke for many when he observed that "belief in supernatural powers is doomed to die out, all over the world, as a result of the increasing adequacy and diffusion of scientific knowledge... the process is inevitable" (Wallace, *Religion*, 264–5). Modern science's evisceration of biblical literalism and its concept of a monotheistic creator god had proven convincing for virtually everyone who studied the issues. As described in chapter 4, science had not only broken free from most of its Christian assumptions, it had completely refuted them.

Most social scientists subscribed to "secularization theory," which held religions would fade, first from government, and then from public life. Religion's last hold-out would be private devotion. In time, even that would be replaced by some variant of modern secularism.

Today, here and in much of the world as a whole, religion is a more potent political force than it has been in many years. Southern Baptists and Pentecostals now form the backbone of the Republican Party, which dominates many states and many of whose leaders want to toss the Constitution aside and replace it with theocracy (Philips, *American Theocracy*). Whenever science disagrees with their beliefs, they reject it.

However, in many ways America's predicted secularization has continued as expected. According to a new Pew poll, between 2007 and 2014 the number of Americans who did not identify with any religion grew from 36.6 million to 55.8 million (Lipka, "A closer look"). When asked their religious affiliation, those who report "none" now total around 25 percent of the populations of both Europe and the United States. In 2015, 34 to 36 percent of those born after 1980 reported having no religious affiliation. As with atheists and agnostics, this percentage has been increasing (Shermer, "Silent No More," 77). In 2007 78.4 percent of Americans identified as Christians. Seven years later the number had dropped to 70.6 percent (Pew Research Center, "America's Changing Religious Landscape"). And the United States is the most religious among developed nations.

In keeping with secularization theory, Americans' growing secularism is most clearly associated with urban living and relatively high levels of education, which would explain the hostility of many conservative religious believers to learning, as well as to cities. The strong countervailing pattern developing in the opposite direction disproportionately includes our country's least educated, least traveled, and least urbanized citizens. A great bifurcation *appears* to be opening between declining numbers of dogmatic believers and a larger, increasingly secular, population.

But appearances can be deceptive.

A complication appears

While the broadest pattern secularization theory predicted is happening, a third development brings the theory itself into question. If we examine the most secular portions of our population, most say they are not atheists or even agnostics, and believe some more-than-human context provides ultimate meaning to life. Only 37 percent of those reporting that they have no religion say they do not believe in God (Alper, "Why America's 'nones' don't identify"). A 2018 Pew study discovered 62 percent of agnostics believe in a higher spiritual force (Pew Research Center, "Most agnostics"). A 2014 survey indicated 32 percent of those calling themselves agnostic thought people experienced consciousness well after death (Shermer, "Silent No More," 77).

These numbers are not what one would expect for the few who identify themselves as atheists. But according to Pew Research Center's findings, 8 percent of atheists say they believe in God or a universal Spirit and 2 percent are "absolutely certain" such exists. Over half, 54 percent, of declared atheists feel "a deep sense of wonder about the universe" (Pew Research Center, "10 facts about atheists"). In marked contradiction to secularization theory, these beliefs in a spiritual dimension are positively related to education. John Michal Greer writes that in 1975 a British national poll found 36 percent reported at least one encounter with "a god, spirit, or sacred entity." The percentages reporting such contacts *increased* with education (Greer, *A World Full of Gods*, 68–9). Other investigations found the same correlation. In a 2011 study of top scientists at research universities, Elaine Ecklund reported that most scientists at major research universities described themselves "as spiritual." In general they considered spirituality as "a substitute for religion" (Ecklund and Long, "Scientists and Spirituality").

There is nothing new about these findings. In his *The Myth of Disenchantment*, Jason Josephson-Storm explored how spiritual and occult ideas have played a consistently important role in the thinking of many of our scientific greats, including Marie Curie, Gregory Bateson, John Dewey, Thomas Edison, William James, Arthur Koestler, Ernst Mach, Alan Turing, and Alfred North Whitehead, and many others (Josephson-Storm, *The Myth of Disenchantment*, 305). Many people are having experiences or intuitions convincing them there is more to life than the secular image of a meaningless, godless, world, but they often lack the vocabulary to describe it, believe organized religions do not connect with it, and so often use the less precise term "spiritual." They are profoundly right.

"Spirituality" focuses on experience whereas "religion" usually refers to institutionalized belief and practice. A 2012 Pew survey on religion and public life reported nearly *half* of all Americans experienced what they report to be a "religious or mystical experience," *double* the number Gallup reported in 1962, when only 22 percent of Americans reported such experiences (Pew Research Center, "Many Americans"). That number increased to 31 percent in 1976, and has apparently remained relatively constant through 1994 when *Newsweek* reported 33 percent.

In 2002, Gallup asked respondents to rate the statement "I have had a profound religious experience or awakening that changed the direction of my life" on a scale from 0 to 5, with 0 standing for "does not apply at all" and 5 for "applies completely." Gallup reported 41 percent of Americans said the statement *completely* applies to them (Gallup Jr., "Religious Awakenings").

While Pew reported "mystical or religious experiences are most common among people who regularly attend religious services," 30 percent of those describing themselves as religiously unaffiliated *also* reported such experiences and 25 percent of people with no religious preference said the statement applied to them completely, as did 27 percent of people who said they rarely or never attend religious services. These percentages are greater than the 22 percent Gallup reported in 1964 for the country as a whole, when a larger percentage of Americans described themselves as Christians. This might reflect a genuine increase in such experiences, for Pew found 55 percent of baby boomer generation Americans reported having had such experiences whereas only 43 percent of seniors had.

The persistence of such phenomena, rooted in experience rather than belief, was not predicted in secularization theory. It is also not linked to traditional American religion. Secularization theory's most abstract prediction is happening, but people's reported spiritual *experiences* reflect something different.

I am one of those for whom this proved true.

My strongest grounds for rejecting the atheists' alternative to monotheism are not historical, philosophical, theological, or scientific, although such grounds exist. They are experiential. Trying to puzzle these experiences out explains why I, a PhD in the very secular discipline of political science, ultimately came to write such a book as this.

A personal account

Growing up in culturally conservative Wichita, Kansas, the only thing I knew about religion was Christianity, along with a vague awareness that Jews and others even stranger existed. Learning the Bible was the word of God, in high school I tried to be a fundamentalist for about a year, before abandoning it in 1964. But the nagging fear that I had made a mistake with eternal implications persisted for some years to come.

Once in college, I read much of the literature explored by intellectually adventuresome young people, including authors such as Alan Watts, Hermann Hesse, and Aldous Huxley. But I found no person or message that truly appealed to me. In graduate school I continued a little exploration, from Carlos Castaneda to Jane Roberts. Watts was perhaps my favorite of all, because of his emphasis on nature as spiritually important. My deepest "spiritual" love was wild nature, and while I occasionally wished something like pantheism was true, I believed it was not. Very rarely, I had strange experiences, like repeatedly seeing an aura around someone, but only that person. Neither that, nor any other such event, persisted or seemed to lead anywhere.

By graduate school, for all intents and purposes I was a devotee of secular social science. I thought there was more to reality than this (I could not deny that aura experience), but I was equally committed to the view that, whatever ultimate reality was, no one knew much about it, and it was irrelevant to the task of living in this world. I did pay attention to books like *The Tao of Physics* and wondered about the meaning of experiences over the years with entheogens. But if I had any religious interests at all, they were in Buddhism and mystical kinds of Judaism because, compared to Christianity, I thought both respected learning. However, I knew very little about either. As for polytheism and pagan deities, I thought such ideas were the beliefs of primitives.

I resembled many who called themselves vaguely spiritual, but not religious.

The bet that changed everything

As a PhD candidate at UC Berkeley, I had a problem. I lacked the money I needed to support myself while I researched and wrote my dissertation, and had discovered there was no security in part-time academic appointments. I also knew if I got an 8-to-5 job, the dissertation I dreamed of writing would probably never get written.

A fellow graduate student suggested I try and sell versions of the envelopes I frequently decorated when sending letters to friends. At my wits' end as to any other alternative, I decided to try it. I decorated stationery and envelopes with my pen and ink art, had them printed, and waited for the world to beat a path to my door. The world paid no attention. I knew nothing about running a business.

To avoid bankruptcy, I ended up selling them as a street vendor on Berkeley's Telegraph Avenue. To my delight, my business began to flourish, and eventually I even had a significant wholesale market. However, I still had to continue as a street and craft fair vendor to cover my own expenses. Slowly, the dissertation took shape, while I was otherwise immersed in an environment very different from traditional academia.

When selling my art, I met people I normally would have never encountered while on the Berkeley campus. In a friendly conversation, one customer—noting my envelopes with dragons and unicorns—asked if I had any wizards or magicians, as he had a personal interest. When I asked him if he performed on stage, he said he "didn't do that kind of magic."

I thought he must be another Berkeley loon, of which there were a great many. Telegraph Avenue's sidewalks were regularly visited by crowds of chanting Hare Krishna devotees, religious fundamentalists with their bullhorns, and simple ranters running on about an amazing variety of bizarre things. But this man was a good customer, didn't rant, and was not interested in the state of my soul, so I just replied, "That's interesting." Still, I was disappointed a person I had taken an immediate liking to turned out to be a nut.

A year or so later, I had finished my dissertation, had it accepted, and thought I would soon leave this world for an academic position. I was wrong. As I remember those events (and I will never forget them), this is what unfolded. When Don, for that was his name, came by to get gifts for the holiday season, I decided to ask him if he could show me some "real magick." I was curious as to how he would weasel out of my request, since I was sure he couldn't.

Instead he replied "Sure, how about tonight?"

Embarrassed, I answered I needed to package more stationery for tomorrow. For us vendors, Christmas season was the equivalent of harvest time for farmers. But I swore when I saw him again I'd ask the same question, and, no matter what, take him up on it if he answered the same way.

I did and he did. In January he showed me "real magick."

I arrived at his south-of-campus apartment around ten at night, as requested. He answered the door wearing a black cloak while carrying a staff. "Let's go up on campus," he said.

"OK," I replied, while thinking, "I hope I don't meet anyone I know."

It was an extraordinary night, and the final, most decisive, event happened at an open-air plaza surrounded by buildings on all four sides. None of the buildings opened out to the plaza. The plaza itself was elevated a story above ground level, and could only be accessed by a spiral staircase within a narrow opening between two buildings, or, on the other side, by outside stairs that disappeared into the ground and entered a basement to emerge on the other side, with still more steps rising up to the plaza. The plaza itself was square, with a circular platform in the middle. There was a sidewalk extending from one entrance to the other. The rest was a "sea" of gravel over which a footbridge arched from the sidewalk to the circle, as if the gravel were water. On the far side, two large chimneys rose, giving the place a kind of spooky temple image. I had been at Berkeley for ten years and never known this place existed, although, like most everyone, I knew where Trader Vic's statue of a saber-toothed tiger stood, near the base of the spiral stairs leading up to it.

We sat on a bench at the plaza's edge. Don had said its strange design and unusual privacy had led some Bay Area occultists to use it for rituals. Sometimes they conjured up entities, and one of them had never been returned to wherever it had originated. Perhaps we could see a six-foot-tall angry something-or-other trapped on the gravel surrounding the plaza.

No such entity ever appeared.

Instead, across the circular plaza, between two juniper bushes growing along the narrow strip between the sidewalk and an adjoining building, I saw something short and almost invisible. It was stationary, transparent, pale, cylindrical, and whiteish. Don asked me whether I saw anything. I decided to give him the minimal information.

"Yes."

"Is it between those two bushes?"

"Yes."

"Is it about three feet tall?"

"Yes."

"Is it white?"

"Yes, but I can barely see it. It's very faint."

"Let me see what I can do about that." With that, Don walked to the center of the circle, placed his staff on the ground, and leaned his head against it. The image glowed much brighter!

"My God," I thought. "This guy's for real."

He returned, and asked if it was easier to see. I said it was, and we sat together on the bench. I wasn't going to walk over to it, and it made no attempt to visit us (which was fine by me). In time, simply sitting, with whatever it was standing motionless between the bushes, became kind of dull, and it had grown very late. We decided to leave. Before we did, Don walked to the center, leaned again on his staff, and the apparition vanished completely.

When we walked past where it had been, I got down on my hands and knees to see whether I could detect anything unusual on the ground between the bushes. Nope. Nothing. Coarse gravel, with a brick wall behind the bushes, was all that was there.

My secular Western worldview collapsed that night, as did my suspicion that, while there was more to the world than the modern outlook acknowledged, no one knew much about it. Don clearly could enter into communication with entities we both could see, but which modern science denied existed.

At that point I could have filed this night away as an amazing experience, as I had with seeing auras around one guy, and returned to living life as I had lived it before, or I could explore further. In a decision whose full implications I did not grasp at the time, I asked to study with him. Don agreed, and we began meeting together weekly.

About six months later he invited me to a Wiccan midsummer sabbat to celebrate the summer solstice.

A sacred encounter

We gathered in a glade surrounded by live oaks in Berkeley's Tilden Park. Perhaps fifty or sixty people were there, maybe more. Hours after the ritual was supposed to have started, it finally began. This was my introduction to "Pagan Standard Time." By then I had shifted from excitement at witnessing an actual sabbat performed by actual Witches, to being fed up with the glacial pace of things and was contemplating leaving.

When we gathered to form a circle in a small clearing, my thoughts were, "It's starting, that means it will end, and I can go home."

After the circle was cast, the High Priestess and High Priest walked to its center. When he invoked the Wiccan Goddess, she came. Powerfully. Overwhelmingly. Beyond anything I could have imagined beforehand.

She was not visible to my eye, and at that time I got no sense of how she looked, but I experienced her presence as *more real* than I was. It was as if my normal experience was one dimension of a multidimensional reality, and what exists in many dimensions was more real than my world, which exists in only a few.

For another sense of this experience, think of a beautifully painted tree or person. Real as it can seem, it only has two dimensions. As a being, an actual three-dimensional tree or person is more real. Another comparison that might help give a sense of my experience is, if life is normally experienced on a two-dimensional movie screen, with her it became three dimensional, no 3-D glasses needed.

But there was an even deeper dimension of inner psychic reality. We can get a small sense of such a presence in unusually close and intimate encounters with those who are special to us, as compared to an encounter structured entirely by social roles, such as a waiter, waitress, or customer. In one case we encounter a Thou; in the other, a role.

She also radiated unconditional love, not just for me, but for everything. It was universal, but also deeply personal. It was as if she had complete access to everything that I was, my many failings included, and still embraced me without reservation. There was nothing impersonal about it.

I had always thought I knew what love was, but that afternoon I discovered I only knew enough to recognize that hers was more real than anything I could have previously imagined. The love I have both given and received was real enough, but diluted by needs and expectations. She was a deity, and therefore free of the limitations of human love. If my capacity for love was a flashlight in the dark, hers was the sun, abolishing all darkness. Again, it was as if what I experienced in a few dimensions, I now experienced in many.

Years later, in another encounter, I told her, "Someday I hope I will be worthy of your love."

She responded, "You have always been worthy of my love."

I had a brief moment of pride, of feeling special, until she added: "All beings are always worthy of my love."

This message and the experience of unconditional love was in keeping with many mystics' reports of God as love, except that encountering the Godhead is experiencing only love; she was feminine, and possessed other individuated qualities.

I am a political scientist by training, and we study power—particularly power in a hierarchical sense. I was both attracted to and repelled by it. Repelled because of the destruction, suffering, and atrocities committed by people caught up in exercising it; and attracted because, if I or those like me had enough of it, we could radically reduce those crimes against humanity and nature. Or so we convinced ourselves. We would be exceptions to the rule, which is an all too common delusion for those attracted by power.

I remember thinking at the time, "With love like this, who needs power?" Another interpretation of my experience would be that love is the most powerful thing in the world, but it is a power of presence, not of hierarchy or control. From that time on, my attraction to power in any hierarchical sense plummeted. This completely unexpected psychological shift on my part occurred in minutes and has now lasted over thirty years.

Today, when I look at Donald Trump and others like him, it seems to me they have become largely vehicles for power, parasitized at the cost of their humanity, and are now withered husks of what they had once been or could have become. Opposing them is necessary for the good of others and the earth, but were they not so powerful, they would be pathetic.

Another distinctive quality accompanied her. As I experienced her, it seemed as if she was accompanied by forests, meadows, and streams. She was somehow integrated with the world of nature. Since that first encounter, whenever I use a name for her, she is my Lady of Forests and Fields.

She was not the Godhead. In time I would experience that as well, but not now. She had personal traits, whereas, as I experienced it, the Godhead was pure love, the source for all that existed, neither male nor female, neither just in the earth or just transcendent to it. She was an individuated and aware being, far closer to this source than I, or anything I had ever experienced.

Finally, she was beautiful. Again, more so than anything I had ever experienced. The Wiccan Charge of the Goddess, which I had not heard at the time, caught her beauty as well perhaps as words ever could: "I, who am the beauty of the green earth, and the white Moon among the stars, and the mystery of the waters, and the heart's desire, call unto thy soul." Precisely.

When she departed I remember thinking "So THIS is a deity! And here is a religion that asks their god to come, and she does."

That afternoon in Berkeley's Tilden Park was my introduction to polytheism, as well as my entrance into Wicca. But much more was to come.

Varieties of polytheistic experience

Initially I thought everyone present had had the same experience I did at that sabbat, or in similar ceremonies. I soon discovered this was not the case. Some had similar ones, others had different kinds of encounters, and some simply felt that at last they had come home.

I did not have many such experiences in the years that followed. She appeared, although less intensely, in two other sabbats, and in one esbat, or full moon ceremony. But for the most part, she did not. It has now been decades since I had my last such encounter.

I wondered why these appearances were so few, and now believe were we to experience her more often, we would live just for those times. And apparently, whatever the purpose of our life, in Wicca at least, it is not for people to become dependent on deities. It is less clear to me why everyone did not have experiences such as mine. But I was to discover that encounters with polytheistic deities took many forms within many traditions, and within each not everyone had similar encounters.

An encounter on Mount Saint Helena

Perhaps a year after that midsummer sabbat, Don asked me whether I was interested in attending a sweat lodge ceremony high up Mount Saint Helena at a former Girl Scout camp. Mount Saint Helena is the highest mountain in what Californians call the North Bay region, rising 4,342 feet, the highest point in both Sonoma and Napa counties. I was not particularly interested in collecting religious experiences; my goddess encounter had been sufficient for me, but I have always loved nature, and it sounded interesting, so I joined him.

Sweat lodges are most often associated with Native American traditions, though they or similar activities have long taken place across the northern regions of the world. To build a sweat lodge today, people construct a framework of willows into a dome too low to stand up in, and canvas tarps are used to cover it except for a small entrance that can be closed. Enough tarps are used so even on a bright day it is completely dark inside. A pit in the center is used to hold red-hot stones, which are brought in at the beginning of each of four rounds. The first round invited in spirits to help with the ceremony; during the second, we asked for healings; the third was the healing round; and the fourth, one of thanksgiving.

That sweat was dark, long, and hot, but for me, not a powerful spiritual event. I was a little disappointed. Once it was over I walked to a nearby stream to dunk myself in its cold waters. I also had a metaphysical question that had long nagged at me: Why were we here? What was the purpose of life?

As I stood knee deep in its cold waters, a feminine presence made herself felt. She was not the Wiccan Goddess—there was no sense of perfect love, of superhuman beauty, or of her being much more real than I was. But she radiated a deep beauty and kindness, and wisdom beyond the human. I also had a vague sense of her appearance. She seemed more European than Native American, which answered another question that bothered me. Was it appropriate for me, a White guy, to engage in practices rooted in a culture that my people had treated with criminal brutality? That a friendly spirit showed up indicated that this was not an issue, at least if my motivations were good.

She gave me a short message: "See what you have been given." To this day, decades later, there are several possible meanings to her message, and I was too surprised to ask her what she meant. But it was friendly, and not obviously Wiccan.

I was learning that the polytheistic world has a variety of entities, from fully superhuman to some who were far closer to us, but wiser and kinder. And some that apparently were neither.

Mount Shasta provides an attitude adjustment

I liked sweats and the sense of being close to nature, especially to the spirits of the land, for sweats were about as earthy a practice as you could do. And I hoped for a repeat visit from that entity, though she never returned, to me at least. In time the group's leader announced he would teach a year-long course he called "Coyote's Kindergarten." It would involve learning more about Native American practices to harmonize and learn from the spirits of the land. It did not conflict with my Wiccan practice, and so I decided to attend.

At the end of that year, during which I had no powerful experiences, we each had a solitary three-day vision quest high up on California's Mount Shasta. Within California's alterative spirituality community, this immense, glacier-clad volcano had a reputation as a place where unusual things happened, from UFOs to Bigfoot sightings to encountering underground "Lemurians," and what have you. Personally, I regarded most of this as nonsense. But the mountain was beautiful, I would spend three days alone high up on it hoping for a vision or something, and I had enjoyed Timothy's teachings, which were now coming to an end. I also had come to believe that while the Spirit world of earthly energies was very real, it was not very powerful, since our society seemed to be destroying every sacred site and practice it encountered. As it continues to do today.

I hiked up to where I would spend three days and nights, a little below timberline, and laid my sleeping bag out in the small spot I would stay for that time. I carried water but no food. And then I sat. Or chanted. Or simply enjoyed the beauty of Northern California's wild mountain country. Once a ptarmigan came within a few feet of me, but I was too dense to ask what that meant. The third night I was supposed to stay up until dawn, praying and chanting for a vision, but decided I would rather get a good night's sleep. I thanked the mountain for my time there, apologized for not staying up, and went to bed.

It took me a while to fall asleep, but eventually I did. Then, around 2 a.m. (I checked my wristwatch after the event) I woke up. Something was nearby, something VERY big. All I felt was a sense of approaching immensity. Suddenly, I was immersed within it, with intense pressures squeezing me from every direction. When I describe it now, I say it was like being at the bottom of the ocean, with the all-important difference that I could breathe.

The scale of this presence was so vast that I have since compared myself to it as an ant would to a bulldozer. It had no discernable personality or individuality. It seemed to be pure power.

I could not move of my own volition, though my body thrashed about within my sleeping bag. I was terrified. Then, suddenly, it departed. I relaxed, thinking it was over.

Only it almost immediately returned for a second round. Panicked, I realized I was in way over my head, and utterly alone. The only force that seemed large enough to handle it was the mountain itself, and so I called out "Shasta! Shasta!"

My voice seemed far away, perhaps like hearing someone scream half a block away on a quiet night. But with my call, that force immediately vanished. Somehow, I knew it would not return, and it did not.

I stayed in my sleeping bag and soon fell asleep, not to awaken until dawn.

When I arose, the events of the night before seemed unreal, and yet I knew beyond doubt they had happened. After a while I gathered my stuff and, profoundly shaken, began walking down to the place we would all gather after finishing our time on the mountain.

Many years later Timothy told me he had noticed my increasingly lacka-daisical attitude toward the Spirit world, and had asked the mountain to pro-vide me an "attitude adjustment." It did.

Brazilian healing

My Mount Shasta experience transformed my spiritual life in another very important way. We ended our vision quests with a fire ceremony, and after I had sung my thanksgiving song, my right foot began vibrating. The vibrating rapidly spread throughout my body, and soon I was flat on my back, with my body arching effortlessly, with only my heels and head touching the ground. It was out of my control, and eventually stopped on its own.

My teacher in these matters told me what was happening was good, but he did not feel able to teach me much. He suggested I explore African Dias-poric traditions, whose leaders knew about such things. Returning to Berke-ley, my Wiccan friends and coven mates did not have any idea what was going on either. When I raised my athame, a ritual knife, within a Wiccan circle, my arm would begin to jerk around, leaving some wondering whether I might accidentally hurt myself, or one of them. I never did, but decided to investigate an African Diasporic group meeting in Oakland, led by the remarkable Luisah Teish.

I enjoyed their rituals and the people were very friendly, but I was uncom-fortable with animal sacrifice. So, I never joined, but for some time remained a frequent guest at their events. It was there that I met a woman who told me of a healing circle in Berkeley, where I lived at the time. It was an eclectic group whose leader, a Brazilian, was deeply involved in Brazilian Umbanda, and in Tibetan Buddhism. The woman was good-looking, and so, for reasons much more earthy than spiritual, I visited the center.

As soon as I walked in the door, I entered into a light trance and felt a bit dissociated. I sat down in a row of chairs, along with the other people who came to receive healing. When my turn came, I went to the central area and sat in another chair. Four mediums dressed in white stood around me and began applying healing energy. As soon as they began, I lost control of my body as had also been the case on Mount Shasta. I fell out of the chair and began thrashing around on the floor. I remained clearheaded, but I had no control over my body.

The center's leader came out of a side room where he had been working with someone, and soon took better control of my body than I had, even though he never touched me. Once I had calmed down, he told me that what was happening could be either a great blessing or a great curse, and asked me to work in the temple, to ensure the former. I asked whether I could still practice Wicca, because my commitment to the Goddess was total.

He said yes.

I stayed for six or seven years, and gradually became a major practitioner of those healing techniques. It was as demanding as getting my PhD at Berkeley, but involved neither reading books nor writing papers. The center's leader told us one time, "I could teach you everything that could be put into words in a weekend, and it would be worthless." Instead, we gradually developed our own capacities to interact with the Spirit world and to move healing energy within our own bodies as well as sending it to others. In time I no longer lost control of my body. In Wiccan circles my athame was steady.

I was so impressed with the knowledge this tradition had that I occasionally told the Wiccan Goddess I would transfer my primary identity to the healing group, if she would show up during one of their sessions. She never did.

However, once a year, our leader would invoke the presence of his major spiritual teacher, an enlightened Buddhist who now existed on a spiritual plane. His name was "Venerable Master Shidha" (pronounced Shi-dee-hah). Usually I felt little to nothing when he was invoked. However, on one occasion his presence was about as strong as had been the case with that first encounter with the Wiccan Goddess. Again, there was a sense of unconditional love, but his presence was masculine and ethereal rather than imbued with a sense of nature and the feminine.

This blessing from VM Shidha was fascinating because, while he radiated perfect unconditional love and I experienced him as somehow more real than I was, he was presented to us not as a deity, but as an enlightened being who had once been human. But he shared those two superhuman qualities with the Wiccan Goddess.

An encounter with the Godhead

Becoming actively involved with Wicca and with healing groups did my academic career no good, not because there was active discrimination against me as a Pagan, though there was some, but because I lacked the single-minded job-at-any-cost attitude beginning academics had to have to get their foot in the door. During the first crucial years I stayed in the Bay Area, teaching as a visiting professor, so I could continue learning from Don and others. Consequently, my professional life became a mix of temporary teaching positions and posts in think tanks rather than a secure academic position. In one case I suddenly lost my position in a think tank because the organization encountered unexpected financial stresses. I was suddenly out of a job.

I moved back to Oakland from Sonoma County, to once again become a full-time street vendor. I was deeply depressed with the course events had taken.

I was driving south through a rural part of Marin County when suddenly I was immersed with the presence of all that is, or the Godhead. This was an experience of unconditional love for all things, but unlike my encounter with the Wiccan Goddess, it was not female. Nor was it male.

It was the Creator in the sense that all that existed in my world seemed to emanate from it, as light might come from the sun. This was a loving emanation, seemingly for the sake of manifesting love in as many ways as possible. All things, even those most objectionable from our perspective, were included.

When I thought about what had happened, it seemed as if love and reality emanated from this source, gradually to become individuated into deities and the like, and still farther from that source, beings like ourselves, although always illuminated by it.

Seeing while healing

While working with the Brazilian healing circle I was offered a visiting professorship at the University of Puget Sound, in Tacoma, Washington. I accepted, and spent two years there teaching American politics. My first year, a student— older than most, and a former Marine—told me he needed to withdraw, and needed my approval because the time for a free withdraw had passed. I told him there was no problem, but asked him why he needed to drop the course.

He told me he had been rear-ended while stopped at an intersection, and had hurt his back. X-rays showed that the impact had crushed a disc in his neck. "I am either in so much pain I cannot pay attention or I am so drugged up I can't pay attention." He was going to need an operation.

My experience with energetic healing work convinced me it was effective, but I still wondered whether this effectiveness was in the work itself, or whether it triggered a placebo effect. Here was a chance, maybe, to help someone and also to clarify my thoughts on that matter. His X-ray indicated a genuine injury causing intense pain.

I suggested that, if he was open to it, he come to my apartment and I would see if I could help him. Somewhat to my surprise, he agreed.

In every session we both stood and I worked behind him, silently. During the first session I "looked" with my mind's eye into his neck, and "saw" what appeared to be a dark spider wrapped around his spine, where the injury was. I tried to "pull" it off psychically, and failed. I then tried to "dissolve" it with energy, and again failed. Finally, I sent a thin beam of healing energy into it, hoping to weaken it from within.

Afterwards, I "looked" elsewhere in his back, and "saw" what seemed to be many small black insects. I envisioned a psychic rake, and "raked" them out. I then tapped his shoulder and said I was done.

He turned and said, "Before you say anything, let me tell you what I experienced." After maybe thirty years I obviously cannot remember his exact words, but he said something like "Around my spine was an eagle's claw, and you tried to take it off, and couldn't. Then you tried to dissolve it, and couldn't. Finally, you managed to weaken it. There also seemed to be something like ants in my back and you raked them out."

"Eagle's claw" and "spider" are different, but of course what we "saw" was neither. What they shared in common was something with appendages wrapped around the injury. He also correctly described the order of my attempts to remove it and their semi-successful outcome. I will always remember his verb "raked" because that was exactly what I envisioned doing.

The most reasonable conclusion was that we interpreted what happened in slightly different but complementary ways. No matter the explanation, clearly minds could access information within another body that there was no way of explaining in secular terms. I no longer worried that what I was doing was somehow energizing a placebo response.

He was never able to repeat that accurate a description again, but after four sessions his pain was largely gone (as was the "spider"). He remained virtually pain free and did not need an operation through at least the final year I taught there.

An unexpected blessing from Yemaya

Our Brazilian group held annual celebrations and made offerings to Yemaya, the Brazilian orisha of the ocean, on a beach every New Year's Day. In time I left the group, on friendly terms, because its focus was becoming increasingly Buddhist, and much as I respect that tradition, it was not mine. However, I and some other friends continued honoring Yemaya every New Year's on the Sonoma coast. Every time I made offerings to her, the water would rise, and I'd get wet.

One January a big winter storm had blown in, and when I tried to contact my friends who also made offerings, no one was home. I decided to go make offerings on my own. I also decided to do it at Coleman Beach, a small rocky beach that was hard to access even in good weather because the stairs down the cliff face were in poor shape. That meant I'd have it to myself.

Once at the bottom, the size of the incoming waves made standing on the beach itself dangerous. So, I looked around at the surrounding huge boulders, trying to find one that was not getting periodically swamped with a big wave, but still jutting far enough out that I could make the offering. One rock seemed perfect.

I figured water would still come over the rock, as it always seemed to whenever I made an offering to her. Consequently, I removed my shoes, walked to its edge, and emptied cornmeal into the water. Suddenly a wave came up well over the top, hitting me waist high. I thought it would knock me over, but as it receded, I remained standing, holding a jar of molasses.

Determined to finish the offering, I unscrewed the top and began pouring the molasses into the ocean. As I emptied the last of the molasses into the sea, I looked up.

And up.

And up.

A wave far above my head was almost to the rock. And then it was on top of me, sweeping me off my feet.

I remember thinking "I'll be a newspaper article tomorrow…"

I was carried back, perhaps twenty feet or so, to the cliff face, and deposited, standing up, into a narrow crack. Had I encountered that crack a few inches in either direction, I would not be writing these words today. But instead of having my head smashed, I had a tiny scratch on a single knuckle.

And the water was *warm*!

I was exhilarated, joyous, and grateful for the event. I felt wonderful. The thought of having barely escaped death was not important.

I had received a blessing, although I was aware that this kind of blessing was not wisely pursued. My subsequent offerings have been in much safer places. But no matter where, the waters come up far higher than they had been—in one case rising high enough to extinguish a beach fire that had been burning for hours, far from the water's edge.

Implications

My experiences, these and others, led me to a decades-long effort to try and find a scientifically respectable way of making sense of them. During the first year or so I kept a small notebook where I recorded them. I was concerned that I would get so "far out there" as to lose touch with reality, whatever that was. So, I wrote down what happened, whether it was expected (usually not), whether there were other witnesses (sometimes yes), and whether I had imbibed or smoked anything at the time (I think never).

I also observed how my life went, and while it was not going the way I had anticipated when getting my PhD, I kept my old friends, ran my business successfully, and published papers in refereed social science journals. Other than having such experiences, nothing was happening in my life to indicate I was losing my mind or otherwise failing to handle consensus reality.

In time I decided it was more irrational for me to doubt the reality of such experiences than to accept that, somehow, I was encountering dimensions of reality most Americans did not experience, or want to.

But I always sought for a way to link them with the world I shared with everyone else. Now, more than thirty years after they began, I think I finally have something to offer.

Patterns?

Based on these experiences, and some others, one observation leaps to the front: the extraordinary variety of encounters. They range from the God-head to spirits that seem small, passive, and anything but superhuman. Some are visible, some are not. Some have an ethical presence dwarfing ours, others seem to consist of pure energetic power, particularly my experience on Mount Shasta. But even this latter responded powerfully to what I did (as well as, perhaps, to what my teacher, Timothy, had earlier requested). And yes, some seem unfriendly.

A second observation is more universal. It was possible to enter into relationship with them. But here, again, variety applies. Some initiated the encounter, others responded when an effort was made to contact them. Some provided a message or teaching, others an experience. Some transformed my life, but most did not. Some could be seen by others, some were purely private encounters, invisible even to people nearby.

A third observation is that the details of these experiences seem largely confined to the cultural context in which they occurred. The Wiccan Goddess never appeared within a Brazilian ceremony. Nor did a *preto velho* or *caboclo*, so central to many Brazilian ceremonies, ever appear in a Wiccan circle, though I admit they were never asked. To a large but perhaps not complete degree, entities from different spiritual traditions, rarely "crossed over." Of those I am told did, the people with whom they interacted had previous experience with one that later showed up in a different context.

Finally, there is no certain way of determining whether an entity is who it says it is in a particular encounter. While some encounters are repeatedly with the same entity, or at least appeared to be, beyond this, only context and perhaps what the entity said was a clue for identity. And there is no guarantee they spoke truthfully. I am reminded of a report of Michael Harner's describing an Ayahuasca experience to an indigenous shaman. He had been told by some entities he encountered that they were the real masters of the planet. His guide responded "Oh, they're always saying that" (Harner, *The Way of the Shaman*, chapter 1). But, as with people, repeated encounters gave a sense of their character, and most were very welcome over the years, like treasured friends.

A key clue for me was the sense of reality in an encounter. In terms of personal presence, many appear as real as an encounter with another human being. However, the most loving manifest as more real than myself. Whereas the Wiccan Goddess, who possesses these qualities, came as a deity immanent with the world, VM Shidha, sharing these same qualities, was in some important sense removed from the world, although in loving relation to it. Further, he had supposedly once been human, whereas the goddess was clearly super human.

For thousands of years, people in every society of which we have knowledge have reported personal experiences with sacred powers. The earliest evidence for modern human beings, or even our earlier Neanderthal cousins, is frequently accompanied by evidence many archaeologists think shows they experienced their world in spiritual terms (Rendu et al., "Intentional Neanderthal burial"). We have no way of knowing how these practices and beliefs arose, but there is no shortage of more recent evidence that competent people in all cultures have experiences that led them to similar conclusions.

Some of history's greatest thinkers, including Socrates, the man who more than any other inspired Western philosophy, had such experiences. Important figures in the history of mathematics and science have either reported such experiences or taken their existence very seriously—figures such as Blaise Pascal, Emanuel Swedenborg, Thomas Edison, Alan Turing, Freeman Dyson, and Brian Josephson—going well beyond describing subjective insights. These examples should dispose of the easy reply that such people are weak-minded or suffering from some mental disease more substantial than simply disagreeing with a skeptic.

A secular culture whose members think about these matters through inherited monotheistic filters would have great difficulty acknowledging the existence of such a reality. The filters need to be removed. Those of us who have had such experiences would also welcome supporting evidence that our encounters are not simply the firing of synapses within our skulls. But if our experiences are in any sense accurately interpreted, the world within which we live is fundamentally different from how the dominant Western consensus about reality conceives it.

In the following chapters I will not argue that I have penetrated to the ultimate truth of spiritual reality. I will argue that the world around us is alive to a far greater extent than we normally imagine, all the way down, and all the way up. In terms of what we can reasonably believe to be true, the evidence for such a reality is stronger than for either a monotheistic view or for a purely secular one. Our world is in some strong sense aware, and there are spiritual entities within it with whom we can enter into beautiful, loving, and transformative relationships.

Chapter 6
SCIENCE AND SPIRIT

*It seems to me immensely unlikely that
mind is a mere by-product of matter.
For if my mental processes are determined wholly by the
motion of atoms in my brain I have no reason to suppose that
my beliefs are true. They may be sound chemically but that
does not make them sound logically. And hence I have no
reason for supposing my brain to be composed of atoms.*
—J. B. S. HALDANE, *POSSIBLE WORLDS*

WHILE ITS DISCOVERIES WERE eliminating any rational support for the existence of a transcendent creator deity, science was creating room for a different view of spiritual reality, one equally far removed from secularism. This alternative's scientific roots were in post-Newtonian physics, many of whose founders had often observed that relativistic and quantum worlds were stranger and more paradoxical than anyone could get their mind around, other than through mathematical equations. Einstein demonstrated that mass and energy were different forms of the same "stuff," sinking the notion that matter was fundamentally inert. But it was quantum mechanics that really divorced our day-to-day experience of the world from its reality at a deeper level.

Quantum theory challenged the last Christian-derived assumption in science: that mind and matter shared nothing in common. In fact, quantum theory suggested their relationship was quite intimate. In 1927, Sir Arthur Eddington wrote that viewing the universe as some kind of mind was "a fairly plausible inference from the present state of scientific theory…[But] Science cannot tell whether the world—spirit is good or evil, and its halting argument for the existence of a God might equally well be turned into an argument for the existence of a Devil" (Eddington, *The Nature of the Physical World*). Max Planck, whose work in physics provided the foundation for quantum theory, wrote, "I regard consciousness as fundamental. I regard matter as derivative from consciousness. We cannot get behind consciousness. Everything that we talk about, everything that we regard as existing, postulates consciousness" (Planck, *The Observer*). These discoveries were very disconcerting to most scientists of the time, and remain so today. Most fields remain dominated by the assumption that consciousness and mind differ radically from matter. This was a matter of faith rather than proof, because it is clear to our daily experience that our consciousness continually affects the physical world, and vice versa. A color, let us say "red," requires consciousness to make any sense at all. A person who saw only in black and white, who suddenly was able to see red, could be said to have learned something new about the world, something that could not be reduced to the wavelengths of light, because such wavelengths previously showed up as a shade of gray.

From science's traditional standpoint, the ideal physics theory should not refer to human beings in any way, and should be the foundation for deriving all of chemistry, biology, and even human life. While accepting this ideal, Nobel laureate physicist Steven Weinberg admitted, "I don't see any way of formulating quantum mechanics without an interpretative postulate that refers to what happens when people choose to measure one thing or another thing" (Folger, "Crossing the Quantum Divide," 32). On the whole, scientists turned their backs on the unsettling implications of modern physics. Quantum phenomena did not seem to matter in the larger world, but only in the realm of the fantastically small. It therefore seemed reasonable to continue applying a mechanistic model to all larger phenomena, from atoms to galaxies.

This approach gained added power with the coming of WWII and the following Cold War. World events drew many scientists' interests away from theory toward addressing more immediately practical matters. The dominant view remains that, somehow, consciousness and subjectivity emerge from matter or, alternatively, that consciousness is in some way an icing on a materialist cake, playing no causal role in the world, and seeming to be a kind of illusion.

Physics' philosophical implications remained unsettling curiosities best ignored in favor of practical research—until the seventies.

During the Cold War, plenty of money was available to train physicists, and many very capable people were attracted to the field. Then, in the 1970s, the bottom fell out of the job market. Many new PhDs, who had been doing cutting-edge research for their doctorates, learned that the positions they anticipated obtaining no longer existed. A group of young physicists in Berkeley had developed common interests in the philosophical implications of what they were studying, rather than the traditional focus on physics' practical applications. Dubbing themselves the "Fundamental Fysiks Group," they picked up where physics' pioneers had left off, and banded together to explore the deeper meaning of its paradoxical phenomena (Kaiser, *How the Hippies Saved Physics*). As they did, many of these scientists were intrigued not only with how quantum physics clashed with traditional Western assumptions about the physical world, but also how the quantum world seemed to support Eastern mysticism, and even the possibility of psychic mind reading. In the late 1970s, a small publishing industry had arisen that explored modern physics' unsettling philosophical implications. I remember in the early 1980s, when two friends quite independently recommended I read Fritjof Capra's *The Tao of Physics* (Capra, *Tao of Physics*). One, a mathematician, told me he was no expert on Eastern thought, but the physics was accurate and exceptionally clearly described. The other, a specialist on early Chinese Neo-Confucianism, told me he knew little about physics, but the description of much Eastern mystical thought was good. Capra's book was the most prominent of many similar volumes appearing during this time, and was by far the most widely read.

Building on insights from quantum physics' "founding fathers," they also incorporated newer discoveries. Quantum entanglement in particular caught their attention. In quantum theory, particles separated by vast distances could retain a connection such that measuring one affected the other, for basic to quantum theory is the assertion that a particle's speed and location cannot *both* be measured. Measuring one influences the other, which is where the issue of consciousness enters in.

Quantum entanglement indicates that different parts of a quantum system are linked in a way such that influencing one part *instantaneously* influences the other, no matter how far away it might be. Classical physics held this to be impossible, and Albert Einstein had used this alleged impossibility to argue that quantum theory was obviously incomplete since nothing traveled faster than the speed of light. In the sixties physicist John Bell developed a theorem that would in principle enable this issue to be tested empirically.

Over the years since, a number of experiments had been performed testing whether quantum entanglement really existed, and it had always survived the tests. But it seemed to some as if alternative "hidden variables" could also explain the observations, supporting Einstein's objections. In 2015, eighty years after Einstein had made his objection and fifty years after Bell had devised his theorem, it finally became possible to conduct loophole free tests of quantum entanglement. Four experiments were conducted and quantum theory triumphed in all (Hanson and Shalm, "Spooky Action," 59–65). Truly, as Haldane observed in 1927, "the Universe is not only queerer than we suppose, but queerer than we *can* suppose" (Haldane, *Possible Worlds*, 286). The implications are profound. As Albert Wendt describes them: "The polarization of entangled photons would be correlated no matter how far apart they were, even across the universe. And since what goes for photons goes for other particles, and since all particles in the universe have at some point been entangled...everything in reality is correlated" (Wendt, *Quantum Mind*, 53–4). Capra and others demonstrated to a wide audience that science no longer stood in contradiction to many of the world's mystical spiritual traditions, and subsequent experiments have supported them. Consciousness was a necessary part of the system, and the universe was connected as a complete whole, and instantaneously. This does not mean the universe is *self*-conscious, or necessarily even conscious that it is conscious, but if quantum mechanics depends on consciousness to complete the theory, it is reasonable now to say the universe in some way is conscious as *experience*. The challenge is to the other side, which denies it.

As Eddington had cautioned, science did not prove Eastern mysticism was correct, but it was compatible with it, "all the way down." Long considered the "hardest" and most exact of all sciences, physics now denied that any account of the universe could be based on purely deterministic laws. The mechanists' promissory note that even consciousness could be reduced to physical phenomena was proving impossible to pay.

However, one last divide separated quantum physics' implications from influencing most of the rest of science. Quantum phenomena are unimaginably small. In any rigorous sense they cannot be measured because they are not really objects. Electrons sometimes act like balls, sometimes like clouds, and sometimes like waves, so measuring one, even in theory, is probably impossible. But *if* it were possible, the *largest* their radius could be is one billionth billionth of a meter. Atoms are about one hundred million times larger, but even an atom cannot be measured exactly because we would need to be able to measure *its* electrons to determine its size. But, again as an approximation, if a hydrogen atom were the size of a golf ball, a golf ball at the same scale would be the size of the earth (EMSB, "Relative Size of Atoms"). This size issue is important because by the time things get big enough to matter in our world, it seems as if quantum phenomena can be ignored. The traditional pre-quantum model works just fine. But recent research suggests this wall is crumbling.

Chapter 6

Overcoming the size barrier

In 2018 the results of an extraordinary experiment were published in *Nature*. Scientists brought the motions of two drumheads into an entangled quantum state. The drumheads were about the width of a human hair, very fine by our standards, but truly enormous in quantum terms (*Science News*, "Einstein's 'spooky action' goes massive"; Ockeleon-Korppi et al., "Stabilized entanglement"). They were on the verge of what we can see unaided, and far larger than many bacteria and other cells. These findings lend substantial credibility to the new field of quantum biology. Nor do they stand alone.

Birds apparently can see the earth's magnetic field to aid them in navigation. Doing so apparently requires their being sensitive to quantum phenomena (Starr, "Quantum Coherence"). Using their sense of smell, fruit flies apparently can detect quantum level vibrations (Courtland, "Fly sniffs"). Perhaps most importantly, in 2018 an experiment with bacteria appears to demonstrate phenomena that were most easily explained by their entering quantum entanglement with photons (O'Callaghan, "Schrödinger's Bacterium").

Photosynthesis is one of the most important abilities life developed, for it enabled it to colonize the planet. In photosynthesis, plants gather photons through special cells which gather and transport the collected energy to where it can be transformed into chemical energy the plant can metabolize. Some researchers have discovered phenomena in this process that they believe indicate quantum level influences (Engel et al., "Evidence for wave-like energy transfer," 782). Again, other researchers deny this, and it is currently a field of active debate (Ball, "Is photosynthesis quantumish?"). Physicist Paul Davies writes in the *New Scientist* that "the transition from living to non-living is marked by a distinctive transformation in the organization of information" where "top-down laws" that "make the flow of information depend on the global state of the system as well as nearby components." There is a "well-known precedent in standard quantum mechanics" where "when a measurement is made of an atomic state—when new information becomes available—a completely different kind of evolution kicks in, sometimes called the collapse of the wave function" (Davies, "What is life?" 31). While work in quantum biology is still early, it is showing great promise at answering some of biology's most perplexing current questions (Perry, "3 of Nature's Greatest Mysteries"). That quantum physics very likely sheds light on larger scale phenomena such as avian migration underlines its implications for claiming consciousness is a dimension of reality.

Evidence and truth

Some years ago, I was discussing the possibility of psychic phenomena with an atheist who finally played what he thought was an unanswerable objection: such phenomena are impossible because consciousness does not exist independently of physical bodies. He knew this to be true because we cannot measure it outside bodies, though he admitted it existed within at least some living ones.

I replied, "So before Marie Curie measured it, radiation did not exist?"

He was silent.

His error grew from misunderstanding an important truth about science. Science's power rests on its ability to expose errors, not to discover truth. As I explained in chapter 4, what we sometimes generalize as the "scientific method" are those criteria scientists as a community have come to respect as fair methods for evaluating a scientific claim. There are two dimensions to this.

First, a scientific claim must be interesting. If I say the sun will rise in the east tomorrow because I have burned an offering to Sol, and it does, no scientist (except maybe some psychologists) will be the least bit interested. If I say I burned an offering to Sol so it will rise in the west, and then it does rise in the west, my claim will attract notice, and Sol may well attract worshipers.

The same principle applies to a scientific claim. Scientists must find it interesting, and then ideally have some means to test whether or not it survives a challenge. Even surviving a test does not prove its truth. It only proves it remains a *reliable* explanation for why something happened. The more it proves to be reliable, the more confidence scientists will have in it. The criteria for evaluating reliability emphasize experiment, measurement, and prediction. So far, quantum mechanics has proven 100 percent reliable.

Scientists continually seek to make their standards ever more exact, reducing uncertainty in interpreting a test's results. But uncertainty about a claim can never be reduced to zero. Measurements still need to be interpreted. Ultimately judgment is still needed, and judgment always has a psychological dimension.

Sometimes a very tiny difference between a predicted outcome and the actual measurement indicates a fundamental flaw within a theory that has worked flawlessly for hundreds of years. A justly famous example involved Newtonian mechanics and Mercury's perihelion. The perihelion is the point in a planet's orbit where it approaches the sun most closely. When measured, Mercury's perihelion shifted annually a little more than Newton's theory of gravity predicted, adding up to less than one thirty thousandth of a full orbit around the sun over a century.

This predictive error disappeared when Einstein's new theory of relativity was applied to the problem. But until Einstein's theory was tested, Newton's theory reigned secure despite the problem, nor was this unreasonable. Newtonian mechanics worked wonderfully well, and perhaps there was an explanation for Mercury's orbit that, once grasped, would solve the problem. After all, this had happened before.

Much earlier, astronomers had discovered a small error in Uranus' predicted orbit as calculated by Newtonian mechanics. The mystery was resolved when Urbain Le Verrier (1811–1877) hypothesized that an unknown planet still farther out would alter Uranus' motion in the way observed. His mathematical calculations predicted where and when astronomers should look to find it. When they did, in 1846, the planet Neptune was discovered. Newtonian theory had predicted where astronomers should look to find the then unknown Neptune, thereby explaining the discrepancy between theory and observations about Uranus.

In short, a predictive error *may or may not* indicate an underlying problem with the larger theory, and when it is first discovered, there is no sure way to tell.

Predicting what has never been observed

Not being able to observe something is not in itself evidence it does not exist, and science has many cases where what had never been seen was accepted to exist because doing so solved otherwise unsolved problems. In the mid-1800s, long before there was experimental proof they existed, many eminent physicists treated atoms as real. Other eminent physicists rejected their existence because they could not be seen. Finally, in the late 1800s, measurements of cathode ray tubes revealed puzzling observations that could apparently only be explained if atoms existed. Atoms themselves were never actually "seen" by scientists until the 1970s, more than one hundred years after physicists and chemists had largely accepted their existence.

Nor were atoms the only unobservable entities important in physics. In 1897, physicist J. J. Thomson argued for the existence of a small unknown particle he called an electron, which was vastly smaller than the still unobserved atom. He won the Nobel Prize for his discovery in 1906. Wolfgang Pauli postulated the existence of neutrinos in 1930. There was no way then to test for their existence, which was only confirmed in 1958.

These "unobservables" solved problems and enabled predictions confirmed by experiments. Nothing else did as well. They did so consistently enough that scientists accepted their reality. Today unobservables such as multidimensions, multiple universes, and dark matter continue to play powerful roles in physics.

As the importance of unobserved entities in science demonstrates, there is no purely impersonal determination of many important scientific theories (Polanyi, *Personal Knowledge*). The facts often do not speak for themselves. Scientists' personal judgment is needed to weigh the various factors that create the context within which these "facts" need to be evaluated, and scientists can differ in their judgment.

Two factors moderate scientists' susceptibility to simply affirming their own desires. First is a personal commitment to truth, but that commitment is an *individual* virtue and differs in degree among scientists, who are also motivated by ambition and other desires. But these individual variations exist within science as a *system*. Scientists at their best seek truth, and the scientific system weeds out their errors, enabling other scientists to build further on what has so far survived as the most reliable knowledge (Ziman, *Reliable Knowledge*). Scientists such as Richard Feynman have pointed out that different theories with identical observational consequences can provide different perspectives on problems, and lead to different answers and different experiments. In addition, as Adam Beckler observes, "it's not just the observable content of our scientific theories that matters. We use all of it, the observable and the unobservable, when we do science" (Beckler, "What is Good Science?"). This history needs to be kept in mind when we explore the question of consciousness.

The hard problem

Today many scientists call exploring the nature of consciousness the "hard problem." No one is quite sure what consciousness is, although quantum mechanics seems to require it. If consciousness in some sense exists, it includes some kind of subjective experience. But, because of the initial mechanistic assumptions largely baked into scientific procedures, scientists seek to minimize subjective experience as far as possible. On many questions these procedures have been successful beyond anyone's wildest dreams. As Steven Weinberg emphasized earlier in this chapter, science relies on what is impersonal and objective as far as it can, and when that dependency breaks down, as it did in quantum physics, a serious philosophical crisis arises. This lack of fit between the tools for scientific investigation and the phenomenon to be investigated is what makes the problem of studying consciousness so hard.

Consciousness is easier to point to than define because defining something requires standing outside it in some sense. But only conscious beings seek to define consciousness (de Quincey, *Radical Nature.* 62). Based on our daily experience, as well as the reports of others, consciousness is an awareness of existing separately from other existing things, *or* it is an experience of an egoless unity, with no sense of separation, which is often called a mystical or unitive experience. "Awareness" and "experience," of course, presume consciousness rather than standing outside it. We end up where we began.

These kinds of experiences arise in one of three ways: in a world where consciousness once did not exist; in a world where, in some sense, consciousness is a basic characteristic of reality; or in a world where consciousness is an illusion that never really existed. Leading scientists can be found arguing all of these positions, though I have a hard time taking the third seriously, since we must first be conscious to experience an illusion, so illusion implies consciousness.

Because of the experiences I related in chapter 5, I believe consciousness in some sense is a basic constituent of reality. If so, then consciousness plausibly exists as some kind of unitive awareness without a subject, because it is easy to imagine a universe where subjects able to experience subjectively did not exist, as after the Big Bang. Physicists Bernardo Kastrup, Henry Stapp, and Menas Kafatos summarize this position, writing, "The dynamics of all inanimate matter in the universe correspond to transpersonal mentation, just as an individual's brain activity—which is also made of matter—corresponds to personal mentation" (Kastrup et al., "Coming to Grips").

What contemporary science enables us to do is to abandon science's last remaining theologically rooted assumption: that consciousness and matter are radically distinct and therefore a scientific explanation is solely in terms of matter without reference to consciousness. Of course, some scientists disagree, but their disagreement is no longer backed by unambiguous evidence; it instead reflects their judgment, a leap of faith, that someday, despite present appearances, their claim will be demonstrated. It has no more evidence in its favor, and I would argue less, than the alternative that awareness in some sense appears to be coexistent with all that exists.

A number of perceptive authors have written excellent books exploring these issues in great depth, and I have benefitted enormously from them. The most important for my purposes have been David Abram, Christian de Quincey, Thomas Nagel, Emma Restall Orr, and Alexander Wendt (Abram, *Becoming Animal*; de Quincey, *Radical Nature*; Nagel, *Mind and Cosmos*; Orr, *The Wakeful World*; Wendt, *Quantum Mind*). To explore these issues more deeply, I recommend reading them. I will give summaries here of some major points in what are careful and subtle arguments. Readers seeking more detail should turn to these authors. Each takes a different route to a similar conclusion: that awareness of some sort exists at every dimension of reality.

Self-organization

In *Mind and Cosmos,* Thomas Nagel argues that in science what needs explaining is subjectivity. Consciousness is not an effect of physiological neurological processes, because they are "*in themselves* more than physical." If I hit a nail into a rock with a hammer, something happens to the rock, but science would say the nail did not know anything happened to it. However, if I hit you with a hammer, you would experience the blow subjectively. You would know something happened to you. If you then wondered why I had hit you, you would be thinking about what had just happened. In a sense you step back from the experience to examine it. In Nagel's terms, thinking "transcends subjectivity and … discover[s] what is objectively the case" (Nagel, *Mind and Cosmos*, 72). As simple consciousness, I experience being hit rather like a worm experiences being hit. Unlike a worm, I might wonder why that happened. In doing so,

I have gone beyond experience to step back and think about it. I then can ask why it happened. Seeking truth enters in to try to understand my experience. As Nagel puts it, "Reason connects us to truth directly—perception to truth indirectly" (Nagel, *Mind and Cosmos*, 82, 83, 87).

Nagel then introduces the concept of "self-organization" to describe how consciousness becomes more complex than simple experience alone. I will frequently make use of this term in the chapters to come, so it is important to get at least an initial idea of what it means. "Self-organization" refers to the ability of ordered patterns to arise without their being imposed by a divine engineer, or through the linear working-out of reductionist laws governing their parts. The pattern emerges from the relations between its various components, and relations are not linear, but mutually influence one another. The pattern could be purely physical, such as the shape of a tornado, or it could involve consciousness, as when organisms reach sufficient complexity to be able to think, as well as experience. It can also refer to unintended patterns arising from actions by many organisms in some kinds of relationship.

The term "self-organization" has important applications in many fields. My first book explored self-organization in democracies (diZerega, *Persuasion, Power and Polity*). The patterns in a market economy, Adam Smith's "invisible hand," emerge out of the independent actions of many people. The same is true for the patterns that enable us to distinguish an ecosystem. Self-organization enables us to describe a whole as greater than the sum of its parts because, at a minimum, the context of their relations shapes the actions of all their parts. The processes generating the pattern transcend what we can deduce from its parts alone. *This perspective will ultimately take us to polytheism, but there are some more steps we need to take along the way.*

If consciousness is in some sense a basic aspect of reality, thinking emerges from conscious processes that are not thinking. Thinking is a pattern of consciousness that cannot be reduced to perception alone. Reason cannot be reduced to perception and desire because it also requires some self-awareness *and* the ability to separate a larger and more important context from the immediate desires of the self. To act beyond the spur of the moment we must anticipate our future situation, imaginatively projecting ourselves into some future circumstance. This future self of ours does not yet exist. It is not a perception, it is a creation.

Not every organism possesses the ability to stand back from experience and analyze its implications within a larger context, and those that do vary greatly in this capacity. However, a sufficiently complex organism can step back from perception and desire, and using reason, evaluate them within a larger context. A new quality, thinking, arises from sufficiently complex relationships among simpler organisms that cannot think. For example, I see something I desire, perhaps a work of art, but my reason tells me if I buy it a future "I" will not be able to pay rent. So, I pass it by.

The *same* capacities enabling us to put ourselves into our future shoes enable us to put ourselves into the shoes of others. In both cases we project our present self into the imagined mind of another self. Sometimes we knowingly sacrifice this future self's well-being for the pleasures of the moment, but when we do not, we make use of our ability to empathize with others. To act in "self-interest" depends on our ability to recognize similarities in beings other than our immediate self, and to care for them (diZerega, "Deep Ecology and Liberalism"). Thinking therefore requires a capacity to step back and view what is immediate from a larger context, and self-interest requires this context to include others that are not me, which requires the capacity for empathy.

Truth

Nagel argues that if reason exists, then *mind independent truths* also exist, truths which require thinking to discover (Nagel, *Mind and Cosmos*, 85). A purely physical being, determined by physical law in every respect, would not be a being where "truth" had any relevance to its actions. Examined carefully enough, it would be an automaton. A nail hit sufficiently hard with a hammer will penetrate wood. But this truthful observation is irrelevant to the nail, and the hammer; it is relevant only to the living being observing it.

Regardless of whether I was raised believing something is true, or convinced myself later that it was, or simply spent my life pursuing it without success, truth exists at a different level of reality than atoms. And as we saw earlier, science is possible only because many scientists pursue truth, even if science as a system can only eliminate errors and confirm what is *provisionally* true. The concept of truth requires awareness of its possibility, and science

Chapter 6

depends for its existence on scientists pursuing truth, even if science can never know whether or not truth has finally been discovered.

Natural teleology

Nagel introduces a concept he calls "natural teleology." Teleology suggests a direction of future development exists that, absent interference, will eventually manifest. That the *telos* or "goal" of an acorn is to become an oak and that of a chicken egg is to become a chicken are teleological observations. It is irrelevant to this truth that most acorns and eggs never become either, because they are eaten. Absent external interference, organisms tend to be healthy. Health is another teleological concept. (The concept of teleology is avoided by reductionists who seek explanations entirely by past causes rather than future outcomes. It is not accidental that reductionists also deny consciousness can exist as a basic quality of reality.)

Similar to health for an organism or becoming an oak is for an acorn, truth is not a cause because it is unknown; rather, it is a goal, an attractor for the mind. Truth is an inherent "goal" for reason to pursue. While science *as a system* can never be sure when truth has been discovered, for it to work by expanding our store of reliable knowledge, *as individuals*, scientists must pursue truth.

While teleology makes sense when applied to living organisms, how can it apply to processes far transcending individual organisms? Nagel's "natural teleology" requires that physical determinism not be total, nor that the universe be random. If determinism is total, all outcomes are the working-out of mechanical processes. If the universe is random, nothing will have an intrinsic direction of development. If we compare the universe to a cosmic dice game, the dice are loaded. Some outcomes are more likely than others. The dice still must be thrown and in any particular case the outcome is not determined, but over time their bias will show. Some outcomes will be more likely than others, and these outcomes will tend to produce increasingly complex systems (Nagel, *Mind and Cosmos*, 92–3). Natural teleology manifests through the self-organization of complex systems, and Nagel holds that these laws of self-organization apply to matter "or of whatever is more basic than matter" (Nagel, *Mind and Cosmos*, 93). Please keep this idea of self-organization in mind as we will return to it again and again.

136

Beyond our valuing of truth, what evidence do we have that such a teleological bias exists? We do not know what consciousness is, nor can we measure it, but we can look for evidence of its impact within the world where there is an absence of the physical structures assumed necessary for its existence. If the evidence is strong enough, the ubiquity of consciousness is a reasonable conclusion, and from it arises thinking and the values it implies.

Reality is not "value free": the iterated prisoner's dilemma game

One clear example suggesting such a bias arises from a contest political scientist Robert Axelrod held for computer programmers. The goal was to discover the program that could win the iterated prisoner's dilemma game (Axelrod, *The Evolution of Cooperation*).

If two people are arrested for a crime, the prisoner's dilemma arises when something like the following happens. They are guilty, but each knows if both are silent they will get a year in prison, because while some evidence of a crime exists, there is not enough to demonstrate its severity. The prosecutor knows a more serious crime occurred, but lacks sufficient evidence to convict on it. The prisoners are then separated, and each is told if they inform on the other, they will get a six-month reduction in their sentence, while the other will get a sentence of four and a half years. However, if each implicates the other, both get four and a half years. They cannot communicate with one another. If the prisoners are self-interested, what do they do?

In the computerized version, "iterated" means the parties involved play this game over and over, with points substituting for years. Axelrod offered a prize for whoever could devise the winning computer strategy. It turned out cooperative strategies fared better than competitive ones, and the one that ultimately won was called "Tit for Tat." It was very simple. Start by cooperating. As soon as the other side fails to cooperate, retaliate once. *Do not escalate.* Return to cooperating when the other side does.

Escalating retaliation risked further escalation in return, leading to unending conflict that depressed both scores. In addition, according to these competing programs, there was no advantage in seeking to lower the other's score. The winning strategy focused only on improving its own score. Cooperative strategies were labeled "Nice."

Next, Axelrod developed an "ecological" approach to make the game more like evolution as it happens in life. Initially the game's environment consisted of many different strategies playing against one another. Some were unsuccessful, and were eliminated from future play. The next round pitted the remaining strategies against one another, and again, the least successful were eliminated. This weeding out continued until a single best strategy emerged. Axelrod's intent was to develop better and better adapted "life forms" that "reproduced" by making it to the next series of games. In his words: "At first, poor programs and good programs are represented in equal proportions. But as time passes, the poorer ones begin to drop out and the good ones thrive. Success breeds more success, provided the success derives from interactions with other successful rules. If, on the other hand, a decision rule's success derives from its ability to exploit other rules, then as these exploited rules die out, the exploiter's base of support becomes eroded and the exploiter suffers a similar fate" (Axelrod, *The Evolution of Cooperation*, 52). Exploitive programs might appear successful at first, but by eliminating the programs they exploit "in the long run it can destroy the very environment it needs for its own success" (Axelrod, *The Evolution of Cooperation*, 52). Interestingly, Tit for Tat was not always the best strategy. When paired with a "mindless" strategy such as "Random," which did not seek to win points, Tit for Tat sank to Random's level. But, as its name suggests, Random sought neither to win nor to hurt its opponent. Random was mindless (Chen et al., "Axelrod's Tournament"). A computer code seeking the most logical way to win a game is about as detached from ethics in our sense as one can get. Yet cooperation proved to have an *intrinsic* advantage over other strategies, an advantage embedded in reality. This is what we would expect if there was a slight natural teleology to reality that would give the advantage, ultimately, to cooperators. If an environment is mindless—that is, random—tit for tat is not successful; on the other hand, the concept of success has no real meaning.

But there is much more.

Mutualism

Traditionally evolution has been considered a purely competitive process, the opposite of tit for tat. But the reality is different. Mutualism arises when relationships between species are beneficial to both. The most immediately obvious examples are plants and their pollinators. But this example, so fundamental to life as we know it, only scratches the surface of mutualism in the plant world.

The vital importance of mycorrhizal fungi and the plants whose roots they link is increasingly recognized as vitally important. For example, Suzanne Simard discovered birch and Douglas fir trees in northwestern forests are connected underground through these mycorrhizal filaments. In the winter, when birch have no leaves, nutrients flow from the firs to the birch. In the summer, especially if the fir is in the shade, the birch benefits the firs. Three very different species are involved: fungi, which are more closely related to ourselves than to any plant; the broad-leafed birch; and the coniferous firs (Gorzelak et al., "Interplant communication"). Once looked for, mutualism appears all over. For example, lichens are not a single organism. They are symbiotic communities of fungi and algae. Legumes, such as beans, exist in close association with rhizobia bacteria, which is why they add nitrogen to the soil. And many animals depend on nutritional or digestive symbiosis with bacteria to flourish—including cows, termites, and ourselves. It is safe to say our world would look entirely different, and be far simpler, in the absence of symbiotic relations.

In keeping with the logic of the iterated prisoner's dilemma, most mutualism seems to have evolved from previously antagonistic relationships (Mayhew, *Discovering Evolutionary Biology*, 114). Successful long-term (iterated) strategies for well-being tended to favor cooperation, and the same holds true in the biological world. The language of competition and zero-sum thinking cannot grasp the principles underlying biological diversity any more than they can the pure logic of a computer program. Again, there seems to be a "natural teleology" at work.

But we are raised to believe that the road to success is through competition. Americans, fortified by economists, like to talk about the market as competitive, and emphasize how competition makes life better for all. *But market competition emerges from cooperation.* People cooperate to form businesses. Competition arises when two or more businesses seek the same customers or buyers seek a scarce product such that there is not enough to go around. From these initially cooperative foundations, a social ecology arises, one of mind-bending complexity weaving together competition and cooperation.

But it would rapidly dissolve if everyone treated their relationships as competitive. A social world based on competition would be an impoverished place, if it could exist at all.

Nor is this truth unique to human beings.

Eusociality

Eusociality challenges the common notion in some biological circles that altruism is genetically advantageous. Mutualism serves all the partners, but how might a kind of altruism arise where an organism sacrifices its own interests for the benefit of unrelated others?

Eusociality exists in species with advanced levels of social organization and where multiple generations perform different functions by means of an altruistic division of labor. Ants, termites, and some bees and wasps are eusocial, as are a crustacean, a rodent, the African wild dog, and we humans. While eusocial species are few, compared to the total number of species, in terms of their biological success they represent what E. O. Wilson describes as *The Social Conquest of the Earth* (Wilson, *The Social Conquest of the Earth*). For example, while amounting to about 2 percent of over nine hundred thousand known insect species, eusocial species make up more than half the insect biomass.

Eusociality developed from earlier, more narrowly individual organisms and apparently arises from a combination of unusual ecological and biological factors. As with the evolution of cooperation in the prisoner's dilemma game, prolonged iteration of interactions within a species seems to be required. Under these conditions the logic of cooperation emerges.

Solitary ancestors of eusocial bees and wasps built nests and cared for their offspring, opening the door to further development of those characteristics. Groups are more effective in defending nests and offspring against predators and parasites, and large groups are better at it than small ones. At this point, group selection begins to dominate individual selection, giving the evolutionary advantage to more integrated and cooperative groups over less integrated and cooperative ones. Wilson points out that while selfish individuals will generally beat altruistic individuals, which supports the individualistic selfish gene model he once accepted, groups of altruists beat groups of selfish individuals (Wilson, *The Social Conquest of the Earth*, 162–3). When those conditions exist, it is not difficult to imagine how group selection could ultimately create cooperative breeding and then caste systems (the defining property of eusociality in the strong sense).

Wilson and Hölldobler argue that eusociality in its strongest sense is dependent on the evolution of an anatomically distinct worker caste (Wilson and Hölldobler, *Eusociality)*. The advantages arising from the division of labor magnify the developing further specialization in a self-organizing process as successes in one kind of cooperation set the stage for successes in others. In insects the first step is a division of labor between those who reproduce and those who serve the group, as with bees. Then the worker caste becomes more diverse and specialized, as in ants. And further specializations then unfold (Hölldobler and Wilson, *The Ants)*. This process can proceed so far that what is considered a single organism can change, and in the most eusocial cases "a colony can most meaningfully be called a superorganism" (Wilson and Hölldobler, *Eusociality)*. The ancestors of ants were once more solitary and less specialized. Today most ants cannot even reproduce. Wilson goes so far as to describe most "individual" ants as "robots" of their queen. It is as if our hands and feet could physically detach from our body, to serve us better. Wilson describes ant colonies as superorganisms based on queens.

Human eusociality arose by different means than in insects, and is not as complete. Even India's caste system never approached the caste distinctions in eusocial insects. Individuals can also have interests that hurt the groups within which they live, and sometimes they act on them. Further, in contrast to eusocial insects, human societies of any size contain different and sometimes overlapping groups with their own group interests. Yet here as well, the triumph of cooperation over other approaches to intraspecies relationships is clear. This truth is hidden from many of us by a deeply flawed understanding of individuality, rooted in Protestant assumptions. I will discuss this in the next chapter.

Eusocial qualities give a species an evolutionary advantage over less social ones, but it takes a particular kind of environment to enable it to arise through group selection. As within the iterated prisoner's dilemma game, certain conditions are necessary for this arrangement to emerge, but once it emerges, it beats all competitors. Again, this condition fits Nagel's discussion of a "natural teleology."

To this point, we have seen that the logic of cooperation appears intrinsic to the logic of a computer program, and reappears in cases of cooperation among living organisms. This also means that truthfulness has an intrinsic long-range advantage over deception for equal organisms in relation to one another.

Mind in unexpected places

We think of mind as existing when an organism can remember past experiences and learn from them; when it can discern relevant differences in its environment, and respond appropriately; and, in some cases, when it can engage in complex communication. Traditionally minds have been thought to be limited to some animals, who have developed complex biological structures such as brains and nerves to facilitate minded activity. A complex brain was supposedly needed for a mind to exist, strengthening the claim that consciousness arises internally within certain organisms.

Scientists have now discovered this is not the case.

In some relevant sense, mind exists far more widely within the world. A hint exists in the previous example of mutualism between three very different species: firs, birch, and fungi. Another stronger one involves "mother trees" in these same forests. Mother trees are old firs who are therefore the most connected by underground mycorrhizal networks with other trees. They feed little firs through these networks, but as Suzanne Simard discovered, they feed those related to themselves more than those that are not. In addition, they reduce competition between their roots and the roots of their smaller kin. On the other hand, if a seedling that is kin to the tree was sick, the mother tree would direct more carbon to neighboring seedlings, regardless of relationship, to encourage better health. In other words, they could distinguish between kin and not kin, assist both, favor kin and refrain from action that might hurt them, but also have a sense of the larger whole as more important than kin alone (Petersen, "Web of the Woods"; Markham, "Trees talk to each other"; Simard, TED talk). What Simard discovered regarding Douglas fir and paper birch seems to apply to plants within natural ecosystems in general (Toomey, "Exploring How and Why"). We would have no problem attributing this behavior to conscious intent if observed among human beings.

Additional research has found something perhaps even more amazing. When environmental conditions deteriorate for one species of tree, its declining members can then feed resources to *another* better-adapted species through these underground networks. This was found to be the case with Douglas fir and ponderosa pine, where declining firs sent resources that assisted the pines. Jennifer Fraser writes: "It wasn't a trivial amount of food, either. The amount transferred and measured by radioactive carbon labelling was about the same as the energetic cost of reproduction—a significant donation by any standard" (Fraser, "Dying Trees"; Song et al., "Defoliation of inferior Douglas-fir").

At least some plants also have memories and can learn from past experiences. This has been proven in experiments with mimosas, whose leaves normally fold up when touched. Australian scientist Monica Gagliano and her colleagues dropped water on mimosa leaves, initially prompting them to close up. The mimosa stopped closing their leaves when repeated disturbance had no damaging consequences, acquiring this learned behavior in a matter of seconds. Further, learning was faster in less favorable environments. These plants also remembered what they had learned for several weeks. The study's authors write: "Astonishingly, *Mimosa* can display the learned response even when left undisturbed in a more favorable environment for a month. This relatively long-lasting learned behavioral change as a result of previous experience matches the persistence of habituation effects observed in many animals" (Gagliano et al., "Experience teaches plants"). Gagliano has continued her research searching for evidence of consciousness in plants such as peas, and in companion planting experiments, and finding it (Gagliano, *Thus Spoke the Plant*).

Still simpler organisms can also learn and, to a point, remember. Slime molds, which in the cases studied are essentially single cells, can solve mazes and other puzzles, escape from traps, and learn that what may once have appeared harmful can be safely ignored. Slime molds were taught to ignore substances that they would normally avoid, such as caffeine. Unlike mimosa, if left to themselves, slime molds "forget" what they learned within a few days, but if carefully dried, so they enter into dormancy, when revived a year later, they will "remember" what they "learned." This finding is all the more interesting because the process of going dormant and then reviving involves substantial physical and biochemical changes (Miskivitch, "Slime Molds"; Yong,

"A Brainless Slime"). On the other hand, this short-term memory can be transferred to naïve slime molds. Separate molds will tend to fuse together, and when they do, the "new" mold obtains memories from the smaller one. These memories were not diluted, but extended equally throughout the larger organism. Experiments evaluating these findings have been applied more than two thousand times, with the same results. As with the discoveries about plants, no one understands how this happens (Yong, "A Brainless Slime"). This kind of learning is called "habituation," and is considered the most primitive form of learning. We learn this way as well. For example, habituation enables people to tune out nonessential stimuli and focus on the things that really demand attention. I once rented an apartment for a summer's research, not knowing it was next to railroad tracks. The first night I was awakened by the noise and vibrations from an approaching train. I wondered how I, a light sleeper, would handle a summer here. Within a week I slept soundly all night and never heard the train again. Below the level of explicit awareness, I remembered this sound and accompanying vibrations were not worthy of attention.

To summarize so far, the world is not devoid of values, and these values privilege cooperation over competition. The elaboration of this cooperative principle requires competition to exist in order to demonstrate cooperation's selective advantage. The value of cooperation appears deeply embedded in life as such, as well as simple logic. Mind appears to be needed for this cooperation to emerge (even in Axelrod's case, programmers needed to write the programs). Mind appears to exist in organisms that do not have the biological structures long thought necessary for mind to exist. Even in the absence of brains and neural tissues, consciousness as perception, decision-making, learning, and memory exist in plants and even in single cells. It becomes more developed as an organism becomes more complex, but exists even at the cellular level.

Memory

Memory is required for a self to exist. A self in the sense that I am using it is simpler than our conception of ourselves. It is a point of awareness in a context where it experiences other things *that are not it*. Here I find Orr's work very insightful. She observes: "As the subject becomes self-defined it asserts a measure of control, adjusting its perception of its external and internal context, honing the coherence of its own part of nature's mind. The inner community of minds develops the capacity to respond as a coherent interiority of mind. It is a development that is happening all the time. It is a process that continues until the perceptive data allows for thought, consideration, and consciousness" (Orr, *The Wakeful World*, 202–3).

We have seen such focused awareness can emerge at the level of a single cell.

A self arises from experiencing what Emma Restall Orr describes as a "flow of moments," whose inner coherence memory makes possible (Orr, *The Wakeful World*, 231). Selves arise as emergent properties from a more diffuse "primal" consciousness when relations between the elements constituting an entity become complex enough to make memory possible, as we have found exists in a simple form in even the simplest cells. With a growing capacity for memory, Orr writes, "what we perceive is the depth and breadth of soul, and every soul is an integral part of nature as a whole" (Orr, *The Wakeful World*, 215). Every soul exists within the all-encompassing field of awareness that is sometimes accessed through mystical experience.

We have tracked crucial dimensions of a self down to the level of single cells. Where life exists, consciousness does not appear to be either emergent or illusory, but life as we understand it, and selves, are. As new qualities emerge with growing complexity within the physical world, the same holds true in the world of awareness. When we have those kinds of experiences where the self disappears into a state of mystical oneness, consciousness is experienced as all-encompassing and beyond the ability of any self to describe.

Awareness precedes complexity, not the other way around. Alternatively, if awareness is a derivative of nonconscious matter, it must arise within the simplest forms of life, without more complex physical structures such as nerves, that were long considered necessary for consciousness to exist. There appears to be no living entity that does not have at least some basic consciousness, and even self.

But if consciousness in some way is a basic quality of reality, how does it become isolated in individuals?

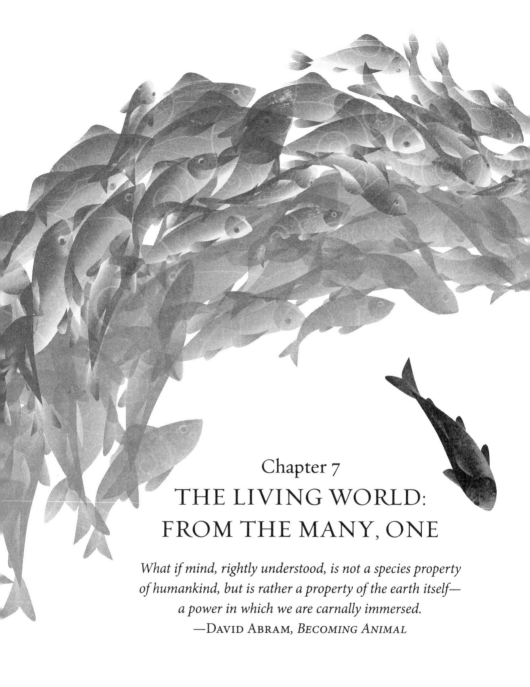

Chapter 7
THE LIVING WORLD:
FROM THE MANY, ONE

*What if mind, rightly understood, is not a species property
of humankind, but is rather a property of the earth itself—
a power in which we are carnally immersed.*
—DAVID ABRAM, *BECOMING ANIMAL*

THE VIEW OF CONSCIOUSNESS I have developed is in harmony with many of our mystical traditions. One general word for this view is "panpsychism": that consciousness in some form is a fundamental and universal dimension of reality. Skeptics challenge those of us making such claims with a puzzle. How can universal mental phenomena produce ourselves and the other individuals we encounter daily, individuals who experience themselves as separate from others?

The "combination problem"

We see the most amazing number and variety of individual entities, as well as experiencing ourselves and those we know as individuals. We see colors, hear sounds, and feel and smell in ways pointing to a world of duality, of me and not me—and not just duality, of a remarkably varied duality. Other beings see colors differently and have senses of smell dwarfing our own. Additionally, some have senses we do not, such as a bat's ability to navigate quickly through echolocation, or a shark's ability to use electrical fields in finding prey. All these beings appear to have selves, and therefore some sense of individuality. But if consciousness is a fundamental dimension of reality, and individuals only became possible after life arose, how does individuality emerge from unitive awareness? In 1890, William James, a pioneering explorer of psychic and religious phenomena from a modern point of view, succinctly described this problem: Take a sentence of a dozen words, and take twelve men and tell to each one word. Then stand the men in a row or jam them in a bunch, and let each think of his word as intently as he will; nowhere will there be a consciousness of the whole sentence. We talk of the "spirit of the age," and the "sentiment of the people," and in various ways we hypostatize "public opinion." But we know this to be symbolic speech, and never dream that the spirit, opinion, sentiment, etc., constitute a consciousness other than, and additional to, that of the several individuals whom the words "age," "people," or "public" denote. The private minds do not agglomerate into a higher compound mind (James, *Principles of Psychology*).

How, then, might such minds emerge from it? More fundamentally, perhaps, how can tiny mental elements become larger ones at any level?

Philosopher David Chalmers suggests: "It may be that the constraints imposed by the combination problem are so strong that the challenge cannot be answered" (Chalmers, "The Combination Problem," 211). Many panpsychists have responded to this challenge, and I think they have done so effectively (Orr, *The Wakeful World*, 165–71; de Quincey, *Radical Nature*, 230–36). Emma Restall Orr offers a clear description of the position I believe solves this issue, and accounts for what we are discovering in the sciences of life. Orr explains: "Every creature, every tree and beetle, every lake and mountain, every atom and galaxy, is its own pattern of being, integrated within the community of its evolving environment. Further, every being is composed of or interconnected with numerous other individual beings, each of these also existent within its own web of communities, while at the same time firmly held within nature's universal soul … the fabric of nature is made up of interactions-internal and external" (Orr, *The Wakeful World*, 238).

As a practical matter the combination problem is continually solved all around us. Orr explains that "there is no need for a theory of aggregation to create coherent minds. What we do need, however, is an understanding of why patterns come into being, as they do within the whole, like eddies and currents within the ocean …" Integral to understanding patterns is the related term of community (Orr, *The Wakeful World*, 191). The connections in meaning between communities and ecosystems are patterned phenomena arising out of relationships: "We are talking about ecosystems, but only if we understand ecosystems as existent at every level of being from the micro to the macro, shimmering with the wakefulness of mind … A community, then, is a pattern of relationships, within each pattern there are countless smaller patterns, and each pattern itself is a part of a larger pattern and a part of other different patterns" (Orr, *The Wakeful World*, 192).

Unitary selves emerge from relationships among simpler unitary selves, and do so "all the way down." Modern science has demonstrated this insight without the need to describe just how this happens. While we may not be sure how it is solved, it is solved, and at many readily observable levels. Once we see how this process unfolds, it is only a small step to apply it to polytheistic experiences. When combined with the discoveries of quantum physics, this argument supports the view our world is alive in some sense "all the way down" *and "all the way up."*

We can begin with William James, who concluded that if consciousness is treated like a thing or a noun, it does not exist. But it clearly does. James suggested the problem was not consciousness, but rather how it was usually described. He preferred describing consciousness as a process or a verb (de Quincey, *Radical Nature*, 64–5). Experience is not a point in time, it is an ongoing process which may or may not be remembered.

But then how might this insight and the rise of life connect?

Scientists' traditional argument for how life arose requires enormous spans of time or a very lucky accident to generate the first living cell out of the almost unimaginably great number of nonliving chemical reactions that could happen in a lifeless world. Conservative monotheists generally claim this is statistically impossible. Therefore a creator god was necessary, at least to begin the process. Such a deity is far removed from most monotheistic conceptions of a personality actively engaged with the world, but fits the deist idea of a god that created the world and then ceased being involved, perhaps observing what arose as we would observe a tank of tropical fish.

Secular scientists countered that, given enough time, and with millions or trillions or even gazillions of planets in an unimaginably big universe, eventually the equivalent of a monkey randomly typing *Romeo and Juliet* would occur, and life would arise. It obviously happened, and here is where it happened. While modern physics demonstrated "matter" was dynamic, most scientists believe mechanistic passivity remained true at scales larger than the quantum level, and life's origins were matters of time and luck.

My last chapter suggests this convenient assumption is as false as the divine engineer supposedly needed to get the ball rolling. Quantum influences can shape phenomena at much larger levels, including living beings. These findings appear to support a smaller number of scientists and philosophers who argue the Creator/lucky accident dichotomy is a false one. Matter does not simply respond passively to laws external to it, and under suitable conditions could spontaneously develop into physical life, and from there, into ever more complex forms of it. One general term for this outlook is "emergence."

Emergence and dissipative structures

"Emergence" refers to how complex orders can arise "spontaneously," without anyone being in charge. Neither chance nor creator are needed, for the dice of the universe are loaded. The *self-organization* of simpler elements in relation to one another leads to the *emergence* of qualities that could not be predicted by examining the qualities of their parts. In this sense the new emergent whole is greater than the sum of its parts.

The term's origins lie in the early social sciences during what we call the "Scottish Enlightenment." David Hume and other Scottish thinkers were equally skeptical of religious claims that order was designed by God and other Enlightenment philosophers' claim that reason alone could create social order and morality. They were challenged to describe how order in society could exist if God did not create it and it was too complicated for us to deliberately design.

Their solution provided a basic foundation for the social sciences. Whether in customs, language, or the economy, complex networks between people shaped by what we today call "feedback" evolved over time, even with no one in charge. There is a direct line of connection between these discoveries and Darwin's applying similar insights to evolutionary theory. "Self-organization" describes the process; "emergence" describes the outcome.

Until Ilya Prigogine's work on what he called "dissipative structures," emergent phenomena seemed confined to the biological world. The division between life and not-life seemed firm and clear. At least beyond quantum phenomena, what was "not life" was understandable purely mechanistically. Then, in 1984, Prigogine (1917–2003) and Isabelle Stengers' (b. 1949) book *Order Out of Chaos* explored emergent processes in the nonliving world (Prigogine and Stengers, *Order Out of Chaos*).

Dissipative structures, as Prigogine called them, are ordered patterns whose elements consist of continual exchanges of energy and matter from their larger environment. In the process, what initially appears disorderly gradually assumes a coherent pattern that persists so long as enough energy is applied, which it then dissipates as heat. This is why these physical or chemical systems were described as creating "order out of chaos." Prigogine ultimately received a Nobel Prize for demonstrating how complex patterns existing far from chemical equilibrium could be generated and maintained in nonliving systems.

According to the second law of thermodynamics, as time progresses, energy tends to disperse or diffuse, increasing what is called entropy. For example, in a cold room, hot coffee cools down, and ice cream melts in a warm one. In both cases the temperature differences between coffee or ice cream and their rooms decline, as heat is dissipated, cooling the coffee or melting the ice cream, while also infinitesimally changing the temperature of the rooms in the opposite direction. With enough hot coffee or ice cream we would also notice the rooms warming up or cooling down. In short, as time progresses, energy tends to spread out and structures dependent on heat differentials within their environment disappear. Over time entropy increases because there are more ways for energy to spread out than for it to be concentrated.

Prigogine discovered that when energy was added to some chemical systems new structures could emerge (hence dissipative structures) due to internal self-reorganization. As the existing energy dissipated out, like a cooling cup of coffee, so long as energy continued being added, new, more complex and stable patterns would arise.

A clear example for most of us would be hurricanes, which maintain their patterns so long as their environment feeds them sufficient energy. When a hurricane no longer travels over warm enough water, it dissipates. Dissipative structures are in sharp contrast to better understood orderly physical structures existing at chemical equilibrium, such as a quartz crystal, which does not depend on external energy to persist in its form. Hurricanes do. External energy enables them to be self-organizing.

Prigogine argued that as long as certain kinds of systems receive energy and matter from an external source, dissipative structures can go through periods of instability after which a coherent pattern emerges, resulting in a more complex system whose specific characteristics cannot be predicted except as probabilities. They do not need to be alive for this to happen.

Living beings such as ourselves are also such systems. We require sufficient energy from our environment to live. In living, we emit heat, and require additional nourishment to replace the energy dissipated as heat, maintaining sufficient internal warmth to live. When we die, this pattern breaks down as the energies associated with life cease shaping its physical components, and our bodies begin to decay back into equilibrium with their environment.

Prigogine and Stengers recognized three similarities between living systems and nonliving dissipative structures:

1. Both require outside energy to maintain their pattern.

2. In both cases overall patterns are predictable but not the precise details. Within a culture or organism, every detail could change, while new energy replaced what had been released, and yet the cultural patterns survive and the organism still flourishes as an individual. Dissipative structures are nonliving patterns maintained in some sense the same way: every physical component within them might change while their patterns continue.

3. Concepts of feedback, instability, perturbations, and chance within complex systems had long been features in the life sciences, and, with Prigogine, now could be applied to the physical sciences.

A long-accepted boundary between living and nonliving phenomena was breached.

New insights into the rise of life

One key difference between living and inanimate things is that living organisms are better at using energy to maintain their structure than are nonliving processes. And living structures are more complex than dissipative physical ones.

Physicist Jeremy England of MIT argues that a group of atoms driven by an external source of energy and surrounded by a heat bath can gradually restructure itself in order to dissipate increasingly more energy. As this happens it becomes an increasingly efficient dissipative structure. England suggests that, under certain conditions, matter inexorably acquires a key physical attribute associated with life, and such an outcome could happen if solar or chemical fuel is surrounded by an ocean or atmosphere, into which energy dissipates.

England believes his work suggests that "clumps of atoms surrounded by a bath at some temperature, like the atmosphere or the ocean, should tend over time to arrange themselves to resonate better and better with the sources of mechanical, electromagnetic or chemical work in their environment" (quoted in Wolchover, "A New Physics Theory of Life"). England's theories can be tested, and as of 2017, the initial tests support his case (Wolchover, "First Support"). These discoveries do not create life, for they still shed no light on how "proto cells" became living cells, or how a genetic code arises. But proto cells, within which life could develop, are not unusual occurrences. What makes England's discovery so important is that it suggests life would arise whenever the appropriate conditions existed for it, rather than depending on a series of extraordinarily improbable coincidences. Biological physicist Carl Franck has been convinced by England's work that "the distinction between living and nonliving matter is not sharp" (Marcus et al., "Three Dimensional Vortices"). England's findings undermine arguments that life emerges from some improbably happy combination of molecules or a deity no longer involved with the universe. The alternative that life emerged from rolls of "loaded dice," as Nagel suggested, rather than by chance or divine interference, has powerful supporting evidence.

Emergence in biology

In biology, "emergence" describes how complex patterns arise "spontaneously" in evolution and ecosystems. Not being controlled "from above," emergent processes possess *decentered* or *distributed authority*. In the human world it explains how languages grow and develop; how the internet remains useful to everyone seeking information on it; how the market economy coordinates billions of people making trillions of exchanges; and how science hangs together and grows even though no scientist knows more than a tiny fragment of the whole—and much more (diZerega, "Outlining a New Paradigm"). This concept will prove central to my discussion of polytheism in chapter 9, but for now let us consider examples somewhere short of the gods.

Think of our language. No one designed English, no one decides to add some new words and not others, or how a word changes its meaning, as "wicked" is doing today, or "democracy" did from the time of our founding to now. Most of us are not even aware of the grammatical rules we follow as we speak. Sometimes we say things we never said before, or hear things we have never heard before, and everyone involved understands what was said. How English maintains itself, and changes, is something over which every

English speaker exercises some tiny influence, but no one exercises much. And yet it all holds together. Order emerges, and we generally have little trouble communicating with one another.

Impressive orders, intricate variety, and spontaneous adaptation occurs without any central authority or directing hand in language, ecologies, science, the market economy, the World Wide Web, and much else. To the degree the term has any meaning at all, "authority" is distributed among all participants within any of these orders. What emerges are kinds of order far too complex for any person to plan deliberately, and they are taken for granted in our daily lives.

Darwin breached the boundary between human beings and the rest of life. Prigogine challenged the boundary between life and non-life, *from the side of life*. England added to the dissolving of this boundary, again by showing that processes associated with life were also present in the nonliving world. Age-old boundaries are dissolving, and doing so by expanding processes associated with living systems into the nonliving world. In all these cases emergent processes were replacing reductionist mechanical ones.

Lynn Margulis, individuality, and symbiosis

Western society is captivated by a particular concept of the individual as some kind of irreducible unit. God created us as individuals, each with a unique soul. Protestantism, and the science it helped enable, strengthened this image, conceiving of human individuals as not only separate from nature, but radically separate from one another. Today this conception of an individual is dissolving before our eyes, at every level.

When I was a student in the 1960s, the usual way biologists viewed multicellular life was as complexes made up of many individual cells, very much like physical things were viewed as ultimately made up of atoms. How these cells came to be was considered one of the mysteries of life. That was then.

Today the accepted picture is much different. Beginning with her dissertation in 1965, and many subsequent books, Lynn Margulis (1938–2011) made a powerful case for what is now called a theory of endosymbiosis. Its central idea is the importance of symbiotic relations rather than competitive ones. Traditionally, evolutionary theory had emphasized the central role of competition, and symbiotic relations were considered rare and relatively unimportant. Margulis argued that they were not rare, and arguably were more fundamental to life as we know it than competition.

Margulis' basic argument explained an important distinction between two different kinds of cells: prokaryotes and eukaryotes. Prokaryotic cells, such as bacteria and archaea, do not have a nucleus or specialized organelles, a term describing a cell's equivalent of organs. Eukaryotic cells, such as those making up our bodies, have a nucleus as well as specialized organelles: the mitochondria and chloroplasts. From ants to redwoods, all multicellular organisms consist of eukaryotic cells, and scientists had long been puzzled how these building block cells ever came to be.

Margulis argued that eukaryotic cells originated out of symbiotic relationships between once separate prokaryotic cells, some of which in time became the eukaryotic cell's mitochondria, chloroplasts, flagella, and other organelles. These new, much more complex cells possessed qualities not found in simpler prokaryotes (Margulis, *Origin*). While her argument was initially mostly rejected, within ten years genetic analysis had convinced most biologists that Margulis was correct.

The individuality of eukaryotic cells emerges from relationships between prokaryotes, who to some degree continued to retain their own individuality. The cells making up our bodies consist of simpler cells that had merged to become more complex organisms while still to some degree maintaining their own identity. Amazing as Margulis' research was at the time, no one then imagined how far this breakdown of what we regarded as irreducible individuality would eventually go.

Tissues, viruses, and jumping genes

There are huge differences beyond scale alone between an amoeba and a fish, although the amoeba is a single eukaryotic cell and a fish is composed of innumerable such cells. Fish, and other complex multicellular organisms such as ourselves, are made possible through their cells' ability to form different tissues. Cells forming muscles, nerves, bone, and skin are very different from one another, even though all had a common origin in a single cell arising from a fertilized egg, and share the same genome. How did this ability to differentiate arise?

Embryonic stem cells are an organism's first cells, from which all more specialized cells eventually descend. When a stem cell divides, each new cell might remain a stem cell or become a specialized cell, such as forms a muscle, red blood, or a neuron. But how can copies of the initial cell "know" that in some cases they may need to develop into a heart, in others into skin, and in others, nerves?

Recent discoveries indicate the origins of cells' capacities to form tissues such as skin and bone are derived from viruses (Slezak, "Origins of organs"). Upon infection by a virus, parts of it were incorporated into a cell, giving it new capabilities, one of which apparently made tissue formation possible. By invading cells in order to reproduce, viruses can change them so dramatically as to be a major force in the evolution of life. Scientists, such as Dmitri Petrov (Genetics Society of America, "Viruses revealed"), believe viruses drive the evolution of cells even more than other evolutionary pressures, such as predation or environmental conditions. As Margulis wrote, "Viruses today spread genes among bacteria and humans and other cells, as they always have … We are our viruses" (Margulis, *Symbiotic Planet*, 64). Viruses, and possibly bacteria, accomplish this by transferring DNA that can copy themselves throughout an organism's genome from one organism to another. This DNA is called a "jumping gene." They were first identified around fifty years ago, in Barbara McClintock's studies of maize (Keller, *A Feeling for the Organism*). Most scientists were initially skeptical of her discovery, but since then jumping genes were found to be in almost all organisms and usually in large numbers. They make up approximately 50 percent of the human genome and up to 90 percent of the maize genome. Initially they were thought to exist only within a species.

Now we know jumping genes sometimes ignore traditional ideas of species separation. In 2005, the same jumping genes were reported to have been found within rice and millet, two different species of plants (*PLOS Biology*, "Jumping Genes"). More recently, one jumping gene first discovered in cows has since been discovered in reptiles, frogs, bats, elephants, and marsupials. They also appear to have had a significant impact on how at least some species evolve, for 25 percent of the genome of cows and sheep came from jumping genes originating elsewhere.

The vector in this transfer may be a virus.

We usually think of viruses as harmful, but scientists have discovered that viruses also apparently play important positive roles in biological evolution. On the borderline of life and not-life, viruses cannot reproduce on their own. They must invade a cell and use its resources to reproduce, using nearly every function of a host organism's cells to replicate and spread. Sometimes the host cells die from viral infection, but if they do not, sometimes elements of viral genomes can become part of its host's genome, and in so doing, change its characteristics.

The transfers probably take place through ticks, mosquitoes, and other organisms that prey on, but do not kill, different species, and thereby spread bacteria and viruses from one organism to another. But investigation of this phenomenon is still in very early stages. David Adelson observed, "Even though our recent work involved the analysis of genomes from over 750 species, we have only begun to scratch the surface of horizontal gene transfer." He explained "There are many more species to investigate and other types of jumping genes" (*Science Daily*, "Jumping Genes"; Ivancevic et al., "Horizontal transfer"). One implication of these discoveries is that the scope for horizontal gene transfer may be the entire biosphere, with bacteria and viruses serving both as intermediaries for gene transfer.

Continuums all the way down

Sometimes, two species will have existed so intimately in relation to one another for so long that at least one member can no longer live independently. This is so with some fungi that ants cultivate, and for the corn we grow. Sometimes, this dependency is mutual, so that each needs the other to reproduce, as is the case with yucca moths and yuccas. But this process can go further.

In some cases, organisms can become so mutually dependent they become a separate individual in their own right, as happened with eukaryotic cells. Consider lichens, composed of a partnership of algae and fungi. In recent years some lichens have been found to include separate species, a fungus, an alga, and more recently discovered, also bacteria and archaea. These kinds of relationships have been discovered to be far more common than once was imagined.

The world's great coral reefs are perhaps the largest structures on the planet produced directly by life. It turns out corals are also collective organisms of algae, the polyps, and a wide variety of bacteria. Among other things, this gives coral the ability to develop immunity to disease, even though the corals do not possess a system of cells that learn what pathogens look like and respond immediately if encountered again (Fraser, 2015). Discoveries such as these support Margulis' "Hologenome Theory of Evolution." She argued the true unit of natural selection is often an organism and *all the symbiotic microorganisms living with it*, not just the organism considered separately from this intimate context (Margulis and Fester, 1991). The holobiont (host organism plus its endocellular and extracellular microbiome) can be considered a distinct biological entity on which natural selection operates. This would seem to be another example of group selection as E. O. Wilson discussed with eusocial organisms (Wilson, *The Social Conquest of the Earth*, 142–7, 170–88). Eugene Rosenberg and Ilana Zilber-Rosenberg report that recent experiments demonstrate microbiota can play an initial role in speciation of organisms. Rapid changes in the microbiome genome could allow holobionts to adapt and survive under changing environmental conditions, thus providing the time necessary for the host genome to adapt and evolve (Rosenberg and Zilber-Rosenberg, "The hologenome concept").

The end of species?

Genesis 1:25 described God as making "the wild animals according to their kinds, the livestock according to their kinds, and all the creatures that move along the ground according to their kinds." Biological science accepted this basic division in kinds, even after it had long left biblical accounts of their genesis behind. But the more biologists examined what made a form of life a species, the more difficult it became to make clear distinctions. Frank Zachos' 2016 book, *Species Concepts in Biology*, listed thirty-two different conceptions of what constituted a species existing in modern biology, and in the years since, Zachos said, two more have arisen (Barras, "The End of Species," 37).

As biologists struggle with the lack of a unifying pattern in what constitutes species, and as the work of Margulis and others suggests a species may be better defined as an organism and its immediate context of microorganisms, perhaps the entire concept should be jettisoned. Some biologists now argue the term be replaced by "clade" which means a "group sharing a common ancestor and so comprising a separate twig on the tree of life"

(Barras, "The End of Species," 39). For example, instead of calling ourselves, Neanderthals, and Denisovans separate species, we should be classified as separate clades, but what constitutes a clade varies with the scientist's intent. Clades are nested, one in another, as each branch in turn splits into smaller branches, so, for different questions, we, Neanderthals, and Denisovans can be considered common members of a clade that split from the great apes. *Lineage, not genetics, is what matters.*

Chimeras

In 1998, Karen Keegan needed a kidney transplant. She was tested for compatible donors within her family, and the results indicated she was not the biological mother of two of her three children, even though she had clearly given birth to them. This seemed impossible.

Additional research revealed that soon after conception, the egg that was to become Karen fused with another female egg that, had this not happened, would have become her twin. The fused egg contained two separate DNA blueprints. She had originated from two different genomes, one of which gave rise to her blood and some of her eggs while the other genome was carried in other eggs. Her "twin" was the biological mother of two of her children, even though, because of this fusion, she didn't have a twin. Biologically, Karen was more than one person, she was a "chimera," a single organism composed of cells with different genotypes.

In 2002, Lydia Kay Fairchild applied for state benefits for herself and her children. DNA tests were made on both her and the father of her children. It turned out their father was who he said he was, but she was not their mother. A normal DNA test proving a mother-child link would show a 50 percent match between their DNA patterns, but Fairchild's DNA did not match theirs at all. The state suspected welfare fraud, and ultimately monitored her third pregnancy, taking a blood sample from the newborn as soon as it arrived. According to the sample, she was not its mother either. Except she obviously was.

We now know many people, particularly women, possess genomes from multiple people. Mothers and fetuses apparently frequently exchange DNA as well. Sometimes when twins begin to develop within a womb, one absorbs the other, as happened to Karen Keegan. As it does, a part of its potential sibling's genome, and the tissues it formed, becomes integrated into its own body. Biological individuality is not the same as psychological individuality (Zimmer, "DNA Doubletake").

But what is psychological individuality?

Even our minds ...

We are now ready to examine the evidence that, however limited our understanding of how the "combination problem" described by David Chalmers may be, it is solved all around us on a daily basis, even to help create our minds.

Scientists recently discovered that certain bacteria can significantly increase the intelligence of mice, once they are exposed to them (*Science Daily*, "Can bacteria make you smarter?"). These bacteria are commonly present in the soil, and so, most mice have been exposed. In a fascinating experiment, specially raised, completely sterile mice were taught to run a maze. After learning how, they were exposed to these bacteria. They ran the maze faster. When the bacteria were eliminated, their speed declined to its previous level. At least with respect to running mazes, the collective organism mouse-plus-bacteria was more intelligent than mouse-minus-bacteria.

The intelligence of mice, and presumably other mammals, can be enhanced by radically different organisms that are also able to live independently from them, in the soil. This discovery adds a fascinating possibility as to why kids like to eat dirt. It also adds an even more fascinating question as to the nature of our own individuality, since what is more "us" than our minds?

Greater apparent intelligence was not the only difference in these mice. Normal mice are social; mice raised to be bacteria free are not. Bacteria free mice preferred isolation to interacting even with mice they already knew (O'Donnell, "Cryan Explains Gut Feelings").

Apparently, we are as open to this kind of symbiotic relationship as are mice. The bacteria within our guts can make good health possible, and can even influence our minds for the better. Bacteria and our brains are intimately connected, and our minds are in part the result. In *Scientific American*, Charles Schmidt writes that scientists increasingly believe "the brain acts on gastrointestinal and immune functions [helping] shape the gut's microbial makeup, and gut microbes make neuroactive compounds, including neurotransmitters and metabolites that also act on the brain" (Schmidt, "Mental Health"). We also know gut bacteria can make the chemicals brain cells use to communicate. As in cases of more traditional coevolution between inter-dependent species, microbes have been within us throughout our evolution-ary history. Human and bacterial cells evolved, as Laura Sanders put it, "like a pair of entwined trees, growing and adapting into a (mostly) harmonious ecosystem" (Sanders, "Microbes").

It's not just bacteria

For good reason, mice are afraid of cats. Wise mice stay out of their sight and actively avoid places where cats have recently been. However, a mouse infected by the parasite *Toxoplasma gondii* is fearless, easily moves out into the open, and is attracted to the smell of cat urine. To complete its life cycle the parasite needs the infected mouse to be eaten by a cat, and because it influences their behavior, infected mice are far more vulnerable to cats (Mcauliffe, "How Your Cat is Making You Crazy"). Is it the mouse that is act-ing? The parasite? Or the relational entity, mouse + parasite?

T. gondii also infects human beings. Unlike cats, those infecting us cannot reproduce, but they can survive. An infected woman can pass the infection to her fetus, and sometimes toxoplasmosis causes neurologic or ocular disease in the child. The threat is not great; about one-third of the world's population is infected, and these dire results are rare. But they can happen. Otherwise, scientists long thought that *T. gondii* did not impact healthy people.

New evidence suggests *T. gondii* may influence human behavior much more than suspected (Mcauliffe, "Your Cat"; Flegr et al., "Induction of changes"; Flegr, "Influence"; *Science Daily*, "How common cat parasite"; Flegr, "Effects of toxoplasmosis"). A recent study indicates infection by toxo-plasmosis is linked with entrepreneurial business activity. Starting a busi-ness is risky, and most new businesses do not survive for long. On balance, entrepreneurs are less averse to taking risks than are non-entrepreneurs. The authors report that *T. gondii* infection influenced both individual- and societal-scale entrepreneurship activities. Students testing positive for *T. gondii* exposure were significantly more likely to major in business and even more likely to emphasize "management and entrepreneurship" over other business-related subjects. Among business professionals examined, *T. gon-dii*-positive individuals were also significantly more likely to have started their own business compared with others.

These findings may shed light on large-scale cultural differences. Depending on the population examined, infection rates among human beings from *T. gondii* range from 20 percent to 80 percent. The parasite might even affect cultural development, altering trajectories between cultures where infection is high and those where it is low (*Medical News*, "Toxoplasma"). Nations with higher infection rates had fewer people citing "fear of failure" in discouraging new business ventures (Johnson et al., "Risky business"). Apparently, this is yet another example of individuals being the unifying mental pattern emerging out of a network of relationships with other individuals, rather than some kind of irreducible entity entering into relationships that remain external to it. Are infected human beings acting as individual human beings as traditionally conceived, or as something more complex? While a parasite in a mouse, *T. gondii*'s status in human beings is more complex. It is dangerous for pregnant women but might benefit would-be entrepreneurs. Might the individual uninfected human plus the individual *T. gondii* collectively create a new, more complex, individual that integrates both?

What is an individual?

We are learning that bacteria form essential components of our own bodies, performing tasks necessary for us to live, such as synthesizing vitamins, digesting food, and protecting us against pathogens (Kolata, "In Good Health?"). They also interact with our nerves. We might not be able to survive without bacteria to perform these tasks, and in turn, many of them cannot survive outside us. Each person has perhaps one thousand species of benign to beneficial bacteria living within us. Collectively they possess far more DNA variability than our strictly mammalian body.

These patterns of relationship are so far from traditional ideas about individuals that many biologists suggest we should be considered ecosystems, which takes us to Emma Restall Orr's observation about communities and ecosystems early in this chapter. An ecosystem reaches a state in which it remains more or less unchanged, in spite of the fact that the species that make it up are continuously substituted by others, even to the point that a complete change of organisms can take place, similar to the change that occurs inside a human organism. "In short: the species change, but the structure does not," comments Professor José A. Cuesta (*Science Daily*, "Species are to ecosytems"). Other biologists prefer describing us as superorganisms (Sleator, "The human superorganism"). I usually prefer this term because, unlike an ecosystem, an organism possesses a center of action. Organisms are in some sense aware. Ecosystems are not passive. They can create and sustain conditions that favor some organisms over others. Given what I have argued so far, an ecosystem might have a systemic "presence" that is in some ways a coherent consciousness, but we have no reason to think ecosystems can act to choose an outcome in any deliberate sense. The issue here rests on the degree of awareness an ecosystem has *as a whole.*

However, as centers of action, we had no awareness of the complexity of our own bodies until this was discovered by science, and in this sense the ecosystem term fits as well. Who we are as an organism emerges from networks of relationships between other organisms that do not themselves intend such an outcome. Individuals at every level are emergent phenomena.

Individuality and relationship

The traditional idea of individuals as having firm boundaries is dissolving in front of us, transforming what we think of as physical individuality, even including our most individual characteristic: our minds. I am not questioning whether individuals exist or not; I am questioning how we think about them/us. We very much exist as individuals, but we are different kinds of individuals in different contexts. In addition, the boundaries of our biological individuality do not match those of our psychological individuality.

In theory, the distinction between individuals is clear. Individuals can possess a coherent sense of self, while communities are simply a form within nature without interiority. Communities do not have unified minds even when they act as a whole. In addition, unlike individuals, their boundaries are often indistinct. But, as evidenced in the question of whether we are organisms or ecosystems, "where nature's actuality is in play, such distinctions blur—because nature is fundamentally a series of interactions, not a population of subjects" (Orr, *The Wakeful World*, 217). We are not simply organisms living in an external environment, we are also constituted out of at least some of the relations making up the environment. We also often think of species and environments as distinct, but species can be the most important part of the environment or ecosystem. They can even transform the original ecosystem into another, as happened on some

Aleutian islands, where introduced foxes ate once-abundant ground-nesting birds. With the birds gone, the islands' soils, once fertilized by their droppings, became impoverished due to frequent rains leaching out these nutrients. In time rich grasslands became scrubby brush.

The linkage between species and ecosystems flows both ways. Given enough time, and geographical separation, an introduced species will diverge from its original migrants, as was demonstrated by the race of dwarf mammoths that once lived on Wrangell Island (Wade, "The Woolly Mammoth's Last Stand"). In fact, a single species can even diverge while coexisting within the same ecosystem if it supplies enough possible niches for them to specialize, as Darwin's finches on the Galapagos Islands memorably demonstrated. Sometimes female preference alone can lead to such differentiation (Mayhew, *Discovering Evolutionary Biology*, 9–12). This distinction does not align with whether the relations are between biological organisms, or between such an organism and abiotic phenomena. Usually an ecologist does not need to pay attention to wind-blown dust from parts of Africa, but sometimes this more inclusive frame is important, because not only is the dust an important source of phosphorus for the Amazonian rainforest (NASA, "Satellite Reveals"), it appears to have made the Caribbean's coral reefs and Bahama islands possible by fertilizing the ocean with otherwise rare nutrients (Main, "Saharan Dust"). Saharan dust nourishes the cyanobacteria that then make nitrogen available for the aquatic ecosystem, enabling them to create the carbonates that corals use to create reefs, and even the Bahama islands.

Individuality at every level is an expression of relationships, some of which are traditionally considered external to the individual examined. Some of these relations are tightly coupled, as in the eukaryotic cell made up of what were once prokaryotic cells. Others are looser but still tightly bound, as with the gut bacteria on which we depend and which depend on us, but, unlike in endosymbiosis, maintain a separate individuality. Then there are bacteria that can live separately from us, and we from them, but which might be essential for a truly human mind, as the mouse and soil bacteria research suggests. Finally, there are very loosely coupled but still connected organisms, such as plants, which create the air we breathe and which we animals in turn help to survive. The division between the tightest and most loosely coupled organism is not a boundary, it is a continuum of connections within a network of breathtaking complexity.

It is clear that, as a practical matter, the combination problem that opened this chapter has been solved. Individual organisms, with their own kinds of awareness, can combine into larger more complex organisms that have new features and forms of individuality not present in their components, and may not even be aware of the individuals that, collectively, make up their own individuality.

This research demonstrates that any individual is itself a kind of community of other individuals. As in a dissipative structure, what makes that community an individual is "a continuity of patterns, provoked by and provoking further repetition of interaction" (Orr, *The Wakeful World*, 224). Life is an entwined network of selves down to the cellular level, and awareness is apparently a feature in some form down to the quantum level, becoming a self as soon as biological individuality emerges at the cellular level.

From the simplest cell to the most complex human individuality, the entire biological world, from our bodies, to our minds, to our selves, to our environments, is constituted out of relationships. Biology demonstrates we are deeply integrated with many forms of life existing in varying degrees of independence and dependence. What seems to distinguish individuals from ecosystems is not that one has firm boundaries and the other does not, but rather that individuals have selves, and ecosystems do not.

Orr explains: "As the subject becomes self-defined it asserts a measure of control, adjusting its perception of its external and internal context, honing the coherence of its own part of nature's mind. The inner community of minds develops the capacity to respond as a coherent interiority of mind" (Orr, *The Wakeful World*, 202–3). We are self-aware, creative, beings made possible by fundamentally cooperative relationships *at every level*. As theoretical physicist Carlo Rovelli puts it, "The world is not a collection of things, it is a collection of events—networks of kisses, not of stones" (Rovelli, *The Order of Time*). If the universe is an interconnected quantum system, and quantum phenomena can influence living beings, as quantum biology suggests, and all individuality emerges from relationships between simpler individuals, the phenomena I and so many others encountered within spiritual and psychic realms are far less confusing.

Chapter 8
THE LIVING WORLD: MIND AND CULTURE

*What if there were creatures, entities, that were made up
entirely of ideas, purely of language or something…*
—ALAN MOORE

HUMAN BEINGS ARE UNIQUE in our ability to have ideas and beliefs. But looked at from a different perspective, ideas and beliefs possess us to a unique extent. It's a two-way road.

Social scientists have long debated the nature of individuals' relationship to the society in which they live, given that individuals exist, *and* every individual seems in some way to be an expression of his or her society and times. For a long time, two approaches have dominated the social sciences. "Methodological individualists" tried to reduce society to the logic of individual human action. Understanding society came from focusing on how individuals interacted for their own purposes, even in cases where unintended social patterns emerged. American society is hospitable to this approach, for it harmonizes with Protestant emphasis on individuals in relation to God and Jesus. Ayn Rand's novels reflect this outlook as well. We encountered it in much more sophisticated forms in David Axelrod's iterated prisoner's dilemma game, discussed in chapter 6.

Others argued individuals' actions and beliefs were expressions of deeper causes. For Marxists, we were shaped by our economic class. For racists, our racial or genetic attributes explained how we thought. National identity performed the same function for nationalists. Others, such as Freudians, reduced individuals to unconscious drives shaped by childhood experiences.

Methodological individualists and their opponents all sought to reduce explanations to a single deepest cause to explain all that was most important in society. Advocates for each view attacked weaknesses in the alternatives, and there were plenty of weaknesses to criticize.

In the early half of the twentieth century some European philosophers began arguing that neither approach adequately grasped these issues. Relying on their insights, two sociologists, Peter Berger and Thomas Luckmann, proposed an alternative perspective: we could understand human action by recognizing how it was embedded within *three always present* "moments" (Berger and Luckmann, *The Social Construction of Reality*, 61). The first two, our being individuals and our being shaped by our society, reflected the traditional dichotomy that society is either a human creation or humans are social creations. The third transformed that dichotomy: society is an "objective reality."

But what does that mean? Understanding it will lead us another big step toward grasping polytheism, and indeed, many occult phenomena, though these were far from their intentions.

By their third "moment," Berger and Luckmann meant we *always experience* our world in socially shaped terms we *usually* take to be objectively true. For the small child, terms like "mother" or "father" are as unquestioned as a "turtle" or "tree." A mother, father, turtle, or tree is an example of different kinds of things. These concepts provide a map of meaning through which children can orient themselves among many mothers, fathers, turtles, and trees (Berger and Luckmann, *Social Construction*, 58). The same is true for everything else we learn to take for granted about society until, at some point, we notice a lack of fit between things we had taken for granted. Trees are tall, but on my vacation to Colorado people told me plants a few feet tall on top of a mountain were trees. Mothers are loving, but my friend's mom is not. Such realizations can provoke our questioning because they contradict what we once took for granted.

Cracks in our seamless view of the world usually happen by adolescence, and sometimes much earlier. But whatever these doubts might be, and however they arise, they always exist within the larger taken-for-granted world we accept as true. We can never stand outside all of our social conditioning and evaluate it as a whole. We can only examine certain elements, while provisionally accepting the rest. No part of social reality is immune to rethinking, but we can only question something from within a perspective at least provisionally accepting the rest.

All three "moments," or processes, Berger and Luckmann described are always going on. We are cultural and psychological individuals shaped by complex relations of meaning, rather like what we previously observed with biological individuals being emergent expressions of complex biological relations. Both societies and the individuals within them are patterns of meaning emerging from relationships, *each helping create the other.*

Although they did not use the term, Berger and Luckmann provided a kind of ecological perspective for studying society. They thought they could somehow reduce this view to methodological individualism, as if you could explain an ecology by the actions of its members (Lewis, "Peter Berger and His Critics"). This was not the first time people uncovered more than they thought, a point important for this chapter, as we shall see.

Socially embedded ideas about the world stand on a kind of edge between the realms of objective public phenomena, like people parading down a street, and those that are purely private and subjective, like what I think about the parade. They are mental, for they consist of meanings (a parade is not a crowd) but they also exist independently from us as individuals, in a field of social meaning giving us the basic conceptual tools we need to make our way in the world. (The people parading also see themselves as in a parade.)

I think Berger and Luckmann's insights go still deeper. They confined themselves to the simple subjective/objective dichotomy to describe a world that is rarely experienced as *purely* objective or subjective. They emphasized that society is a world of meaning and presence *independent* of our individual preferences, and it is sustained by the ongoing *collective* mental affirmations and actions of those living within it.

Society is not objective in the sense that a rock or tree is objective. If this third "moment" has any "objective reality" at all, it is in the realm of meaning that grows out of relationships, and the more complex the relationships, the more complex the meaning.

For a small child, "mother" is *not* like "rock," nor is she simply a social role, let alone a description of a biological connection. The child knows nothing about either. The word refers to an intimate relationship. In time, as the child learns more, the social role (mothering is one thing some people do among other things, like "work") and biology (she gave birth to me) are *added* to the term. "Mother" is a very complex term in a way a rock is not. As *objects* a woman and a rock are equally objective, but as carriers of meaning, a woman-as-mother carries far more complex "social objectivity" than a rock.

Meanings imply more than what is meant

Ideas often have content that those who initially had them did not imagine. Consider the belief that marriage should be about love. Until recently, people never imagined this ideal would become a reason for institutionalizing gay marriage. As recently as 1996, in a Gallup poll, only 27 percent of

Americans supported gay marriage, yet virtually all of them would approve of marrying for love alone. However, if love is a reason for marriage, and gay people love one another, the legitimacy of gay marriage is clearly implied. When this implication was repeatedly pointed out, many more Americans came to favor gay marriage. As of 2018, a majority, 67 percent, do (Madhani, "Poll"). Another important example concerns slavery. As an institution, slavery was thousands of years old, practiced on every inhabited continent, and largely taken for granted. When the Declaration of Independence was written, only a few people thought about its implications regarding slavery. However, the arguments for freedom from British rule, when put in terms of universal human rights, took on a life of their own. John Jay, a founder and first chief justice of the Supreme Court, wrote: "Prior to the great Revolution . . . our people had been so long accustomed to . . . having slaves, that very few of them even doubted the propriety and rectitude of it. Some liberal and conscientious men had indeed, by their conduct and writings, drawn the lawfulness of slavery into question . . . Their doctrines prevailed by almost insensible degrees, and was like the little lump of leaven which was put into three measures of meal" (Kurland and Lerner, eds., *Founders' Constitution*: "John Jay to the President").

Well before the Civil War, a majority of American states peacefully abolished slavery.

This process worked both ways. Once Southern leaders recognized the tension between the Declaration and slavery, they repudiated the document their ancestors had endorsed and risked and sometimes given their lives for. As John C. Calhoun, a senator from South Carolina and a US vice president, emphasized, "nothing can be more unfounded and false" than "the prevalent opinion that all men are born free and equal" (West, *Vindicating the Founders*, 33). Any particular meaning can be isolated and examined within the larger context of meanings in which it finds itself, and which we provisionally accept as true. When we do, we can be surprised because we can find new meanings no one suspected until they were discovered there, and sometimes when we do our world changes. *But they were "there" in some sense all along, awaiting discovery.* We often say more than we know, not just through psychological slips but through offering insights with implications of which we are unaware. Afterwards their existence can seem obvious.

Philosopher of science William Bartley writes: "What is distinctive about an item of objective knowledge … is its potential for being understood or identified in some way that has not yet been imagined … Objective knowledge interacts with the individuals living in that ecological niche, and may transform the niche itself. And it adapts in a way analogous to, though not identical with, biological evolution" (Bartley, *Unfathomed Knowledge*, 60–1). What makes a book an example of objective knowledge is not its physical characteristics, nor the marks on a page, but the meaning of the words they depict. But this meaning is not akin to the meaning of a physical rock. It has "fuzzy edges" where what is most obvious bleeds out into Bartley's potentialities waiting to be discovered. What does "love" imply for marriage? What does "equality" imply for society? What does "inequality" imply for society? And so on. Often every interpretation of an idea that seems clear upon reflection just opens up new questions.

All this meaning exists in the realm of consciousness, not in the marks on a page or the physical book. If we treat consciousness or awareness as in some way a fundamental dimension of existence, as I have argued we should, the nature of Berger and Luckmann's third "moment" of society as an objective reality takes on greater substance.

Cultures as ecosystems

Analyses based on networks provide a common framework to unite understanding biological ecosystems with understanding their cultural equivalent. As Bartley noted above, objective knowledge interacts with individuals living in their "ecological niche." *A culture is an ideational ecosystem as the natural environment is a biological ecosystem.* One exists at the level of biological reproduction, innovation, and adaptation, the other at the level of mental reproduction, innovation, and adaptation.

Patterns equivalent to biological ones exist within the ideational social world. The market economy is the network of products and production incorporating all that is bought and sold. Like a biological ecology, some ways of producing, some professions, and some products will be more successful than others. When successful, they often create new niches for other ways of making a living, as cars created a niche for drive-in movies. New products can then change that economic ecosystem. In the 1950s there were around four thousand drive-in movie theaters, but today maybe three hundred survive. Among the causes of their decline was the rise of digital projectors, which are much more expensive than celluloid ones, combined with film increasingly going digital. Compared to indoor theaters, drive-ins have a smaller window to recoup their expenses (you don't go to one in the afternoon or during a snowstorm) nor can they offer many screens each showing a different feature. Like a life-form encountering competition it is ill prepared to handle, drive-ins are dying out, or surviving in very specialized niches.

Similar patterns exist throughout the cultural world. The "ecology of science" is the scientific community as a whole, its different fields, organizations, and projects all given coherence by their relation to one another. Science grows in complexity as new discoveries open up additional fields for exploration. At the same time, when a theory is replaced by a more reliable one, insights once regarded as basic to our understanding are abandoned, or confined to a much smaller niche, as happened to Newtonian physics, the longest-lived major scientific theory of all time.

Cities can be usefully considered social ecologies of intricately meshed economic and other cultural relationships. They also grow and decline and transform themselves in unexpected ways, by adapting or failing to adapt to environmental changes. We can select out social ecosystems such as markets or science or cities for study, but in reality, as with natural ecosystems, they interpenetrate. The particular ecological boundaries that matter to us arise from our questions, whether they probe the other-than-human world or the social ideational world.

If the human world as a whole consists of the social ecosystem, different societies will be the equivalent of rainforest, savannah, and tundra ecosystems. As with these biological systems, different customs, languages, and even psychological attitudes are more in harmony with some than are others. I have described how the attitudes of Protestant monotheists shaped early science, which in time shaped the human world as a whole, ultimately undermining Protestantism. Like the biosphere, a cultural world as a whole is unimaginably complex, virtually all of it linked—sometimes closely, sometimes more distantly—with other cultural ecosystems. As residents of one such social ecosystem, or perhaps as migratory members of several, our sense of who we are and how we think is influenced by the social networks in which we participate.

A culture provides a structure shaping how its members interact. It also responds to changes in how people relate, and often does so independently of anyone's intentions. As it does, in response, people may change the way they relate, as the automobile and now the smartphone transformed how young people related socially and romantically. In biology the term often used for this kind of perpetual mutual responding between organisms and their environment is called "coevolution." The same holds for cultures. We and our cultures coevolve.

Cultural innovations may gradually spread in unexpected ways, such as the tattoos so common in America today. Once-prominent cultural features may largely disappear, such as disco music and crew cuts. An innovation may shape future generations in ways unforeseen by anyone at the time the initial change was made, as did marriage for love. Sometimes a culture can change so dramatically as to become something quite different, as when hunter-gatherers took up agriculture, or agricultural societies transformed into urban technological ones (diZerega, *Faultlines*, 197–8). But cultural ecosystems have one important difference from biological ecosystems. Biological adaptation takes place through generational change. Social adaptation can happen with the speed of changing minds. My grandparents grew up when horses were common on city streets. Most lived to see the first man walk on the moon, live, on television.

Social organisms: human and otherwise

Just as we are not alone in biological ecosystems, sharing them with other organisms, neither are we alone in cultural ecosystems. Recognizing this takes us a major step toward freeing ourselves from inherited monotheistic assumptions about human cultural life. It also helps us understand how we live in an animate world "all the way down" (and, as chapter 9 will argue, all the way up).

Biological ecosystems are diverse collections of many organisms. A cultural ecology obviously depends on people and exists at the level of consciousness, but are there other kinds of organisms? I think there are at least two: organizations and memes.

An organism is the expression of its genome in relation with its environment. An organization is an expression of its sustaining ideas in relation with its environment. In the biological world, the genome adapts or dies, and with it, the organism that is its expression. In the social world, ideas adapt or die, and with them, the organizations and ways of life that are their expression. We now know that the genome expresses itself differently depending on its physical environment. This is called "epigenetics" (Hughes, "Epigenetics"). The ideas helping create organizations also change depending on their environment.

Over and over, we read of organizations established to achieve some goal subordinating that goal to serve their own prosperity and power. In 2010 the Red Cross raised hundreds of millions of dollars to help Haitians devastated by a large earthquake. About one quarter of the money went to its internal expenses, and its actual accomplishments helping Haitians were embarrassingly small (Sullivan and Elliott, "Report"). This is why I no longer contribute to them. Or consider police departments so corrupt that a major Hollywood movie was made about an exception, Frank Serpico, an honest cop in New York's far less than honest police force (Maas, *Serpico*). The movie led to important reforms, but the reforms did not last (Serpico, "The Police Are Still Out of Control"). The organization had a life of its own.

Organizations as organisms have interests that can conflict with the reason they were formed. Over time they will become increasingly independent actors, subordinating or even sacrificing the original goals they were established to pursue as well as shaping their human elements to be in harmony with those of the organization itself. I have written some scholarly analyses of why this happens in so many economic, political, religious, and charitable organizations, but for now, I will simply say they often shape their human members to serve the organization, even at the cost of why they originally joined (diZerega, "Not Simply Construction"). But important as organizations are, the other ideational organism with which we share the social world is even more so.

Memes as ideational organisms

Richard Dawkins coined the term "meme" to refer to ideas or actions *in their social context* (Jordan, "What's in a meme?"). Comparing memes to genes,

Dawkins wrote that they adapt, flourish, and die, through our success or failure in using them, for we are their carriers (Dawkins, *The Selfish Gene*, 192). As memes, ideas adapt, spread, die or mutate through their interaction in social ecosystems in ways analogous to genes in a natural one. Ideas manifest in the material world through their ability to influence behavior. As elements within a culture, ideas influence the world through the actions of the people guided by them. Particularly powerful ideas often do this through their ability to inspire, create, and preserve organizations.

Memes are not my private thoughts, that live or die with me. *Broadly defined*, a meme is any mental creation that is a unit of cultural transmission. Public ideas such as "America," "democracy," "justice," "equality," "God," "vegetable," and "marriage" are memes. Some memes are not words. The opening chords of Beethoven's Fifth Symphony is a meme we would all probably recognize. Shaking hands is a meme. The internet images uniting a picture with a message are memes. Symbols, such as our flag, are memes, and as the flag demonstrates, sometimes a meme's meanings can be many and contradictory.

Memes survive, decline, adapt, or mutate over time, depending on the mental energy people supply them. To succeed, a meme need only be adopted by others. It does not need to be understood intellectually, and many are not, or are understood differently by different people. For example, "democracy" means different things to different people, even when all use it in the same general way. Memes' meanings are shaped by their cultural context—that is, by their relationship to other memes. For example, "vegetable" is not just a plant. It can also refer to a kind of person or health condition, and in so doing also emphasize certain supposed qualities of plants. As we saw in the last chapter, sometimes meanings that make up the meme "vegetable" describe some people better than some vegetables.

Memes shape the cultural ecosystem within which we live because we usually think with and through them. Without memes, our thinking would be vastly simpler. Most of the time, our thinking flows effortlessly within an existing network of memes, without our thinking much about them. The same is true for nonverbal memes. If you want to experience the force of a powerful meme, refuse to shake someone's hand when they extend it to you, while still seeking to come across as friendly.

Our minds use memes as naturally as a fish uses water. Normally words and customs emerge "spontaneously," giving our thinking coherence while relying on the networks of other memes surrounding us to provide needed contexts. Because memes' meanings can be complex, we can have a conversation with another person, using common memes we understand differently, like "democracy" and never actually communicate, even when we think we did, because each weighs the elements in their "penumbra of meaning" differently.

While we cannot stand aside and evaluate every meme comprising important parts of our cultural ecosystem, we can step back from particular ones. Singling a meme out for examination is one way to begin distancing our thought from it. Rather than thinking with and through it, we examine it from a distance. As we do, it becomes our tool rather than a taken-for-granted part of our world. However, when we examine a meme, such as our flag, we rely on other memes to do so, such as America, democracy, justice, imperialism, and racism. The flag-as-meme connects with all these other memes, and more, in an ideational field. In normal kinds of awareness, we can never stand outside all memes.

We can create new memes, as Dawkins did, *although once in the public sphere they are free to flourish or not, independently of our intent.* Dawkins' term evolved in ways he never anticipated, such as how it is now usually applied in the internet. Dawkins is not alone. When Robert Heinlein coined the term "grok" in his novel *Stranger in a Strange Land*, he never imagined it would play a role in the future Neopagan Church of All Worlds (see bibliography), or be employed in the field of computer programming.

A meme exists independently of each of us, but not from all of us. A single meme needs a larger ideational context in which it "lives," just as a lion needs a larger ecological context within which it lives. In both cases this ecological context shapes its characteristics. In turn, it influences its ecosystem.

Along with people, memes populate the cultural ecosystem, enabling us to be social beings with a language and customs providing common meanings enabling us to communicate beyond simple signals. When we uncritically accept them, as we usually must, *from a meme's perspective we are their hosts.* We give them mental energy, helping them replicate. Memes constitute part of the reality within which we live, and in living, we reproduce some of them by using them. People and memes each need one another.

Chapter 8

Are memes alive?

The answer to this question depends on how we regard consciousness. My own perspective adopts Orr's ecological framework. Emma Restall Orr writes of language: "…the verbal element of human language can be understood as a flow of interactions with deeply rooted yet evolving word forms, and as such it is not a creation of the human intellect, but another series of relationships which go to create the mind, the subject, and the self" (Orr, *The Wakeful World*, 241).

Is a meme always locked up within a physical body as a private reality or illusion, or is it a basic constituent of the world? I find it striking that secular scientists consistently describe memes as if they were alive. For example, James Gleick writes: "Memes emerge in brains and travel outward, establishing beachheads on paper and celluloid and silicon and anywhere else information can go. They are not to be thought of as elementary particles but as organisms. The number three is not a meme; nor is the color blue, nor any simple thought, any more than a single nucleotide can be a gene. Memes are complex units, distinct and memorable—units with staying power" (Gleick, "What Defines a Meme?"). Mark Pagel, another evolutionary biologist, writes "the feature of memes we have to bear in mind is that there is no necessary reason they have to help us: whatever form makes them likely to be transmitted, they are likely to adopt." The idea that the arts and religion serve humankind "must confront the simpler idea that these cultural elements might exist for no other reason than that they have evolved to be good at manipulating, exploiting, or taking advantage of *us* to aid *their* transmission" (Pagel, *Wired for Culture*, 135).

From this perspective, memes are "organisms" needing mental rather than physical energy to flourish. We feed organisms food for nourishment. We feed memes our attention for nourishment. Memes replicate by attracting the attention they need to survive and increase. They do this within individual minds and then spread to other minds through people's words or other actions.

But is a meme "alive"? The frequent comparison of memes with viruses is a good place to start. Physical viruses exist on the borderline of life and nonlife. Because they cannot reproduce on their own, viruses are not considered alive by most who study them. They depend on host cells for that. Yet viruses can mutate and evolve, as we discover to our sorrow every flu season. Like a virus, a meme can mutate and evolve, and, as a virus needs a cell to replicate, a meme needs a mind to do so. To persist and flourish, memes must "infect" hosts and then overcome barriers to their spread. Like a virus, a meme contains many, but not all, of the characteristics usually attributed to life.

Like a virus, the evolution of a single meme can be a powerful force in shaping a society. I will return to my marriage-for-love example. At one time in the West, people usually married to create a family, to make an alliance between families, out of religious duty, or to assure security in old age. *Love didn't matter*. As Montesquieu once observed in 1712, a "husband who loves his wife is a man who has not enough merit to engage the affections of some other woman" (Montesquieu, *Persian Letters*, Letter LV). In such a context, gay marriage was unthinkable.

Once the meme "marriage" incorporated love as a reason for its existence, the stage was set for a major transformation. In time, love came to dominate all other reasons for marriage. A meme thousands of years old changed its central characteristics, and as it did, the once unthinkable became thinkable. In the United States, marriage for love legitimized marriage between classes, then interracial marriage in places where it had long been outlawed. Finally, it legitimized gay marriage, an idea once almost inconceivable. Marriage primarily for love was a memetic mutation that ultimately changed the meme's cultural ecosystem.

We are neither the products of forces we do not control, nor the lords and masters of society. We are organisms sharing a mental ecological realm with memes, and, like organisms within a biological ecosystem, our independence is real, *but partial*. We *and* memes are interactive agents connected through our mental energy, and over time, both they and we coevolve together.

This view is not as counterintuitive as it might seem when we realize even our private mentality itself is shaped by more than our biological genome. The evidence connecting entrepreneurship with toxoplasmosis, and the discovery that gut bacteria able to influence our minds also exist in our brains suggests our individuality, real as it is, is a most complex thing.

We no more own our cultural ecosystem than a California bay laurel tree owns its ecosystem.

Consciousness is independent of physical form

Ideas, and the organizations through which they sometimes act, are like organisms needing mental rather than physical energy from people to flourish. Ideas compete for this support and the most successful often have symbiotic relations with other ideas and organizations, the better to obtain and maintain that support. When no one supports an idea, it "dies," or perhaps goes dormant, becoming a kind of ideational spore of meaning, awaiting a more supportive environment.

I have argued that modern physics supports the possibility that consciousness in some sense can be considered a fundamental property of reality. While for years and years people have provided anecdotes supporting this view, they have been casually dismissed by those committed to a mechanistic view of the world. Beyond our personal experiences, such as those I described in chapter 6, and suggestions by quantum physicists, what other evidence exists?

Very interesting scientific research is in considerable harmony with the argument that mental phenomena need not be confined to physical bodies. In addition, some research indicates our minds can be creators, but once we create something, to some degree it becomes separate from us physically. Our minds are always operating to some degree beyond our physical bodies.

The most thoroughly studied and best verified example of the mind not being confined to our bodies has been done while investigating extrasensory perception. For ESP to work, consciousness cannot be limited to within the skulls of humans or other conscious entities. By its very nature ESP is difficult to test through traditional scientific methods, methods assuming physical reality is not changed by the attitudes of the observer.

Russell Targ, who once oversaw remote viewing experiments at Stanford Research Institute, argues the existence of ESP is no longer reasonably in doubt (Targ, *The Reality of ESP*). Remote viewing experiments are one example. In the early 1970s the SRI began testing whether a person could perceive visual information about a faraway location to which they had never been. The research was convincing enough to interest the military, leading to one of the most powerful demonstrations of this capacity.

In 1979 the Soviets had constructed a very large building a quarter-mile from the Baltic Sea. No one in American intelligence had any idea what it was for. It was near the coast, but no channel connected it to the sea. Satellites had discovered it, but of course could tell nothing about what was inside. A remote viewer, and member of the military, was asked to investigate. He reported they were building a huge submarine, bigger than any ever before constructed. He also gave details of its unusual construction. At the time, the military found this unbelievable since the building was inland. But somewhat later, the Russians constructed a channel to the building and the first Typhoon-class submarine was launched. At five hundred feet long, it was much larger than any submarine then in existence (Smith, *Reading the Enemy's Mind*; Targ, *The Reality of ESP*, 115–16; Jacobsen, *Phenomena*, 233–6). Similar techniques enabled Americans to find a crashed Soviet bomber in Africa before the Russians were able to, and so obtain valuable cryptographic information (Targ, *The Reality of ESP*, 116).

Older readers might remember that it was during this time the Pentagon hatched plans to build railroad loops in Nevada and western Utah where trains would transport real and fake MX intercontinental missiles. The idea was that no one could tell which missiles were real and which were fake, and with thousands moving around to forty-six hundred different missile shelters, a surprise attack would be impossible.

Using a computer to generate a randomized pattern, Charles Tart at the University of California, Davis, used psychics to try and beat the game. Marbles were used in place of missiles. An average score would get about 10 percent of the guesses right as to where the marbles might be. Remote viewers trained in SRI methods averaged 25 percent and one scored 80 percent. The MX system was never built (Jacobsen, *Phenomena*, 216–20).

I will provide one more example. Dr. Elizabeth Mayer was a psychologist at the University of California, Berkeley. She had a daughter, a talented young harpist, who sometimes gave public performances. Over the weekend of one performance, she left her very valuable Celtic harp where she had performed. Returning the next day, she found it had been stolen.

Her daughter was devastated, and so Mayer explored every avenue she could think of seeking to get the harp back. None succeeded. Then a friend recommended she try a dowser. Mayer scoffed, until her friend reminded her that she said she'd try "anything." She decided to try—and tracked down the head of a dowsing society, who lived in Arkansas. She called him to describe the problem. He told her, "Just a moment." He returned, to tell her the harp was still in Oakland, and if she sent him a map, he'd tell her where it was. She did, and he did. She put up fliers around the neighborhood where the dowser had pinpointed a particular house, and soon received a telephone call. In a late-night meeting in a Safeway parking lot, the harp was returned.

As she drove back to Berkeley, once she relaxed enough from her excitement at retrieving the harp, Mayer realized, as she put it, "This changes everything." Given her worldview, what just happened could not have happened. As a result, the scientific papers she had been working on remained in her desk for years, while she explored this radically different reality she could no longer reasonably doubt (Mayer, *Extraordinary Knowing*).

The long history of investigations into distance healing, remote viewing, and other phenomena suggests that our minds, our consciousness, are not simply confined to our physical body (Radin, *Supernormal*). Our consciousness is also open to another dimension, in which we are potentially able to access information physically unavailable to us. Consciousness is not localized and information can be acquired without there being a physical connection in any currently understood sense.

But what about *memes?*

A living world: language, memes, and thought forms

In an unusually inclusive discussion, Stephan Schwarz reported a number of experiments supportive of the existence of nonlocal ways of knowing. While he does not discuss them, memes are consistent with the existence of nonlocal perception since they exist in a socially objective realm in some way independent of individuals (Schwarz, "Nonlocal Consciousness"). The experimental results are consistent with the existence of memes as I have described them.

Most experiments involved using words in creative ways, but one used the same approach to investigate symbols, which are also memes. It was conducted by Robert Schorn, Gottfried Tappeiner, and Janette Walde, professors at two Austrian universities. They tested the hypothesis "People are more likely to respond to symbols that were or have been widely known but that they are not consciously familiar with, as compared to similar symbols (control symbols) that have been artificially created for the test" (Schorn et al.,

"Analyzing 'spooky action,'" 46). The investigators picked symbols once well known that were now largely forgotten, or alternatively, symbols familiar to some people but not those selected as subjects. For each real symbol, they created a corresponding fake one. Subjects were shown pairs of symbols, one real and one fake, and asked to judge which "had more 'spirit.'" In a follow-up study they repeated the experiment using real words and anagrams in Cyrillic. They concluded "both in the test with the symbols and that with the Russian words, the original stimuli were selected significantly more often than the artificially created control stimuli. The result concerning the symbols is even more unambiguous than that regarding the Russian words" (Schorn et al., "Analyzing 'spooky action,'" 54). Emma Restall Orr writes of language: "Animistically, the verbal element of human language can be understood as a flow of interactions with deeply rooted yet evolving word forms, and as such it is not a creation of the human intellect, but another series of relationships which go to create the mind, the subject, and the self" (Orr, *The Wakeful World*, 241). Think about how we informally talk about ideas. If the idea is meaningful enough, we often speak of it as if we encountered an independent entity.

- I am *captivated* by an idea.
- I am *obsessed* with an idea.
- I am *intrigued* by an idea.
- I am *revolted* by an idea.
- I am *infatuated* with an idea.
- I am *in love* with an idea.
- I am *loyal* to an idea.
- I am *interested* in an idea.
- I cannot get an idea *to leave me alone.*

An idea can be powerful, grand, subtle, boring, comforting, fascinating, repellant, tantalizing, upsetting, or difficult to get hold of. So can people. We refer to ideas as if they are alive and exist independently from us, *because we experience them that way.* And here is where things get interesting.

We usually think of ideas as tools that empower us in our lives, but in return, they shape our lives. Think of the old adage that when the only tool you have is a hammer, everything is looked at in its capacity to be a nail. Like other tools, ideas shape our perceptions.

Serious trouble arises when we identify too closely with an idea. When we experience it as a part of us, as when I am a ____ or I must be loyal to ___, we "fall under its spell." The term "spell" is revealing. *We become the idea's tool, rather than it being ours.* Not all memes are like this. I doubt anyone identifies with shaking hands or the opening notes of Beethoven's Fifth. But ideas and symbols are another matter.

There is one way we talk about concepts and ideas that we do not use regarding human beings: an idea can be "in the air." Public ideas are memes, and not only do we describe memes as if they were alive, we speak of them as if they existed in some realm other than the purely physical. They do.

Thought forms and egregores

Those of us who have done healing work with energy know intention and focus influence not only our actions, they can also influence what happens in others' bodies. Mind-plus-energy-plus-will can influence others physically separate from us. Consider my own discovery related in chapter 6 that healing energy was not the placebo effect. The same point applies to many kinds of magick. One such magickal creation is commonly called a thought form.

In magickal terms, thought forms are deliberately created centers of focused mental energy possessing a semiconscious existence that can act independently. Thought forms are usually created to carry out some task, often protection. When not "fed" with mental energy, thought forms eventually dissipate. Thought forms are also commonly thought to have access to the contents of the minds that sustain them, at least insofar as they relate to their reason for existence.

One fascinating account of creating a thought form is described in Iris Owen's *Conjuring Up Philip: An Adventure in Psychokinesis.* Sadly, it is out of print, and pricey when purchased used, but you can easily watch a YouTube copy of a television broadcast made in Toronto. It is titled "The Philip (Phillip) Experiment" (YouTube, "The Philip Experiment"). A group of Canadian researchers created a fictional character, Philip. To do so, they wrote a fictional biography and one member drew an imaginary portrait. The group focused intently on him as described, seeking contact through classical séance methods. They wanted to see whether their efforts would gradually give Philip some psychic reality. In time they succeeded. While created by the group, once in existence, Philip was independent of particular members, for if someone was absent he still "came through." If thought forms are to last, they must be able to renew the energy that gives them power—and often, as in Philip's case, this is through being "fed" by those who created them.

But not all such phenomena are deliberate creations. In occult terminology, an *egregore* is a mental field that arises from the more diffused focus of many people in a common context. It was apparently developed to describe the group mind, a kind of personality that a group takes on independently of its members. Egregores are not so much deliberate creations as the result of many minds sharing a common focus. The best discussion I have found is in Greer's *Inside a Magical Lodge*: "Groups of every kind tend to develop personalities of their own—personalities that have their roots in the individual personalities of the group members, but grow and evolve into something that is much more than the sum of its parts" (Greer, *Inside a Magical Lodge*, 101).

Egregores are neither good nor bad, they are rather coherent patterns of group psychic energy, and as such can arise during a football game, a Nazi Party rally, or even the "feel" of a city or neighborhood (Orr, *The Wakeful World*, 204–5).

We can take this insight further. The egregore that arises from a reasonably tightly knit organization, be it a team, a police department, or a political party, can shape its members to behave in ways they otherwise would not. Anyone who creates a successful organization with a strong sense of identity also creates the conditions for an egregore to arise.

An egregore usually refers to a psychic force far less focused than a personality. But can something as focused as Philip also arise spontaneously? I think it depends on the nature of the collective focus.

Early in my Wiccan years I was on the periphery of a group investigating such phenomena as manifesting in the form of Darth Vader (diZerega, "Darth Vader"). Vader was certainly a widespread and popular meme. He also attracted considerable mental and emotional energy, particularly while people watched the original Star Wars series. In time, Vader as thought form could cause considerable harm to others' lives if they were open to this kind of psychic influence. This is what led to the investigation I observed.

Memes are rarely deliberate creations, and, once in existence, are open to use and influence by an open-ended number of people for many different purposes. They arise through a selective process that incorporates many minds in their maintenance, many more than are involved in creating thought forms. Vader was a kind of force sustained as an egregore would be, but with more focus as a personality than a traditional egregore.

If I am right here, the Vader example is hardly alone as a malign psychic influence. The young girls who attempted to murder a classmate a few years ago due, they said, to the influence of "Slenderman," would probably be another (Richmond, "12-year-old Wisconsin girls"). More generally, fan fiction and devoted cult readers could generate such thought forms, be they beneficial or malevolent.

If this is true, memes are a kind of "wild" thought form gaining strength as do egregores, but with much more focus for good or bad.

Memes can lodge in our minds in order to promote their own survival, even at our expense. They have interests separate from, and sometimes even antagonistic to, ours. Mark Pagel argues, "The nature of cultural evolution means that some memes evolve as parasites that live at our expense" (Pagel, *Wired for Culture*, 135). Memes do not care about us, but only for their own flourishing. From their perspective, we are valuable insofar as we serve them by attending to them. I am not importing this way of speaking into scientific discussions; again, this is how the discussions are framed by scientists like Pagel. The difference is that what he would call a metaphor, I call a description of something much more real.

If we take memes, thought forms, and egregores seriously—and I do— one more step emerges from this line of thought. While created by consciousness, and part of our mental ecosystem, the underlying ground of consciousness that gives them, and us, shape, is pure awareness. For example, as I was first developing insights that ultimately led to this argument, I asked a former Zen abbot, and friend, whether the usual popular understanding of mindfulness meditation might be mistaken. Rather than our minds creating thoughts we are taught to passively observe, these thoughts enter our awareness, and we give them energy by attending to them. He told me that was actually how they saw the matter, but rarely spoke in those terms to Westerners. It was too far removed from Western patterns of understanding the world. Better just to meditate.

But in terms of how I have described memes and thought forms, the practice of mindfulness meditation and the experience of ideas operating independently on our minds take on additional significance. Like the biological world around us, the ideational world of culture considered at its most inclusive is also contained within, shapes, and is shaped as an ecosystem. We are inhabitants of both biological and cultural ecosystems. We share biological ecosystems with the enormous diversity of other biological beings, engaged in a complex process of coevolution. We share the ideational ecosystem with memes/thought forms and organizations, again, in a complex process of coevolution.

The living world

We now return again to biological ecosystems. Ecosystems are complex interrelations of living organisms at all levels, from single cells to the largest plants, animals, and fungi. We know the connections between them are extraordinarily complex. Additionally, even plants have qualities that, when identified in animals, are claimed as evidence they have minds. I have made the case in this chapter that our own consciousness is not confined to our bodies. There is no reason to believe consciousness is similarly confined in other organisms.

For years I taught a workshop on energy healing. In this workshop I taught people how to see the densest of the energy fields around the human body. This energy is malleable by consciousness, and I would teach simple methods for doing so.

The same techniques for viewing energy fields can also be used to see them around trees and other things (diZerega, "Energy Fields"). As our own energy fields can be influenced by our intentions, there is no reason to doubt they are also permeated with awareness. And this insight returns us to the larger world within which we live.

Many of us feel differently when we are in wild nature. As David Abram describes the spirit of place: "Each place has its rhythms of change and metamorphosis, its specific style of expanding and contracting in response to the turning seasons, and this, too, shapes—and is shaped by—the sentience of that land ... the spiders and the tree frogs no less than the humans—all participate in and partake of the particular mind of the place" (Abram, *Becoming Animal*, 133).

Much recent research indicates that human beings enter into more healthy and centered frames of mind when they leave the artificial environments of streets, buildings, and parking lots for even the bit of nature found in a lawn. I think it is particularly significant that these signs of better mental and physical well-being continue to increase as a person enters into even more complex natural environments. It was within these complex natural environments, with their complex fields of interrelationship at every level, that we evolved (Dobbs, "Green Space Cure"; van der Wal et al., "Do natural landscapes"; Frumkin and Louv, "The Powerful Link"; Williams, *The Nature Fix*).

While I believe I have made a good case for the world being alive from us "all the way down," what about all the way up? What about those beings we call gods, as well as other manifestations of an ultimately spiritual reality? What about my experiences described in chapter 5, as well as similar experiences by so many others, now and through recorded history?

We turn now to the case for polytheism.

Chapter 9
THE CASE FOR POLYTHEISM

Today Pagan thinkers need to create an intellectual structure which allows diverse Pagan cultures to communicate with and to lend strength to one another ... Above all else the distinctness of Gods and of pantheons must be respected.
—EDWARD BUTLER, *THE THEOLOGICAL INTERPRETATION OF MYTH*

WE HAVE REACHED A point where the many threads developed in this volume can be woven together to defend, and advocate, viewing our spiritual world as polytheistic. Previous chapters have made the following points:

1. Chapters 1 and 2 demonstrated that religions claiming to be monotheistic are based on political power, not spiritual experience, and as soon as a degree of religious liberty exists, and sometimes even in the face of its absence, monotheism decays into polytheism.

2. Chapter 3 argued the idea of monotheism is incoherent and has led to endless strife and slaughter by combining its incoherence with demands that some version of it dominate all other religious points of view. With religious freedom, monotheism fragments into many different deities with devotees of each claiming theirs is the only one.

3. Chapter 4 argued that despite early scientists' all but universal desire to demonstrate Scripture's truth through gaining more knowledge about the material world, science ultimately devastated all rational arguments for scriptural monotheism. Scientists abandoned all of their scripturally derived assumptions about the world except for distinguishing mind from matter. This dogma remains, even though evidence consciousness permeates the world is as strong or stronger than any alternative view.

4. Chapter 5 argued that, despite predictions by secularization theorists and the steady decline of organized religion, there has been no decrease in the considerable number of people reporting powerful spiritual experiences.

5. Chapter 6 argued that, beginning with quantum physics, many leading scientists argued that science is compatible with, and even actively supports, the view that consciousness is in some sense a basic quality of the world. The remaining assumption dividing consciousness from the material world no longer has persuasive power.

6. Chapter 7 demonstrates how modern biology shows that individuality is an emergent property of still simpler individuated entities. As soon as consciousness is localized in an entity, the potential for ever more complex individuality emerges. From basic cells to the most complex life-forms, what are individuals at one level contribute to more inclusive individuality at another. Biological and psychological individuality is contextual and relational. Neither describes a discrete thing able to be separated from its context.

7. Chapter 8 explains how the human world exists in at least biological and cultural ecologies. As an ideational ecology, the world of consciousness includes at least human beings, memes, and organizations. From an occult perspective, memes are thought forms, and organizations tend to develop egregores.

8. For those open to the possibility, there is powerful evidence that some individuals can access information unavailable from the perspective of secular views of reality. Work at Stanford Research Institute and by the US military are examples, as are some dowsers' ability to find lost objects.

These observations provide the context for my argument that polytheism is in *harmony* with modern science, and with all forms of reported spiritual experience. But it is not a powerful argument for the existence of different deities. And it is the extraordinary abundance of an enormous range of spiritual experience within a broadly polytheistic context that I hope this chapter will demonstrate is a reasonable expansion of the argument to date.

Divine variety

I described a variety of my own experiences which in themselves illustrate a puzzling diversity of polytheistic and related phenomena. I did so to outline at least some of the challenges that making a case for polytheism must address. My experiences are hardly all-inclusive, but neither are most or all unique to me. What kind of world makes them possible? Let me recapitulate the challenge.

1. Some superhuman entities exhibit qualities of love and completeness that are close to reported mystical experiences of the Godhead, but within the context of an individual personality distinct from other personalities. I have experienced beings with these qualities as being somehow "more real" than I am. These qualities are clearly superhuman.

2. Some reports are of beings demonstrating superhuman power, apparently without any kind of individualized self as we normally use the term. I described such experiences in my own life, as with that on Mount Shasta and with Yemaya.

3. Some spiritual encounters are completely unexpected. On the other hand, entities sometimes respond when an effort is made to contact them. Wiccan ritual provides many examples of both, as do other experiential polytheistic traditions.

4. Sometimes entities can temporarily "take over" a person's body, causing them to do or say things they normally would or could not. Some people remember what happened, and others do not, relying on observers for that information. This is particularly the case today with African diasporic traditions, but is found in many others as well.

5. Many polytheistic traditions are *based* on personal encounters with their deities rather than sacred Scriptures or others' accounts. Practitioners rarely wonder whether the gods exist, a common concern in monotheism.

6. Sometimes healers in altered states of awareness can "see" into their client, and perceive foreign elements that are then removed or dissolved. On occasion these visions can be verified by the client.

7. In my experience as well as those of many others, as a general rule, deities and spirits associated with one tradition do not show up in very different traditions. Pagan deities normally appear wedded to particular contexts. We do not often (if ever) see the same deity *independently* manifesting in very different cultures, unless in the most general terms, such as Mother Earth.

8. Despite this, syncretism is often encountered in polytheistic traditions. When practitioners have prior experience of deities from dif-

ferent cultures, those deities can accompany them into a new context. For example, Voudon combines spirits of African origin with entities specific to Haiti's Taino Indians. It also includes the Irish goddess Brigid, who apparently arrived in Haiti with Irish deportees (Beyer, "Vodou Spirits").

9. Some deities or superhuman beings were reportedly once human, such as Chango among orishas and Hercules for the Greeks. But within the same traditions others were apparently never human, such as Yemaya among the orishas and Poseidon for the Greeks.

10. There is a wide variety of spirit entities from the clearly superhuman, to beings apparently more like ourselves, down to still "smaller" entities. Deities can be all embracing, even cosmic, and they can be very local. Some appear well disposed toward all or some human beings, other entities appear actively hostile.

Ideally, any attempt to defend polytheism should be able to incorporate this wide variety of polytheistic experience.

Of aspects and individuality

Some polytheists argue that their most important deities are the same as analogous deities with different names in different traditions. This view goes back at least as far as Apuleius' claims about Isis in *The Golden Ass* (Apuleius, *The Golden Ass*, 228). But a great deal rests on what we mean by "the same."

While sharing important similarities, deities within one culture differ from those within another. For example, in many ways the orishas of Cuban Santeria and Brazilian Candomblé resemble the Greek and Roman gods. In all these cases, myths abound of their sometimes not so harmonious relations with one another, along with other similarities. But when we look more closely, we find that, while the similarities are quite real, so are the dissimilarities. The myths often varied within a given culture, with differing stories about how the same deity originated. For example, Aphrodite was both a child of Zeus and the goddess Dione, and also arose from ocean foam when Cronos castrated Uranus and threw his genitalia into the sea.

The frequent equation of Roman with Greek deities turns out to be less straightforward than usually thought, even though common themes appear among different deities. Mars is a Roman god of war and Venus' lover. Ares, the Greek god of war, is similarly linked to Aphrodite. In the very different Yoruba culture, Ogun is the orisha of war and the lover of Oshun, the orisha of feminine beauty. So far, they would seem to be the same deities or powers, under different names, as the English "tree" and the German "*Baum*" refer to the same thing.

However, Ogun combines war and metallurgy whereas Vulcan oversaw these skills for the Romans, and Hephaestus for the Greeks. Both these classical deities were crippled and ugly, which is not the case with Ogun. While a god of war, Mars could be merciful and was committed to protecting Rome. Ares was filled with bloodlust, and apparently could take any side in a conflict to increase its lethality. Unlike Ares or Ogun, Mars was also a god of agriculture, sharing a connection with vegetation with his wife, Venus.

Aphrodite is a goddess of beauty, sexual love, and romance. Venus shares many of her qualities, but she is also a goddess of gardens, pure love, fertility, and domestic bliss. Oshun is associated with fresh flowing water, Aphrodite is connected with the sea. Oshun is associated with witches, whereas it was Hekate and Diana who had this association in the Greco-Roman world.

Oshun is sexually associated with Ogun, and Aphrodite is married to Hephaestus and had affairs with Hermes and Dionysus as well as Ares, while Venus is married to Vulcan, as well as being Mars' lover, sharing a common connection with metallurgy. There seems to be a connection between beauty and metallurgy, as well as with war and strife, but the depictions of these qualities as deities differs.

There are many suggestive connections here, but important exceptions continually appear as well.

Similarly, the functions over which a deity presided could change with time. Apparently, Hekate was originally not associated with the underworld. That came later. She also appears to have become increasingly associated with theurgy, magick, ensouling the cosmos, and facilitating certain communications between people and gods, in Hellenistic and Roman times (Johnston, *Hekate Soteira*; von Rudloff, *Hekate in Ancient Greek Religion*).

Aspecting?

Some Neopagans offer an alternative take on polytheism, arguing that individuated deities are aspects of an all-inclusive goddess or god, returning us to

Apulieus' problem regarding Isis. We can safely presume that many a classical devotee of Hekate would not consider her an aspect of a single universal goddess. This effort at categorization would also not impress present day practitioners of Santeria or Candomblé. Is Yemaya an "aspect" of the Great Mother? Alternatively, many Wiccans, myself among them, believe our goddess is the goddess of the *Witches*, and there are other deities connected to people in other ways. My encounter with the Celtic goddess Brigid shared little in common with my encounters with the Wiccan Goddess, wonderful as both were.

In addition, many polytheistic deities manifest in very different ways while being in some sense the same deity. Christopher Scott Thompson makes this point within a Hindu context. Kali can be a wrathful manifestation of Parvati, Shiva's wife. She can also be a manifestation of Durga, who battles demons. In some myths she is Shiva's loving and obedient wife; others treat Shiva as being powerless without her, and still others describe Kali as the supreme reality, with no need of Shiva. She can also vary in characteristics from village to village and even oppose the Kalis of different villages. "So, which of these versions is correct and authentic? They all are" (Thompson, "Polytheistic monism"). John Michael Greer makes a similar point regarding the Greek gods (Greer, *World Full of Gods*, 106–7). James Kugel writes that ancient Middle Eastern treaties listed deities as witnesses and enforcers. One such treaty includes Ishtar of Arbela, Ishtar of Nineveh, and the planet Venus, which was associated with Ishtar, in this regard. Kugel points out that treaties were not theological discussions, but about as down to earth as an agreement could be (Kugel, *The Great Shift*, 85). Thompson points out how Ellegba, an important deity in Santeria, can manifest in 101 different ways. In some cases, as female, and in others, male. But Ellegba's capacity in this regard is not unique. Many classical deities were similarly of variable sex, depending on what they were doing (G. Clark, "Augustine's Varro," 186).

Infinite in number?

The pre-Socratic philosopher Thales famously wrote "all things are full of gods." Hesiod wrote "upon the bounteous earth Zeus has thrice ten thousand spirits, watchers of mortal men, and these keep watch on judgments and deeds of wrong as they roam, clothed in mist, all over the earth" (Hesiod, *Works and Days*, 248–64). A classical Christian critic of pagans scoffed that the emperor Julian loved three hundred thousand deities (Kahlos, "Refuting and Reclaiming Monotheism," 168).

The same holds for the very different cultures honoring the orishas in Africa and the New World. A small number, those who made it over to the Caribbean during slavery, dominate rituals in African Diasporic traditions such as Santeria and Candomblé. However, in African Yoruba culture the number can be "as many as you can think of, plus one more—an innumerable number" (Falola, *Encyclopedia of the Yoruba*, 84–85).

But, *in some sense* Isis *does* refer to more than the personal goddess to whom Apuleius was devoted. Like the Wiccan Goddess as I have experienced her, she also was considered the goddess of Nature. From Europe to China to the Americas there have been many ways across both millennia and cultures for acknowledging the power and reality of the earth as feminine. Amidst enormous variety there also seems to be points of connection.

Christopher Scott Thompson writes that some Hindus consider Shiva to be God; others consider Vishnu to be God and still others consider a goddess such as Kali, Durga, or Lalita to be God. But, most followers respect the validity of other Hindus considering "one of the other gods as the supreme god, even though the gods as separate deities remain distinct" (Thompson, "Polytheistic monism"). In classical Greece, whereas Zeus was most commonly referred to as the chief among Greek deities, Edward Butler notes "Empedocles decenters Zeus in favor of a demiurgic Aphrodite, and his system differs accordingly" (Butler, "Polycentric Polytheism," 70). The same pattern, which Thompson describes as "divine fluidity," appears in Egyptian religion (Hormung, *Conceptions of God*, 235–6).

Such a seemingly disordered variety of gods/spirits/daimones reinforces many secularists' views that all deities are cultural constructs, without any reality beyond their followers' imaginations. At first take, this secularist debunking seems well taken. But, and here is the rub, it only makes sense to people who have never *experienced* the actual presence of a deity.

Hierarchies or something else?

Such divine variety and complexity are enough to drive anyone who loves tidy categorizations to complete distraction. This is especially the case if they think of divinities in terms of a political hierarchy with God or a major deity as king. This hierarchical model was often employed in polytheistic contexts in classical times. Order was obvious to all, but how could it arise? Aristotle described God as like a general (Frede, "Monotheism and Pagan Philosophy," 46). Other writers treated God as the head of a divine monarchy (Frede, "Monotheism and Pagan Philosophy," 57), or, in a deeply patriarchal world, father (Gasparro, "One God and Divine Unity," 42). Many writers compared the abundance of deities with the abundance of human administrators needed to govern empires (Athanassiadi and Frede, "Introduction," 9; West, "Towards Monotheism," 39; Gasparro, "One God," 54). It seemed as if some higher power was needed to impose order on an otherwise disorderly material world, as kings and emperors claimed to impose it in the human realm (Frede, "Monotheism and Pagan Philosophy"). This concept of a hierarchy of divine power seems to have been a way for solving a problem arising from earlier, less hierarchic, polytheisms. For example, in the *Iliad* and *Odyssey*, different deities took up different sides in human conflicts and even fought among themselves, as when Athena severely wounded Ares. Greek philosophers, and others, bothered by the apparent chaos, sought to discern some ultimate principle that gave order to the world. Over time, for many, Zeus grew in power relative to the other Olympian deities. This pattern of growing hierarchy apparently also existed in the Middle East (West, "Towards Monotheism," 21–40).

Within polytheistic traditions, the specific claims associated with monotheism were largely absent (Frede, "Monotheism and Pagan Philosophy," 63). Most Platonists argued that God could not be regarded as an individual, even one standing at the apex of all that is (Frede, "Monotheism and Pagan Philosophy," 50).

Use of hierarchy in these contexts seems connected to relations of power, both politically, and with regard to the rest of the world. Jordan Paper observes the Sámi people, who herd reindeer on Russia's Kola peninsula, regard individual *wild* reindeer as numinous, whereas *domesticated* reindeer are the gift of the Mistress of the Reindeer Herds (Paper, *The Deities Are Many*, 91). Wild reindeer are independent of the Sámi whereas domesticated reindeer are under their control. The second relationship is more hierarchical than the first.

My own experience supports this interpretation. When I come across edible wild mushrooms, I give thanks, whereas I did not feel the same degree of gratitude to my individual plants, when I cultivated a vegetable garden, but gave thanks to the spirits of the land and weather. Hierarchy and power relations seem intimately connected, reaching a pathological form in monotheism. The image of monarchy or other hierarchy cannot come close to comprehending the reality of polytheism in practice.

But what can?

Returning to emergence

Ancient times were limited in their understanding of complex orders because so many agricultural societies were extremely hierarchical. Apparently earlier hunting societies were far less hierarchical in their outlook, perhaps because social hierarchies were largely absent, and so that frame for making sense of order was lacking. That is certainly the case today (Brody, *The Other Side of Eden*). Only with the rise of cities and the hierarchies they created did this image begin to make sense for people. It was easy to think order came from the top down, and the elites encouraged such thinking.

We are better off today when trying to understand this divine multiplicity because we have a richer understanding of how order can arise in our world.

Both evolution and the ecosystems within which it takes place are ordered patterns that emerged without anyone being in charge. Of course, some monotheists say their deity "guides" evolution, but if so, it is a poor sort of guide, leading to many dead ends and poorly thought out ways of solving design problems (as anyone with a bad back will recognize). Human "anatomy isn't what you'd design from scratch," said anthropologist Jeremy DeSilva. "Evolution works with duct tape and paper clips" (Gibbons, "Human Evolution").

Another alternative to explaining biological order by divine incompetence is more promising, and returns us to two concepts I introduced earlier: self-organization and emergence. Only now we will view them from a larger context, one embracing the sacred.

As previously described, Scottish philosophers sought to understand how social order could arise if God did not impose it and human geniuses did not create it. Their solution was to describe circumstances where no one was in charge and everyone reacted to the local changes around them, insights that led later scientists to discover biological evolution, and from it, ecology. I described in chapter 4 how modern science itself is also such a phenomenon.

"Polycentricity" is a technical term for these systems, and refers to their not being hierarchies, but rather having many independent centers of action, each making its own decisions (Polanyi, *The Logic of Liberty*, 170–84). "Polycentric" means "many centers." The patterns they manifest emerge out of multiple relationships *where no one is in charge*.

To unite this term with two others many readers might not have known before reading this book, *self-organizing* processes are characterized by order *emerging* from *polycentric* networks. It is the opposite of patterns being created by controlling hierarchies, human or divine.

Hierarchies can exist *within* polycentric systems, as organizations exist within a market or research teams exist within science. But no one controls the system as a whole. Every internal hierarchy is subordinate to a system no one controls, and the collective patterns arising from within all actors in a system are examples of emergence.

My discussions of individuality in biology described biological emergence, where individuals emerging from relationships with simpler individuals could, in a more complex set of relations, generate different individuals of a more complex kind. Two kinds of the simplest cells generated the first cell with a nucleus. Some of them together perhaps with viruses made the existence of multicellular individuals possible. Some multicellular and single celled individuals made more complex multicellular individuals possible, as when bacteria common in dirt made mice more intelligent, and some multicellular individuals made even more complex multicellular individuals possible, as when *toxoplasmosis* was discovered to encourage different kinds of thinking in human beings. Each level in this and other examples possessed characteristics not reducible to the sum of its parts. As explored in chapter 7, unified individuals arise from relationships existing between different subordinate but also unified individuals.

Chapter 8 took this argument a step further into the cultural realm, where we, as individuals, are also the results of our collective cultural as well as biological relations, relations of which we are usually not aware. Memes as thought forms and egregores are the most important here.

Chapter 9

Selves with and without bodies

If consciousness is universal, once awareness has become self-conscious in some sense, it does not necessarily disappear when the material form that originally enabled it to emerge disappears. Awareness as an individual arises from being able to integrate conscious relationships over time—past, present, and potentially future.

Consider our own selves. Our bodies shape the consciousness that arises from their involvement with the cultural and biological worlds we inhabit. But once we are sufficiently self-aware, we can direct our consciousness not only in ways that heal our own bodies, as with the placebo phenomenon, we can also heal others, as with energy healing. Self-awareness emerges from our embodied experiences, but once it does, we can to some degree act separately from the body. The conscious self is an emergent outcome of its constituent relationships.

Anyone who has encountered a disembodied spirit or deity, or astral-projected, should have little difficulty granting this possibility. The being I first saw on the Berkeley campus, after I made that challenge to Don, was not material, at least as we think of the term. The same insight holds for anyone who has astral-projected, or experienced awareness of places closed to normal perception, such as inside a person being healed energetically, or from remote viewing or dowsing, where no physical connection exists in any sense recognized by materialism. Perhaps material existence in our sense is a necessary precondition to the development of individuated consciousness such as ours, but once developed, is not necessary for it to persist.

These considerations may shed light on a view common in many polytheistic cultures, that souls are multiple. For example, in shamanistic cultures shamans leave their bodies to retrieve souls that have become separated from their own bodies (Paper, *The Deities Are Many*, 63). This commonly encountered view in traditional cultures makes more sense to us if we consider some element of soul remains behind, maintaining physical life, even as another leaves, but when together they are a unified self. Astral projection would be another example for some, even in the modern West. With death, all are disconnected from the material body.

It may also make sense of experiences of reincarnation. While many reports of past lives have proven accurate in their details, often those reporting them can do so only under hypnosis, or at a very young age after which they forget what they reported. Where are our past lives when we have no recollection? Are we really the same being as what appears to be another living in a different time and place? If individuals in our usual sense are in turn elements in a still more complex entity, this somewhat strange feature of our not being able to remember past lives except in rare or unusual circumstances makes sense. A prosaic biological example is a lichen, which is a collection of an algae and a fungus that makes something possible present in neither alone. The same could be true in the psychic realm, and if so, boundaries will sometimes be more fluid than at other times.

Even our usual sense of individual distinctiveness is fluid, depending on how aware we are of the varied relationships we weave together into a self. Selves in the modern sense of conscious individuality are not things, they—we—are active nodes of conscious relationship that can include more or less of our network of connections. Some linkages are very strong, others are much weaker but can matter in the right context. Sometimes our "self" is quite narrowly focused, as when I hit my thumb with a hammer. Other times it grows far beyond my physical body, as when I empathize with the pain or joy of a loved one, or of strangers.

Each of us is a hub where our experiences come together to create a world of individuated awareness. To some degree we can choose our present and future relationships even as we are constituted from out of them. We have some say in just how far we will seek to acknowledge and shape the relationships out of which we emerge. Each of us is a node where experiences come together to create a conscious individual awareness, linked at the same time with other nodes.

If the One or the Godhead is pure unconditional love, as I and many others have experienced it, the more we expand our hearts, the more links with other nodes enter into our sense of self. As many wise spiritual teachers of virtually all traditions have said, if your path does not have heart in it, it is not for you. This assumption, which I believe is true, leads to a coherent model of the deities able to explain why they are so varied, and why the ways of connecting with them so varied as well.

The gods

If all of reality is considered in some sense a unified One, all conscious nodes emerge from the ultimate source of connections of greater or lesser complexity. Deities can be thought of as "super hubs in this network." The confirmation problem described by William James and David Chalmers is solved at the more-than-human level as it was solved at the biological, psychological, and cultural levels (James, *Principles of Psychology*, chapter 6).

This perspective sheds light on two largely universal dimensions of polytheistic religions. First, they are experiential. Polytheists encounter their deities in relationship, and so faith in their existence is analogous to the faith I have in a currently unseen friend's existence. This has no similarity to faith as described applying to a monotheistic deity.

Polytheistic religions *decenter* spiritual reality, rather like spirituality decenters the self and modern biology has decentered the individual. *There are many deities and no point short of the One at which they all converge.* All share a common root, but manifest in their own ways. Polytheism focuses on relationship, and so, in general, the ideal connection with the sacred is harmony, of respecting "all our relations," rather than salvation or enlightenment. There is no mountaintop toward which all paths climb. Instead there is an eternally opening flower of constantly renewed petals, each a manifestation of the One as well as unique in itself. (This flower metaphor seems implicit in careful thinking about polytheism. Greer uses it in a complementary way. *A World Full of Gods*, 139–40.)

Of webs, nets, and drops

The modern metaphor of a web echoes the Hindu one of Indra's net where every jewel mirrors all the others. Often this image is used to point to the nondual character of ultimate reality, for everything is mirrored in everything else. Without in any sense denying this dimension of the metaphor, each jewel reflects all others from a *different* place within the net. Each jewel *is also an individual expression of the net as a whole.* All are represented, but in each case from a different perspective, explaining the diversity of spirit entities, for the nodes are innumerable.

This perspective enables me to understand how at least some deities can be "more real" than I am. Modern human beings often report feeling disconnected from life; life has no meaning. Even in earlier times, when the world was more commonly regarded as deeply meaningful, many myths explored how we came to feel so separate from our origin. There was a time when animals and people could talk, and even change places, but today this sense of connectedness is often thin or absent.

Even so, the more positive connections we experience with others, the richer and deeper our lives become. In other words, the richness of life arises out of connections and the quality of those connections. This may be true "all the way down" for, as de Quincey explains, "The hierarchical depth of internal relations experienced by any particular entity … is the relative value of that entity within its hierarchical network … a cell is more valuable than a molecule or an atom, and a dog or fish more valuable than a single cell, because it literally incorporates more reality, more complex nestings of levels of internal relations" (de Quincey, *Radical Nature*, 169). Major deities are "super hubs." They are larger, more inclusive foci of relationships within the divine network. *In this sense* they are more real and more important than less inclusive hubs, be they other spirits or beings like us. Might we ourselves grow in wisdom to become more like these deities? I think a poem by the Sufi, Rumi, gives us a clue:

> Let the drop of water that is in you
> become a hundred mighty seas.
> But do not think that the drop alone
> Becomes the Ocean—
> the Ocean, too, becomes the drop!
> (Rumi, *A Garden Beyond Paradise*, 149)

The more drops of which we are aware, the more we are the entire ocean viewed from our unique place within it, and so manifest the unconditional love at the center of everything. (I have quite a way to go in this regard, BTW.)

Divine individuality

Divine and human individuality alike are self-aware focal points integrating multiple relationships into larger wholes. The richer the integration, the richer the individuality. I am the same person but manifest different dimensions of who I am when I am enjoying music with friends, hiking in nature, lecturing in a class, or creating a work of art. In each context, my friends might not be the same as in another. But a complete description of who I am has room for all of this.

Human beings exist in intimate relationship with their culture, including the memes and egregores comprising the ideational ecology within which they exist. And we manifest differently depending on the contexts we encounter. So do our religions. Consequently, in any religion, the identifying features of a god may reflect the worshipers as well as the god (Greer, *A World Full of Gods*, 107).

Like ourselves, deities can have many of the same qualities and not be reducible to one another. Oshun and Venus and Aphrodite share important elements within this web. All are, among other things, goddesses of beauty, and so are profoundly connected. But they also each partake of other different elements, and so are individual. As do people who have lived a rich and multifaceted life, they will also manifest different dimensions in different contexts (Thompson, "Polytheistic monism," part two).

Existing between the One and the world of humans, to the degree they are closer to the One, they will also be better able to manifest unconditional love.

As with larger deities, lesser deities, daimones, and spirits can be self-aware entities that are no longer embodied or perhaps never were. What maintains them is access to energy. Apparently it can come from two directions: more directly from the One, or from individuals in ways we have already discussed with regard to egregores and thought forms. John Michael Greer observes: "Any symbolic pattern that has served as a focus for human emotion and energy will build up an egregore of its own over time … The gods and goddesses of every religion, past and present, are the centers of vast egregores charged with specific types of power" (Greer, *Inside a Magical Lodge*, 106–7).

Greer's observation leads to these questions: Are the gods human creations? Is the Wiccan Goddess an egregore?

If all that is in the world makes up a field of interwoven networks, the more linked a "hub" is, the more real it becomes. From this follows the experience I and others have had of encountering entities *more real than ourselves*.

We are not the apex of awareness or individuality, and to the degree an egregore is in harmony with more fundamental dimensions of reality, it is not simply the result of human consciousness. The gods are not our creations.

But neither need they be divorced from us. How I manifest as a person is not solely determined by me. It is also shaped by those around me and their expectations. Perhaps the same holds for deities. Did the entity I now experience as the Wiccan Goddess exist during the Jurassic? I have no way of knowing. But I am quite sure that, if she did, she did not appear to whoever perceived her in a (super) human form, such as she did to me. Greer seems to be getting at the same thing, writing the most powerful egregores are "built up on the basis of the living patterns of the realm of meaning, outside space and time. These patterns are what some religions call gods, and what others call aspects of god. They…use the egregores the way people use clothing" (Greer, *Magical Lodge*, 109–10). There is no contradiction between arguing an unimaginably huge number of individual deities can exist, and honoring the existence of an ultimate Source from which everything emerges, including the gods. Nor is there any contradiction with honoring one of these multiple deities in particular, while recognizing in others an equal right to honor different deities. We do this in the purely human realm every day. When we love another person, we do not look askance at others who love different people. Nor do we think the person we love is the only lovable person, or that others' love for other people is somehow inferior to our own. Each case of love is irreducibly individual, and a manifestation of the unconditional love that ultimately pervades reality.

Some could misread me as reducing the Gods to very powerful egregores or thought forms. Egregores exist due to their connection with human consciousness. So do thought forms such as Philip. If humans did not exist, these entities would not exist. However, the world and the energies that enliven it existed long before we did. For example, beauty is intimately associated with the sacred. Today we usually consider beauty as rooted in our subjectivity. But beauty long pre-existed human beings. It influences the evolution of many creatures and is also, for many of us, intrinsic to our experience of the world (Prum, *Evolution of Beauty*). And beauty is rooted in consciousness. From this perspective, the core qualities of the sacred and the major Gods pre-existed us. Perhaps it is in relationship with us that they took on dimensions more accessible to minds such as our own.

Neoplatonist polycentrism

As it happens, Neoplatonism pioneered an understanding of polytheism at least broadly compatible with the view I am developing. Mine is rooted in evolutionary biology and ecology, theirs in philosophy and in ancient, and perhaps unbroken, spiritual traditions extending back to the dawn of humanity. That both paths lead to similar insights adds to the credibility of their general conclusions.

Edward Butler, one of Neoplatonism's most important contemporary figures, emphasizes the importance of polycentrism for understanding polytheism (Butler, "Polycentric Polytheism"). Butler writes: "The importance of the philosophical formulation of polycentric polytheism by the Neoplatonists lies in having disaggregated individuality from the logic of part and whole (Butler, "Polycentric Polytheism," 35; "Bhakti and Henadology"). Individuality can partake of a whole, but be individualized because some dimensions are more dominant than are others. Butler is explicating an ancient form of thought that, at the same time, is remarkably modern, as Butler appears to recognize (Butler, "Polycentric Polytheism," 74).

It seems to me Neoplatonism describes the same pattern I have described as existing in the spiritual world. Butler provides a clarifying passage by Olympiodorus (quoted in Butler, "Theological Interpretation of Myth," 34–5): "If the virtues reciprocally imply each other, nevertheless they differ individually…all [of the virtues] are in courage simultaneously courageously, in another [temperance] temperately; and so to all the Gods are in Zeus zeustically. In another [Hera] herically; for no God is imperfect. And as Anaxagorus said all things are in all things, but one is superabundant [in each], in this way also we speak of things divine" (Butler, "Polycentric Polytheism," 34–5). This insight brings us back to a weakness of any monotheistic view of God as a personality. There is no single perfect personality. Personality implies relationship. In polytheism, *each* of the gods can serve as a center to which all else is linked. But, as Butler emphasizes, "there can be no unique center" (Butler, "Polycentric Polytheism," 6).

As Rumi observed, the ocean becomes the drop and, as implied by the image of Indra's net, each jewel reflects all the others from its own place. If these examples still fail to give you a sense of this insight, let me risk a mundane example: Each of my readers can read English, but each brings his or her own way of interpreting my words to this manuscript. If "English grammar" is the One (which it clearly is not), then hopefully the point above is clarified: we all share it, but employ it differently.

Monism and abundance

People having the most complete mystical experience describe a total *but temporary* annihilation of their self, entering into a state of awareness without differentiation, a divine "Nothingness." One account of such a classic mystical experience is Alfred Lord Tennyson's (1809–1892) description of one that he experienced: "[I]ndividuality itself seemed to dissolve and fade away into boundless being, and this not a confused state but the clearest, the surest of surest, utterly beyond words—where death was an almost laughable impossibility" (quoted in Paper, *The Mystic Experience*, 94).

I think this experience is not the "ultimate spiritual realization." I think there is no ultimate spiritual realization other than, perhaps, the *gradual* expansion of the links to which one is connected to include all of them, as Rumi suggested. And as he observed, individuality does not disappear, it is transformed. If this latter is the case, it is not a situation we can reasonably expect to attain this time around.

Many mystics experience what is often called the Godhead, and not pure nonduality. They report that love and compassion are among the most basic elements of the divine. This was my experience when it happened to me. And my own and others' experience of gods emanating unconditional love as being more real than anything else supports this argument. *There is both unity and diversity within the very structure of existence as human beings experience it.*

Only through a rich and varied individuality can the maximum opportunities for realizing love and compassion be attained. If love is the recognition and cherishing of inner beauty manifesting through someone or something, there is no love in nonduality because there is nothing separate to love. If, as the Wiccan Goddess once told me, "All beings are worthy of my love," then the greater the number of such beings, the greater the opportunity for love to manifest. Love cherishes particularity. Divine love cherishes *all* particularity.

In a way, we could say transcendence exists only in and through immanence. We always encounter it from within a particular context. Particular descriptions of this experience often differ in their details shaped by who we are and when and where we have the experience. Significantly, all who experience it say it cannot be described. But we try. The problem is not the experience, it is the always inadequate effort to communicate it, because words, even poetic ones like Rumi's, cannot quite get us there, though he gets closer than arguments like mine. An argument by its nature distances us so we can evaluate it whereas great poetry draws us in.

Transcendence versus immanence is a false dichotomy. Duality versus nonduality is false as well. This world is always monist, always dualist, and always individuated (Paper, *The Deities Are Many*, 129; *The Mystic Experience*, 75–135).

Do I believe I have found the truth?

I do not argue my explanation for the near universal experience of a living and polytheistic world is the truth. I am a human discussing the more-than-human, using concepts developed largely in Western thought, and especially contemporary science. I have sought to clear away the errors of monotheism, leaving us free to rethink the nature of the divine. Combining what I have learned in the sciences with my own experiences, I hope I have presented a good road map to important dimensions of the more-than-human that lack the debilitating weaknesses of monotheism, and honor the rich spiritual history of diverse cultures and peoples. To do so I have employed insights rooted in modern science, but as I argued earlier, this approach has been used at least since the invention of the clock.

My argument relies on apparent similarities between very different phenomena, enabling them to shed light on one another. I believe it captures a part of the truth better than any other model I have encountered, and relies on concepts proving themselves increasingly important in the sciences. As in science, the test is not truth, for we do not know the full truth, but reliability compared to alternatives. Better ones can always emerge.

I am suggesting a way of understanding that honors the experiences of people in the midst of their different spiritual practices, recognizes the reality of the sacred, of the diversity of forms in which it manifests, and that we live within a universe that is most appropriately conceived of as a Thou rather than It.

But the superhuman is beyond human power to grasp. No words can fully describe even individual experience. Try describing an orgasm. That is why the best poetry is so important. It takes us as far as words can go, and then opens the door to where they cannot. How much more true must this be for the more-than-human?

I am offering one more finger pointing at the moon, hopefully a more reliable one than many.

BIBLIOGRAPHY

Abram, David. *Becoming Animal: An Earthly Cosmology.* New York: Pantheon, 2010.

Aiken, Henry, ed. "Introduction, David Hume." In *Moral and Political Philosophy.* New York: Hafner, 1948.

Alexe, Dan. "The influence of Sufi Islam in the Balkans." *The EUobserver* (December 1, 2010). https://euobserver.com/news/31390.

Allen, Karma. "'I have been a terrible husband and father': Pastor who praised Pulse nightclub shooting resigns after admitting to drinking, gambling, hiring prostitutes." *ABC News* (January 10, 2019). https://abcnews.go.com/US/terrible-husband-father-pastor-praised-pulse-nightclub-shooting/story?id=60280311.

Alper, Beka A. "Why America's 'nones' don't identify with a religion." *Pew Research* Center (August 8, 2018). https://www.pewresearch.org/fact-tank/2018/08/08/why-americas-nones-dont-identify-with-a-religion/?.

Apuleius, Lucius. *The Golden Ass.* Translated by Robert Graves. Middlesex, England: Penguin, 1950.

Aquinas, Thomas. *Summa Theologica.* Translated by the Fathers of the English Dominican Province. http://www.newadvent.org/summa/index.html; http://www.newadvent.org/summa/5094.htm.

Assmann, Jan. *The Price of Monotheism.* Translated by Robert Savage. Palo Alto, CA: Stanford University Press, 2010.

Associated Press. "Judge tosses Detroit schools case, says no right to literacy." *The Washington Post* (July 3, 2018). https://www.usnews.com/news/best -states/michigan/articles/2018-07-01/judge-dismisses-detroit-schools -literacy-lawsuit.

_____. "Lutheran Panel Re-instates pastor After Post 9/11 Interfaith Ser- vice." http://www.nytimes.com/2003/05/13/nyregion/lutheran-panel -reinstates-pastor-after-post-9-11-interfaith-service.html.

Athanassadi, Polymnia, and Michael Frede. "Introduction." In *Pagan Mono- theism in Late Antiquity.* Oxford: Clarendon Press, 1999.

Augustine of Hippo. "Letter 185." Chapter 6: 23. *New Advent.* http://www .newadvent.org/fathers/1102185.htm.

_____. "On Genesis." In *The Works of St. Augustine: A Translation for the 21st Century.* Brooklyn: New City Press, 2014.

Axelrod, Robert. *The Evolution of Cooperation.* New York: Basic Books, 1984.

Ball, Phillip. "Is photosynthesis quantumish?" *Physics World* (April 10, 2018). https://physicsworld.com/a/is-photosynthesis-quantum-ish/.

Barras, Colin. "The End of Species." *New Scientist* (Jan. 26, 2019): 36–9.

Bartley, W. W. III. *The Retreat to Commitment.* LaSalle, IL: Open Court Pub- lishing, 1984.

_____. *Unfathomed Knowledge, Unmeasured Wealth.* LaSalle, IL: Open Court Publishing, 1990.

Batme, Steven. "Embracing Academic Torah Study: Modern Orthodoxy's Challenge." In *The Torah: A Historical and Contextual Approach.* http://thetorah.com/embracing-academic-torah-study-modern -orthodoxys-challenge/.

Beckler, Adam. "What is Good Science?" *Aeon* (2018). https://aeon.co /essays/a-fetish-for-falsification-and-observation-holds-back-science.

Berger, Peter L. *The Heretical Imperative: Contemporary Possibilities of Reli- gious Affirmation.* NY: Anchor, 1979.

Berger, Peter, and Thomas Luckmann. *The Social Construction of Reality.* New York: Anchor Books, 1966. http://perflensburg.se/Berger%20 social-construction-of-reality.pdf.

Beyer, Catherine. "Vodou Spirits." *ThoughtCo* (Aug. 18, 2018). https://www .thoughtco.com/spirits-in-african-diaspora-religions-95926.

Biblicalunitarian. "Trinitarian or Unitarian: Does it really matter?" http:// www.biblicalunitarian.com/articles/faq/trinitarian-or-unitarian -does-it-really-matter.

Borg, Marcus. *The God We Never Knew.* San Francisco: Harper San Francisco, 1997.

Boyd, James W. and A. Donald. "Is Zoroastrianism Dualistic or Monotheistic?" *Journal of the American Academy of Religion,* Vol. XLVII, 4 (December, 1979): 557–88.

Brecht, Martin. *Martin Luther, Volume 3: The Preservation of the Church, 1532–1546.* Minneapolis: Fortress Press, 1999.

Bringhurst, Robert. *A Story as Sharp as a Knife.* Vancouver: Douglas and MacIntyre, 1999.

Brody, Hugh. *The Other Side of Eden: Hunters, Farmers, and the Shaping of the World.* New York: North Point Press, 2000.

Brooks, Michael. "Quantum time: Is this where the flow of existence comes from?" *New Scientist* (April 21, 2018). https://www.newscientist.com /article/mg23831740-200-quantum-time-is-this-where-the-flow-of -existence-comes-from/.

Brown, Peter. "Between Two Empires." *The New York Review of Books* (Jan. 17, 2019).

Brummett, John. "Mark Pryor and theocracy." *Arkansas News* (July 25, 2009).

Bullard, Gabe. "The World's Newest Major Religion." *National Geographic* (April 22, 2016). http://news.nationalgeographic.com/2016/04/160422 -atheism-agnostic-secular-nones-rising-religion/.

Burton, Tara Isabella. "The biblical story the Christian rights uses to defend Trump." *Vox* (March 5, 2018). https://www.vox.com/identities/2018/3/5 /16796892/trump-cyrus-christian-right-bible-cbn-evangelical -propaganda.

Butler, Edward P. "Bhakti and Henadology." *Journal of Dharma Studies* (July 25, 2018).

_____. *Essays on a Polytheistic Philosophy of Religion.* New York: Phaidra Editions, 2012.

_____. "Polycentric Polytheism and the Philosophy of Religion." *The Pomegranate: The International Journal of Pagan Studies* (2008).

_____. "The Theological Interpretation of Myth." *The Pomegranate: The International Journal of Pagan Studie*s, Vol. 7, No. 1 (2005): 27–41.

Calvin, John. "Sermon on 1 Corinthians 10:19–24." *Calvini Opera Selecta, Corpus Refomatorum,*Vol. 49, 67. Translated by Robert White in *Calvin and Copernicus: the Problem Reconsidered.* Calvin Theological Journal 15 (1980). https://biologos.org/blogs/guest/john-calvin-on-nicolaus-copernicus-and-heliocentrism/.

Capra, Fritjof. *The Science of Leonardo: Inside the Mind of the Great Genius of the Renaissance.* New York: Anchor, 2007.

_____. *The Tao of Physics.* New York: Random House, 1975.

Ockeloen-Korppi, C. F., et al. "Stabilized entanglement of massive mechanical oscillators," *Nature* 556 (7702), 2018.

Chalmers, David. "The Combination Problem for Panpsychism." In *Panpsychism: Contemporary Perspectives.* Edited by Godehard Brüntrup and Ludwig Jaskolla. Oxford: Oxford University Press, 2017.

Chen, Janet, Su-I Lu, and Dan Vekhter. "Axelrod's Tournament." *Game Theory* (Stanford University, Palo Alto, CA 1998–9). https://cs.stanford.edu/people/eroberts/courses/soco/projects/1998-99/game-theory/axelrod.html.

Christianity Today. "Editorial: The Evil in Us" (July 1, 2004). https://www.christianitytoday.com/ct/2004/july/2.22.html.

Chrysostom, John. *Treatise On The Priesthood*, Book 1. Translated by Graham Neville. New York: St Vladimir's Seminary Press, 1984.

Church of All Worlds. Home page. http://caw.org/content/.

Church of Jesus Christ of Latter-Day Saints. "Introduction" (2013). https://www.lds.org/scriptures/bofm/introduction?lang=eng.

Cillizza, Chris. "Vladimir Putin's popularity is soaring among Republicans." *The Washington Post* (Feb. 21, 2017). https://www.washington post.com/news/the-fix/wp/2017/02/21/vladimir-putin-so-hot-right -now/?utm_term=.dddf83251a50.

Clark, Gillian. "Augustine's Varro and Pagan Monotheism." In *Monotheism Between Pagans and Christians in Late Antiquity*. Edited by Stephen Mitchell and Peter Van Nueffelen. Walpole, MA: Peeters, 2010.

Clark, Ken. "Lying for the Lord." *MormonThink*, http://www.mormonthink .com/lying.htm.

Clement of Alexandria, *The Stromata, or Miscellanies*, 7.16. http://www .earlychristianwritings.com/text/clement-stromata-book7.html.

CNN. "Franklin Graham conducts services at Pentagon." CNN.com (April 18, 2003). http://www.cnn.com/2003/ALLPOLITICS/04/18/graham .pentagon/.

Commins, David. *The Wahhabi Mission and Saudi Arabia*. London: I. B. Tauris, 2009.

Cooper, Richard T. "General Casts War in Religious Terms." *Los Angeles Times* (October 16, 2003). http://articles.latimes.com/2003/oct/16 /nation/na-general16.

Courtland, Rachel. "Fly sniffs molecules' quantum vibrations." *New Scientist* (Feb. 14, 2011). https://www.newscientist.com/article/dn20130 -fly-sniffs-molecules-quantum-vibrations/.

Davies, Paul. "What is life?" *New Scientist* (Feb. 2, 2019): 28–31.

Dawkins, Richard. *The Selfish Gene* (2 ed.). Oxford: Oxford University Press, 1989.

de Quincey, Christian. *Radical Nature: The Soul of Matter*. Rochester, VT: Park Street Press, 2010.

Descartes, Rene. *Fourth Meditation*, Truth and Falsity (1647). https://www .colorado.edu/philosophy/potter/meditation%20iv.pdf.

diZerega, Gus. "Darth Vader, Luke Skywalker and Thought Forms." *Patheos* (Jan. 11, 2013). https://www.patheos.com/blogs/pointedlypagan /2013/01/darth-vader-luke-skywalker-and-thought-forms/.

_____. "Deep Ecology and Liberalism: The Greener Implications of Evolutionary Liberalism." *Review of Politics,* 58:4, (Fall, 1996).

_____. *Faultlines: The Sixties, the Culture War, and the Return of the Divine Feminine.* Wheaton, IL: Quest, 2013.

_____. "From Methodological Individualism to Emergence, Ecology, and the Fluid Self." in *Austrian Economic Perspectives on Individualism.* Edited by Guinevere Nell. London: Palgrave MacMillan, 2014.

_____. "Not Simply Construction: Exploring the Darker Side of *Taxis.*" *Cosmos+Taxis*, Vol. III, No. 1 (2015): 17–37. https://cosmosandtaxis.files .wordpress.com/2015/11/dizerega.pdf.

_____. "Outlining a New Paradigm." *Cosmos and Taxis*, Vol. 1, No. 1 (2013). http://www.sfu.ca/cosmosandtaxis.html.

_____. *Persuasion, Power and Polity: A Theory of Democratic Self-Organization.* Cresskill, NJ: Hampton Press, and Institute of Contemporary Studies (Oakland, CA), 2000.

_____. "Seeing and feeling Energy Fields." http://www.dizerega.com/fault lines/appendices/seeing-and-feeling-energy-fields/.

Dobbs, David. "The Green Space Cure: The Psychological Value of Biodiversity." *Scientific American* (Nov. 13, 2007). https://blogs.scientificamerican .com/news-blog/the-green-space-cure-the-psychologi/.

Eagan, Margery. "Are 'Trump Christians' really Christian?" *The Boston Globe* (April 2, 2018). https://www.bostonglobe.com/opinion/2018/04/01 /are-trump-christians-really-christian/loTMwQyqRBYgOoovmYA7eI /story.html.

Ecklund, Elaine Howard, and Elizabeth Long. "Scientists and Spirituality." *Sociology of Religion*, Vol. 72, No. 3 (2011): 253–74.

Eddington, Arthur S. *The Nature of the Physical World: Gifford Lectures of 1927: An Annotated Edition.* Annotated by H. G. Callaway. Newcastle -upon-Tyne, UK: Cambridge Scholars Publishing, 2014.

Edelstein, Ludwig. *The Idea of Progress in Classical Antiquity.* Baltimore, MD: Johns Hopkins Press, 1967.

Edwards, David. "Alabama Lawmaker pushing 'personhood' because 'aborted babies' might go to Hell." *Rawstory* (Feb. 6, 2013). http://www

.rawstory.com/rs/2013/02/06/alabama-lawmaker-pushing-personhood -because-aborted-babies-might-go-hell/.

Edwards, Jonathan. "The Eternity of Hell Torments" (April 1739). http:// www.biblebb.com/files/edwards/eternity.htm.

_____. "Sinners in the hands of an Angry God" (1741). http://www.iclnet .org/pub/resources/text/history/spurgeon/web/edwards.sinners.html.

Ehrman, Bart. "An Interview About My Agnosticism." *The Bart Ehrman Blog* (May 10, 2014). https://ehrmanblog.org/an-interview-about-my -agnosticism/.

Eisenstein, Elizabeth L. *The Printing Press as an Agent of Change*. Cambridge: Cambridge University Press, 1979.

_____. *The Printing Revolution in Early Modern Europe*. Cambridge: Cambridge University Press, 1993.

EMSB. "Relative Size of Atoms and the Universe." http://laurenhill.emsb .qc.ca/science/relative.pdf.

Engel, Gregory S., Tessa R. Calhoun, Elizabeth L. Read, Tae-Kyu Ahn, Tomáš Mančal, Yuan-Chung Cheng, Robert E. Blankenship, and Graham R. Fleming. "Evidence for wavelike energy transfer through quantum coherence in photosynthetic systems." *Nature*, Vol. 446 (April 12, 2007): 782.

Fact Checker, *The Washington Post*. https://www.washingtonpost.com /graphics/politics/trump-claims-database/?utm_term=.9e6d52c61bc8.

Falola, Toyin. *Encyclopedia of the Yoruba*. Bloomington: Indiana University Press, 2016.

Finocchiaro, Maurice A. *The Galileo Affair*. Berkeley: University of California Press, 1989.

Flegr, J. "Effects of toxoplasma on human behavior." *PubMed*. National Library of Medicine, NIH.

_____. "Influence of latent *Toxoplasma* infection on human personality, physiology and morphology: pros and cons of the *Toxoplasma*—human model in studying the manipulation hypothesis." *The Journal of Experimental Biology*, January 1, 2013. 216: 127–133. http://jeb.biologists.org /content/216/1/127.full.

Flegr, J. and S. Ztkovai, P. Kodym, D. Frynta. "Induction of changes in human behavior by the parasitic protozoan *Toxoplasma gondii*." *Parasitology*, 1996 Jul., 113 (Pt 1): 49–54. http://www.ncbi.nlm.nih.gov /pubmed/8710414.

Folger, Tim. "Crossing the Quantum Divide." *Scientific American* (July 2018).

Forward. "In Spain, Inquisitors Tracked Conversos by their Foodways." *Forward* (Jan. 24, 2003). https://forward.com/articles/9216/in-spain -inquisitors-tracked-conversos-by-their-fo/.

Franklin, Benjamin. *Poor Richard's Almanac* (1750).

Fraser, Jennifer. "Dying Trees Can Send Food to Neighbors of Different Species." *Scientific American* (May 19, 2015). https://blogs.scientificamerican .com/artful-amoeba/dying-trees-can-send-food-to-neighbors-of -different-species/.

———. "Swapping Symbionts Enabled Mediterranean Lichen to Conquer the Arctic." *Scientific American* (June 3, 2015). https://blogs.scientific american.com/artful-amoeba/swapping-symbionts-enabled -mediterranean-lichen-to-conquer-the-arctic/.

Frede, Michael. "Monotheism and Pagan Philosophy in Later Antiquity." In *Pagan Monotheism in Late Antiquity*. Edited by Polymnia Athanassadi and Michael Frede. Oxford: Clarendon Press, 1999.

Friedrich, Carl, and Zbigniew Brzezinski. *Totalitarian Dictatorship and Autocracy*. Cambridge, MA: Harvard University Press, 1965.

Froese, Paul, and Christopher Bader. *America's Four Gods: What We Say About God & What That Says About Us (Updated Edition)*. Oxford: Oxford University Press, 2015.

Frumkin, Howard, and Richard Louv. "The Powerful Link Between Conserving Land and Preserving Health." *Land Trust Special Anniversary report* (2007). https://www.americantrails.org/files/pdf/FrumkinLouv. pdf.

Gaddis, Michael. *There Is No Crime for Those Who Have Christ: Religious Violence in the Christian Roman Empire*. Berkeley: University of California, 2005.

Gagliano, Monica. *Thus Spoke the Plant*. Berkeley: North Atlantic Books, 2018.

Gagliano, Monica, Michael Renton, Martial Depczynski, and Stefano Mancuso. "Experience teaches plants to learn faster and forget slower in environments where it matters." *Oecologia*, Vol. 175 (May 2014): 63–72. https://link.springer.com/article/10.1007%2Fs00442-013-2873-7.

Gallup, Jr., George H. "Religious Awakenings Bolster Americans' Faith." *Gallup* (Jan. 14, 2003). http://news.gallup.com/poll/7582/religious -awakenings-bolster-americans-faith.aspx.

Gander, Kashmira. "White House Bible Study Led By Pastor Who Is Anti-Gay, Anti-Women and Anti-Catholic." *Newsweek* (April 11, 2018). http:// www.newsweek.com/white-house-bible-group-led-pastor-anti-gay-anti -women-anti-catholic-881860.

Gasparro, Giulia Sfameni. "One God and Divine Unity. Late Antique Theologies Between Exclusivism and Inclusiveness." In *Monotheism Between Pagans and Christians in late Antiquity*. Edited by Stephen Mitchell and Peter van Nuffelen. Leuven, Netherlands: Peeters, 2010.

Gaukroger, Stephen. *The Emergence of a Scientific Culture: Science and the Shaping of Modernity 1210-1685*. Oxford: Oxford University Press, 2006.

Gay, Peter. *The Enlightenment, an interpretation: The Science of Freedom*. New York: W. W. Norton, 1969.

Genetics Society of America. "Viruses revealed to be a major driver of human evolution." *PhysOrg* (July 13, 2013). https://phys.org/news/2016 -07-viruses-revealed-major-driver-human.html.

Gibbons, Ann. "Human Evolution: Gain Came With Pain." *Science* (Feb. 16, 2013). https://www.sciencemag.org/news/2013/02/human-evolution -gain-came-pain.

Gleick, James. "What Defines a Meme?" *Smithsonian Magazine* (May, 2011). https://www.smithsonianmag.com/arts-culture/what-defines-a-meme -1904778/.

Gorzelak, Monika A., Amanda K. Asay, Brian J. Pickles, and Suzanne W. Simard. "Inter-plant communication through mycorrhizal networks mediates complex adaptive behavior in plant communities." *AOB Plants, NCBI Resources*, May 15, 2015. https://www.ncbi.nlm.nih.gov/pmc/articles /PMC4497361/.

Got Questions? "What is Arianism?" https://www.gotquestions.org/arianism
.html.

_____. "What is Monophysitism/Eutychianism?" https://www.gotquestions
.org/monophysitism.html.

Gottlieb, Anthony. "Think Again? What did Descartes really know?" *The New Yorker* (Nov. 20, 2006). https://www.newyorker.com/magazine
/2006/11/20/think-again-2.

Greer, John Michael. *Inside a Magical Lodge: Group Ritual in the Western Tradition*. St. Paul, MN: Llewellyn, 1998.

_____. *A World Full of Gods: An Inquiry into Polytheism*. Tucson, AZ: ADF Publishing, 2005.

Gushee, David. "5 Reasons Torture is Always Wrong." *Christianity Today* (Feb. 1, 2006). https://www.christianitytoday.com/ct/2006/february/23.

Hadot, Pierre. *The Veil of Isis: An Essay on the History of the Idea of Nature*. Cambridge, MA: Harvard University Press, 2006.

Haldane, J. B. S. *Possible Worlds*. London: Chatto & Windus; London: Routledge (reprint), 1927.

Halper, Evan, and Jordan Rau. "Pastor's Remarks Spark Furor." *The Los Angeles Times* (May 21, 2004). http://articles.latimes.com/2004/may/21/local/
me-pastor21

Hanson, J. W. *Universalism*. San Diego: St. Alban Press, 2002.

Hanson, Ronald, and Krister Shalm. "Spooky Action." *Scientific American* (December 2018): 59–65.

Harner, Michael. Author Quotes, http://www.greatthoughtstreasury.com/
author/michael-harner from *The Way of the Shaman* chapter 1.

Harrison, Peter. "The Bible and the Emergence of Modern Science." *Science & Christian Belief,* Vol. 18, No. 2 (2006).

_____. *The Bible: Protestantism and the Rise of Natural Science*. Cambridge: Cambridge University Press, 1998.

_____. "The Bible, Protestantism and the Rise of Natural Science: A Rejoinder." *Science and Christian Belief,* Vol. 21, No. 2 (2009).

Hartford Institute for Religion Research. "Fast Facts about American Religion." http://hirr.hartsem.edu/research/fastfacts/fast_facts.html#denom

Hartshorne, Charles. *Omnipotence and other Theological Mistakes.* Albany: State University of New York, 1984.

Henry, John. "Magic and the origins of modern science." *The Lancet,* 2000, 354 (Dec. 1999). https://www.thelancet.com/pdfs/journals/lancet/PIIS0140-6736(99)90366-5.pdf?code=lancet-site

Herbjørnsrud, Dag. "The African Enlightenment." *Aeon,* https://aeon.co/essays/yacob-and-amo-africas-precursors-to-locke-hume-and-kant

Hertz, Todd. "Benke Suspended for 'Syncretism' after 9/11 Event." *Christianity Today* (July 1, 2002). https://www.christianitytoday.com/ct/2002/julyweb-only/7-29-31.0.html.

Hesiod. *Works and Days.* Translated by Hugh G. Evelyn-Whyte (1918): II 248–64. http://www.sacred-texts.com/cla/hesiod/works.htm.

Hinn, Costi. "Benny Hinn is my Uncle, but Prosperity Preaching Isn't for Me." *Christianity Today* (Sept. 20, 2017). https://www.christianitytoday.com/ct/2017/october/benny-hinn-costi-uncle-prosperity-preaching-testimony.html.

Hobbes, Thomas. *Leviathan* (1668). (For image of the frontispiece: https://en.wikipedia.org/wiki/Leviathan_(Hobbes_book)#/media/File:Leviathan_by_Thomas_Hobbes.jpg).

Hölldobler, Bert., and E. O. Wilson. *The Ants.* Cambridge, MA: Harvard University Press, 1990.

Hooper, Rowan. "Magic and science fuel Middle England cult hero." *New Scientist* (Dec. 8, 2018).

Hormung, Erik. *Conceptions of God in Ancient Egypt: The One and the Many.* Translated by John Baines. Ithaca, NY: Cornell University Press, 1982.

Hughes, Virginia. "Epigenetics: The sins of the father." *Nature* (March, 2014). https://www.nature.com/news/epigenetics-the-sins-of-the-father-1.14816.

Hume, David. "An Inquiry Concerning the Principles of Morals" (appendix II). In *Moral and Political Philosophy.* Edited by Henry D. Aiken. New York: Hafner, 1948.

Islamweb. "Allah gets angry with those that do not supplicate him." (July 8, 2018) https://www.islamweb.net/emainpage/index.php?page=showfatwa&Option=FatwaId&Id=346606

Ivancevic, Atma M., and R. Daniel Kortschak, Terry Bertozzi, David L. Adelson. "Horizontal transfer of BovB and L1 retrotransposons in eukaryotes." *Genome Biology* (2018): 19 (1)

Jacob, J. R. "Boyle's Atomism and the Restoration Assault on Pagan Naturalism," *Social Studies of Science* 8, no. 2, May 1978.

Jacobsen, Annie. *Phenomena: The Secret History of the U. S. Governments Investigation Into Extrasensory Perception and Psychokenesis.* New York: Little, Brown, 2017.

James, William. *Principles of Psychology.* New York: Henry Holt and Company, 1890. ("Chapter 6: The Mind-Stuff Theory," accessed via The University of Adelaide on June 12, 2019, https://ebooks.adelaide.edu.au/j/james/william/principles/chapter6.html)

Jefferson, Thomas. "Chapter 17: Query XVII: The different religions received into that state?" In *Notes on the State of Virginia*, 1782.

_____. "Thomas Jefferson to Uriah Forrest, with Enclosure, 31 December, 1787." https://founders.archives.gov/documents/Jefferson/01-12-02-0490.

Jenkins, Jack. "Group of nearly 80 evangelical leaders publish letter condemning Trump." *Think Progress* (Oct. 6, 2016). https://thinkprogress.org/trump-evangelicals-letter-d86c70f05194/

Jenkins, Philip. *Jesus Wars: How Four Patriarchs, Three Queens, and Two Emperors Decided What Christians Would Believe for the Next 1,500 Years.* San Francisco: HarperOne, 2010.

Jewish Virtual Library. "Christian-Jewish relations: The Inquisition." *AICE*, https://www.jewishvirtuallibrary.org/the-inquisition

Johnston, Sarah Iles. *Hekate Soteira*, Atlanta: Scholars Press, 1990.

Johnson, Stefanie K. and Markus A. Fitza, Daniel A. Lerner, Dana M. Calhoun, Marissa A. Beldon, Elsa T. Chan, Pieter T. J. Johnson. "Risky business: linking *Toxoplasma gondii* infection and entrepreneurship behaviours across individuals and countries." *Proceedings of the Royal*

Society B: Biological Sciences, July 25, 2018. http://rspb.royalsocietypublishing.org/content/285/1883/20180822

Jonas, Hans. *The Phenomenon of Life: Toward a Philosophical Biology.* Chicago: University of Chicago Press, 1966.

Jones, Levi. "Pentecostals: Demon Possessed gibberish speakers for Satan." Landover Baptist Church. http://www.landoverbaptist.net/showthread.php?t=79413

Jordan, Mark A. "What's in a meme?" *The Richard Dawkins Foundation* (Feb. 4, 2014). https://www.richarddawkins.net/2014/02/whats-in-a-meme/.

Josephson-Storm, Jason A. *The Myth of Disenchantment: Magic, Modernity and the Birth of the Human Sciences.* Chicago: University of Chicago Press, 2017.

Kahlos, Maijastina. "Refuting and Reclaiming Monotheism: Monotheism and the Debate Between 'Pagans' and Christians in 380–430." In *Monotheism Between Pagans and Christians in Late Antiquity.* Edited by Stephen Mitchell and Peter Van Nuffelen. Leuven, Netherlands: Peeters, 2010.

Kaiser, David. *How the Hippies Saved Physics: Science, Counterculture, and the Quantum Revival.* New York: W. W. Norton, 2012.

Kastrup, Bernardo, Henry Stapp, and Menas Kafatos. "Coming to Grips with the Implications of Quantum Mechanics." *Scientific American* (May 29, 2018). https://blogs.scientificamerican.com/observations/coming-to-grips-with-the-implications-of-quantum-mechanics/

Keller, Bill. "Liveprayer's Bill Keller calls Out Beck." *Christian News Wire*, July 7, 2019. http://www.christiannewswire.com/news/8322914324.html

Keller, Evelyn Fox. *A Feeling for the Organism: The Life and Work of Barbara McClintock.* New York: Henry Holt and Company, 1983.

Kelly, David. "DNA Clears the Fog Over Latino Links to Judaism." *L.A. Times*, December 5, 2004. http://articles.latimes.com/2004/dec/05/nation/na-heritage5; http://www.cryptojews.com/

Koestler, Arthur. *The Sleepwalkers: A History of Man's Changing Vision of the Universe.* London: Arkana Books, 1989.

Kolata, Gina. "In Good Health? Thank Your 100 Trillion Bacteria." *New York Times* (June 13, 2012). http://www.nytimes.com/2012/06/14/health/

human-microbiome-project-decodes-our-100-trillion-good-bacteria. html?pagewanted=all&_r=2&

Ku, John Baptist. "Interpreting Genesis 1 with the Fathers of the Church." *Thomistic Evolution*. http://www.thomisticevolution.org/disputed-questions/interpreting-genesis-1-with-the-fathers-of-the-church/

Kugel, James L. *The Great Shift: Encountering God in Biblical Times*. Boston: Houghton Mifflin, 2017.

Kurland, Philip B. and Ralph Lerner, eds. *The Founders' Constitution, Vol. I: Major Themes*. Chicago: University of Chicago Press, 1987.

Latourette, Kenneth Scott. *A History of Christianity, Vol. I: Beginnings to 1500*. San Francisco: Harper, 1975.

Lent, Jeremy. *The Patterning Instinct: A Cultural History of Humanity's Search for Meaning*. Amherst, NY: Prometheus Books, 2017.

Leveillee, Nicholas P. "Copernicus, Galileo and the Church: Science in a Religious World." *Inquiries*, Vol. 3 No. 05 (2011). http://www.inquiriesjournal.com/articles/1675/copernicus-galileo-and-the-church-science-in-a-religious-world

Lewis, Paul. "Peter Berger and His Critics: The Significance of Emergence." *Society* (2010) 47:207–13.

Lipka, Michael. "10 facts about atheists." *Facttank*, Pew Research Center, June 1, 2016. http://www.pewresearch.org/fact-tank/2016/06/01/10-facts-about-atheists/

———. "A closer look at America's rapidly growing religious 'nones.'" *Pew Research* Center, May 13, 2015. https://www.pewresearch.org/fact-tank/2015/05/13/a-closer-look-at-americas-rapidly-growing-religious-nones/

Liphshiz, Cnaan. "What made Muslim Albanians risk their lives to save Jews from the Holocaust?" *Jewish Yelegrahic Agency* (Jan. 16, 2018). https://www.jta.org/2018/01/16/news-opinion/world/what-made-muslim-albanians-risk-their-lives-to-save-jews-from-the-holocaust

Locke, John. *A Letter Concerning Toleration*. Edited by Kerry Waters. Peterborough, Ontario: Broadview Editions, 2013.

Bibliography

Luther, Martin. *Table Talk, Vol. 54 of Luther's Works.* Edited by J. J. Pelikan, H. C. Oswald and H. T. Lehmann. Philadelphia: Fortress Press, 1999. https://www.quotescosmos.com/people/Martin-Luther.html

Maas, Peter. *Serpico: The Cop Who Defied the System.* New York: Viking, 1973.

MacAllister, D. C. "Yes, Christians Can Support Torture." *The Federalist* (Dec. 17, 2014). http://thefederalist.com/2014/12/17/yes-christians-can-support-torture/

Machiavelli, Niccolo. *The Prince*, Chapter 18 (1532).

MacIntosh, J. J. and Anstey, Peter. "Robert Boyle." In *The Stanford Encyclopedia of Philosophy* (Fall 2014 Edition). Edited by Edward N. Zalta. https://plato.stanford.edu/archives/fall2014/entries/boyle/

Maddison, Angus. *Growth and Interaction in the World Economy: The Roots of Modernity.* Washington: AEI Press, 2005.

Madhani, Aamer. "Poll: Approval of same sex marriage in U.S. reaches new high." *USA Today* (May 23, 2018). https://www.usatoday.com/story/news/nation/2018/05/23/same-sex-marriage-poll-americans/638587002/

Madison, James. *The Writings of James Madison, comprising his Public Papers and his Private Correspondence, including his numerous letters and documents now for the first time printed.* (Volume 9, to W. T. Barry, Aug. 4, 1822). Edited by Gaillard Hunt. New York: G.P. Putnam's Sons, 1900. Vol. 9. 8/31/2018. http://oll.libertyfund.org/titles/1940

Mai, Tram. "Pastor calls for killing gays to end AIDS." *USA Today* (Dec. 6, 2014). https://www.usatoday.com/story/news/nation/2014/12/04/pastor-calls-for-killing-gays-to-end-aids/19929973/

Main, Douglas. "Saharan Dust Helped Build the Bahamas." *Smithsonian.com.* July 28, 2014. http://www.smithsonianmag.com/smart-news/saharan-dust-helped-build-bahama-islands-180952173/

Marcus, Philip S. and Suyang Pei, Chung-Hsiang Jiang, and Pedram Hassanzadeh. "First Support for a Physics Theory of Life." *Quanta Magazine* (July 26, 2017). https://www.quantamagazine.org/first-support-for-a-physics-theory-of-life-20170726/

_____. "Three-Dimensional Vortices Generated by Self-Replication in Stably Stratified Rotating Shear Flows." *Physical Review Letters* 111, no. 8: 084501. Published 20 August 2013.

Margulis, Lynn. *Origin of Eukaryotic Cells*. New Haven: Yale University Press, 1970.

_____. *Symbiotic Planet: A New Look at Evolution*. New York: Basic Books, 1998.

Margulis, Lynn and René Fester. *Symbiosis as a Source of Evolutionary Innovation: Speciation and Morphogenesis*. Cambridge, MA: MIT Press, 1991.

Markham, Dereck. "Trees talk to each other and recognize their offspring." *treehugger* (July 29, 2016). https://www.treehugger.com/natural-sciences/ trees-talk-each-other-and-recognize-their-offspring.html

Mayer, Elizabeth. *Extraordinary Knowing: Science, Skepticism and the Inexplicable Powers of the Human Mind*. New York: Random House, 2008.

_____. YouTube talk https://www.youtube.com/watch?v=AClVSWvNsW w&list=PL34B98DEB7C27301F.

Mayhew, Peter. *Discovering Evolutionary Biology: Bringing Together Ecology and Evolution*. Oxford: Oxford University Press, 2006.

Mcauliffe, Kathleen. "How Your Cat Is Making You Crazy." *The Atlantic* (March 2012). http://www.theatlantic.com/magazine/archive/2012/03/ how-your-cat-is-making-you-crazy/308873/

McCloskey, Pat. "The Rift Between Jews and Samaritans." *Franciscan media.* https://www.franciscanmedia.org/the-rift-between-jews-and-samaritans/

McEvilley, Thomas. *The Shape of Ancient Thought*. New York: Allworth Press, 2002.

McLennan, Scotty. *Jesus Was a Liberal: Reclaiming Christianity for All*. New York: Pallgrave Macmillan, 2009.

Medical News. "Toxoplasma may be affecting human behavior on a mass scale." *Medical News*, August 3, 2006. http://www.news-medical.net /news/2006/08/03/19237.aspx.

Mehta, Hemant. "Kevin Swanson: We Can Stop Hurricane Irma by Banning Abortion and Gay Marriage." *Friendly Atheist* (September 7, 2017).

https://friendlyatheist.patheos.com/2017/09/07/kevin-swanson-we-can-stop-hurricane-irma-by-banning-abortion-and-gay-marriage/

Merchant, Carolyn. *The Death of Nature.* San Francisco: Harper and Row, 1980.

Metzger, Paul Louis. *Connecting Christ.* Nashville: Thomas Nelson, 2012.

Meyer, Holly. "Congregation, Tennessee Baptist Convention split over church's first female pastor." *Tennessean*, Nov. 14, 2017. https://www.tennessean.com/story/news/religion/2017/11/14/tennessee-baptist-convention-church-woman-pastor-cannot-vote-annual-meeting/861855001/

Miskvitch, Katia. "Slime Molds Remember—But do they Learn" *Quanta Magazine* (July 9, 2018). https://www.quantamagazine.org/slime-molds-remember-but-do-they-learn-20180709/

Mollenkott, Virginia Ramey. *The Divine Feminine: The Biblical Imagery of God as Female.* New York: Crossroad, 1987.

Montesquieu, Charles-Louis de Secondat. "Letter LV, Rica to Ibben at Smyrna." *Persian Letters.* http://www.bartleby.com/167/55.html

Moore, Alan. Interviewed by Rowan Hooper in "Magic and science fuel Middle England cult hero." *New Scientist* (Dec. 8, 2018): 44.

Morrison, Larry R. "The Religious Defense of American Slavery Before 1830." *Journal of Religious Thought* (Fall 1980/Winter 1981): 37.

Moss, Candida. "Interpreting the Bible Just Got More Complicated." *Daily Beast.* (September 3, 2017). http://www.thedailybeast.com/interpreting-the-bible-just-got-more-complicated

_____. *The Myth of Persecution: How Early Christian Invented the Story of Martyrdom.* New York: Harper, 2014.

Myers, Brendan. *The Earth, the Gods, and the Soul.* Alresford, Hants, UK; Moon Books, 2013.

Nagel, Thomas. *Mind and Cosmos.* Oxford: Oxford University Press, 2012.

NASA. "NASA Satellite Reveals How Much Saharan Dust Feeds Amazon's Plants." *NASA* (Feb. 22, 2015). https://www.nasa.gov/content/goddard/nasa-satellite-reveals-how-much-saharan-dust-feeds-amazon-s-plants

Nietzsche, Friedrich. *The AntiChrist*. Lexido: The Full and Free Nietzsche Portal. http://www.lexido.com/EBOOK_TEXTS/THE_ANTICHRIST_.aspx?S=45&WSD_HL=319#WSD_HL

Nixey, Catherine. *The Darkening Age: The Christian Destruction of the Classical World*. London: Macmillan, 2017.

Nyman, Monte. "The Most Correct Book." *The Church of Jesus Christ of Latter-Day Saints* (June 1984). https://www.lds.org/study/ensign/1984/06/the-most-correct-book?lang=eng

O'Callaghan, Jonathan. "'Schroedinger's Bacterium'" Could Be a Quantum Biology Milestone." *Scientific American* (Oct. 29, 2018).

Ockeloen-Korppi, C. F. and E. Damskägg, J.-M. Pirkkalainen, M. Asjad, A. A. Clerk, F. Massel, M. J. Woolley, M. A. Sillanpää. "Stabilized entanglement of massive mechanical oscillators." *Nature* (2018): 556 (7702).

O'Donnell, Ellen. "Cryan Explains Gut Feelings, Thoughts and Behaviors." *NIH Record*, Vol. LXVII, No. 5 (Dec. 4, 2015).

Ofek. Hillel. "Why the Arabic World turned away from Science." *The New Atlantis*. Winter, 2011.

Origen. De Prinicipiis, 3.6.3. *New Advent*. http://www.newadvent.org/fathers/04123.htm

_____. *On the First Principles*. In *Readings in the History of Christian Theology, Vol. I*. William C. Placher, author. Louisville, KY: Westminister John Knox Press, 1988.

Orr, Emma Restall. *The Wakeful World*. Winchester, UK: Moon Books, 2012.

Orthodox Church in America. "Original Sin." http://www.oca.org/QA.asp?ID=3&SID=3

Otterman, Sharon. "Pastor Apologizes to his Denomination for Role in Sandy Hook Interfaith Service." *The New York Times* (Feb. 7, 2013).

Overby, Dennis. "How Islam Won, and Lost, the Lead in Science." *The New York Times* (Oct. 30, 2001).

Owen, Iris M. *Conjuring Up Philip: An Adventure in Psychokinesis*. New York: Harper and Row, 1976.

Pagel, Mark. *Wired for Culture: Origins of the Human Social* Mind. New York: Norton, 2012.

Palast, Gregory. "I don't have to be nice to the spirit of the Antichrist." *The Guardian*, May 23, 1999.

Paper, Jordan. *The Deities Are Many: A Polytheistic Theology.* Albany: State University of New York Press, 2005.

_____. *The Mystic Experience: A Descriptive and Comparative Analysis.* Albany: State University of New York Press, 2004.

_____. *The Spirits are Drunk: Comparative Approaches to Chinese Religion.* Albany: State University of New York Press, 1995.

Patai, Raphael. *The Hebrew Goddess, 3rd enlarged edition.* Detroit: Wayne State University Press, 1990.

Paul, as quoted in "Why do Franciscans Take a Vow of Poverty?" *Franciscan Discernment* (Dec.1, 2015). http://franciscandiscernment.org/index. php/2015/12/01/why-do-franciscans-take-a-vow-of-poverty/

Perry, Barbara and Debbie Nathan. "Mistaken Identity? The Case of New Mexico's 'Hidden Jews.'" *The Atlantic* (December 2000).

Perry, Phillip. "3 of Nature's Greatest Mysteries May Be Solved Thanks to Quantum Biology." *Big Think* (Sept. 3, 2017). https://bigthink.com/ philip-perry/3-of-natures-greatest-mysteries-may-be-solved-thanks-to-quantum-biology

Petersen, Allura. "Web of the Woods." *The Planet Magazine* (March 16, 2016). https://theplanetmagazine.net/web-of-the-woods-350f64b7f637

Pew Research Center. "10 facts about atheists" (June 1, 2016). https://www. pewresearch.org/fact-tank/2016/06/01/10-facts-about-atheists/

_____. "America's Changing Religious Landscape." *Religion and Public Life* (May 12, 2015). http://www.pewforum.org/2015/05/12/americas-chang-ing-religious-landscape/

_____. "Many Americans Mix Multiple Faiths." *Religion and Public Life* (Dec. 9, 2009). http://www.pewforum.org/2009/12/09/many-ameri-cans-mix-multiple-faiths/#6

_____. "Most agnostics, those whose religion is 'nothing in partic-
ular' believe in a higher power or spiritual force." (April 23, 2018)
Pew Research Center: Religion and Public Life. http://www.pewforum.
org/2018/04/25/when-americans-say-they-believe-in-god-what-do-they-
mean/04-25-18_beliefingod-00-06/

_____. "Sharp Partisan Divisions in Views of National Institutions." July
10, 2017. http://www.people-press.org/2017/07/10/sharp-partisan-divi-
sions-in-views-of-national-institutions/

Philips, Kevin. *American Theocracy.* New York: Viking, 2007.

Planck, Max. "Interviews With Great Scientists VI.—Max Planck." *The
Observer* (25 January 1931).

Plato. "Phaedrus." http://classics.mit.edu/Plato/phaedrus.html

PLOS Biology. "Jumping Genes Cross Plant Species Boundaries." *PLOS Biology* (January 2006): 4 (1). https://www.ncbi.nlm.nih.gov/pmc/articles/
PMC1310658/

Polanyi, Michael. *The Logic of Liberty.* Chicago: University of Chicago Press,
1951.

_____. *Personal Knowledge.* Chicago: University of Chicago Press, 1975.

Poole, David C., Michael J. White and Brian J. Whipp. 2017. "The Discovery of
Oxygen." *Hektoen International: A Journal of Medical Humanities* (2017).
https://hekint.org/2017/01/22/the-discovery-of-oxygen/

Prigogine, Ilya and Isabel Stengers. *Order out of Chaos: The Evolutionary
Paradigm and the Physical Sciences.* New York: Bantam, 1984.

Prum, Richard. *The Evolution of Beauty: How Darwin's Forgotten Theory of
Mate Choice Shapes the Animal World—and Us.* New York: Doubleday,
2017.

Quakers (Society of Friends). "The Abolition project." http://abolition.e2bn.
org/people_21.html

Radin, Dean. *Supernormal: Science, Yoga and the Evidence for Extraordinary
Psychic Abilities.* New York: Random House, 2013.

Reeves, Nicholas. *Akhenaten: Egypt's False Prophet.* London: Thames and
Hudson, 2001.

Religious Tolerance. "Liberal-Conservative Conflict Within the Lutheran Church-Missouri Synod." http://www.religioustolerance.org/div_lcms .htm.

_____. "Religious Society of Friends, Quaker Beliefs and Practices." http://www.religioustolerance.org/quaker2.htm

Rendu, William, Cédric Beauval, Isabelle Crevecoeur, Priscilla Bayle, Antoine Balzeau, Thierry Bismuth, Laurence Bourguignon, Géraldine Delfour, Jean-Philippe Faivre, François Lacrampe-Cuyaubère, Carlotta Tavormina, Dominique Todisco, Alain Turq, and Bruno Maureille. "Evidence supporting an intentional Neanderthal burial at La Chapelle-aux-Saints." *Proceedings of the National Academy of Sciences of the United States of America* (Dec. 16, 2013). https://doi.org/10.1073/ pnas.1316780110

Reyes, E. Christopher. *In His Name, v. III.* Bloomington, IN: Trafford, 2014.

Richmond, Todd. "12-year old Wisconsin girls charged in stabbing." *AP News* (June 3, 2014). https://www.apnews.com/ed892d67a63347718b535 3aba8b689a3

Robertson, Pat. *The 700 Club* (January 14, 1991). http://en.wikiquote.org/ wiki/Pat_Robertson

Rosenberg, Eugene and Ilana Zilber-Rosenberg. "The hologenome concept of evolution after 10 years." *Microbiome* (2018): 6:78. https://micro-biomejournal.biomedcentral.com/articles/10.1186/s40168-018-0457-9.

Rovelli, Carlo. *The Order of Time.* New York: Penguin Random House, 2018.

Rudloff, Robert von. *Hekate in Ancient Greek Religion.* Victoria, BC: Horned Owl, 1999.

Rumi, Jalal-al-Din. *A Garden Beyond Paradise, The Mystical Poetry of Rumi.* Translated by Jonathan Star. Edited by Jonathan Star and Shahram Shiva. New York: Bantam Books, 1992.

Rupar, Aron. "Trump religious adviser: Hush money to adult film star 'doesn't matter' because god forgives all." *Think Progress* (March 9, 2018). https://thinkprogress.org/robert-jeffress-trump-stormy-daniels-evangeli-cals-176d228a1c55/

Rwakakamba, Morrison. "Uganda's 'Kill the Gays' bill: Pastor Martin Ssempa and the anti-gay lobby." *Transformation: Where love meets social justice* (March 25, 2014). https://www.opendemocracy.net/transformation/morrison-rwakakamba/ugandas-kill-gays-bill-pastor-martin-ssempa-and-antigay-lobby

Sales, Ben. "Israel's Conversion laws Are About To Get Stricter." *The New York Jewish Week* (June 1, 2018). https://jewishweek.timesofisrael.com/israels-conversion-laws-are-about-to-get-stricter/

Sanders, Laura. "Microbes can play games with the mind." *Science News*, Vol. 189, No. 7 (April 2, 2016): 23. https://www.sciencenews.org/article/microbes-can-play-games-mind

Schmidt, Charles. "Mental Health May Depend on Creatures in the Gut." *Scientific American* (March 1, 2015). https://www.scientificamerican.com/article/mental-health-may-depend-on-creatures-in-the-gut/

Schorn R., G. Tappenier, J. Walde. "Analyzing 'spooky action at a distance' concerning brand logos." *Innovative Marketing*, Vol. 2, Issue 1 (2006): 45–60.

Schrödinger, Erwin. *Mind and Matter*. Cambridge: Cambridge University Press, 1959.

Schwartz, Penny. "Lost diary of tortured Mexican 'converso' features in early American-Jewish exhibit." *The Times of Israel* (December 18, 2016). https://www.timesofisrael.com/lost-diary-of-tortured-mexican-converso-features-in-early-american-jewish-exhibit/

Schwarz, Stephan. "Nonlocal Consciousness and the Anthropology of Religions and Spiritual Practices." In *The Oxford Handbook of Psychology and Spirituality*. Edited by Lisa Miller. Oxford: Oxford University Press, 2019.

Science Daily. "Can bacteria make you smarter?" (May 25, 2010). http://www.sciencedaily.com/releases/2010/05/100524143416.htm

_____. "Einstein's 'spooky action' goes massive: The elusive quantum mechanical phenomenon of entanglement has now been made a reality in objects almost macroscopic in size." (April 25, 2018). https://www.sciencedaily.com/releases/2018/04/180425131858.htm

_____. "How common cat parasite gets into human brain and influences human behavior." (Dec. 6, 2012). http://www.sciencedaily.com/releases/2012/12/121206203240.htm

_____. "Jumping genes: Cross species transfer of genes has driven evolution." (July 9, 2018). https://www.sciencedaily.com/releases/2018/07/180709101216.htm

_____. "Species are to ecosystems as cells are to the human body, according to a mathematical model." (May 16, 2011). https://www.sciencedaily.com/releases/2011/05/110516080132.htm.

Science News. "Einstein's 'spooky action' goes massive: The elusive quantum mechanical phenomenon of entanglement has now been made a reality in objects almost macroscopic in size." (April 25, 2018). https://www.sciencedaily.com/releases/2018/04/180425131858.htm.

Science News. "Mimosa Plants Have Long Term memory, Can Learn, Biologists Say." (Jan. 16, 2014). http://www.sci-news.com/biology/science-mimosa-plants-memory-01695.html

Serpico, Frank. "The Police Are Still Out of Control." *Politico* (Oct. 23, 2014). https://www.politico.com/magazine/story/2014/10/the-police-are-still-out-of-control-112160_full.html

Sharlet, Jeff. "Sex and Power inside the C Street House." *Salon* (July 21, 2009). https://www.salon.com/2009/07/21/c_street/

Shasha, David. "Killing Off Rational Judaism: The Maimonidan Controversy." *Huffington Post* (May 25, 2011). http://www.huffingtonpost.com/david-shasha/killing-off-rational-juda_b_498846.html

Shaw, B. D. *Sacred Violence. African Christians and Sectarian Hatred in the Age of Augustine.* Cambridge: Cambridge University Press, 2011.

Shaw, Gregory. *Theurgy and the Soul, The Neoplatonism of Iamblichus.* University Park, PA: Pennsylvania State University Press, 1995.

Shermer, Michael. "Silent No More." *Scientific American* (April, 2018): 77.

Simard, Suzanne. TED talk; see https://www.ted.com/talks/suzanne_simard_how_trees_talk_to_each_other?language=en

Sleator, R. D. "The human superorganism—of microbes and men." *Med Hypotheses* (Feb. 2010): 74(2): 214–5. DOI: 10.1016/j.mehy.2009.08.047. http://www.ncbi.nlm.nih.gov/pubmed/19836146

Slezak. Mark. "Origins of organs: Thank viruses for your skin and bone." *New Scientist* (Feb.26, 2014). http://www.newscientist.com/article/mg22129583.300-origin-of-organs-thank-viruses-for-your-skin-and-bone.html#.U5fWOC_1_x8

Smith, Paul. *Reading the Enemy's Mind.* New York: Forge, 2005.

Song, Y. Y., Suzanne W. Simard, Allan Carroll, William W. Mohn & Ren Sen Zeng. "Defoliation of interior Douglas-fir elicits carbon transfer and stress signaling to ponderosa pine neighbors through ectomycorrhizal networks." *Scientific Reports, 5* 8495 (2015). DOI: http://dx.doi.org/10.1038/srep08495

Sonneborn, T. M. "Paramecium in Modern Biology." *Bios*, Vol. 21, No. 1 (Mar., 1950): 31–43.

Spanu, Nicola. "The Magic of Plotinus' Gnostic Disciples in the Context of Plotinus' School of Philosophy." *Journal for Late Antique Religion and Culture* 7 (2013): 1–14. https://www.academia.edu/9189369/Plotinus_and_Iamblichus_on_Magic_and_Theurgy

Stanford Encyclopedia of Philosophy. "Natural Philosophy in the Renaissance." (August 30, 2016). https://plato.stanford.edu/entries/natphil-ren/

_____. "Newton's philosophy." (May 6, 2014). https://plato.stanford.edu/entries/newton-philosophy/#AftPriIIDebLei

_____. "Perfect Goodness." (Oct. 1, 2013). https://plato.stanford.edu/entries/perfect-goodness/#DivFre

Starr, Michael. "Quantum Coherence Underlying Magnetoreception in Avian Species Confirmed." *Science News*, Resonance Science Foundation, https://resonance.is/quantum-coherence-underlying-magnetoreception-avian-species-confirmed/

Stewart, Matthew. *Nature's God: The Heretical Origins of the American Republic.* New York: W. W. Norton, 2014.

Stice, Elizabeth. "What Ruined Frederick Douglass as a Slave?" *History News Network* (July 1, 2018). https://historynewsnetwork.org/article/169230

Sullivan, Laura and Justin Elliott. "Report: Red Cross Spent 25 Percent Of Haiti Donations On Internal Expenses." *NPR* (June 16, 2016). https://www.npr.org/2016/06/16/482020436/senators-report-finds-fundamental-concerns-about-red-cross-finances

Swanson, Kevin. "Kevin Swanson: Death to Gays." https://www.youtube.com/watch?v=qTNymA9mRq4

Targ, Russell. *The Reality of ESP, A Physicist's Proof of Psychic Abilities.* Wheaton, IL: Quest, 2012.

Tertullian. *De Spectaculis*, as quoted on *Tentmaker* "Quotes from Christian Perpetuators of the Mythology of Hell." http://www.tentmaker.org/Quotes/hell-fire.htm

Thompson, Christopher Scott. "Polytheistic Monism: A Guest Post by Christopher Scott Thompson (Part Four)." *Dowsing for Divinity* (May 19, 2014). https://www.patheos.com/blogs/sermonsfromthemound/2014/05/polytheistic-monism-christopher-scott-thompson-part-4/

_____. "Polytheistic Monism: A Guest Post by Christopher Scott Thompson (Part One)." *Dowsing for Divinity* (May 19, 2014). http://www.patheos.com/blogs/sermonsfromthemound/2014/05/polytheistic-monism-christopher-scott-thompson-part-1/

_____. "Polytheistic Monism: A Guest Post by Christopher Scott Thompson (Part Two)." *Dowsing for Divinity* (May 19, 2014). https://www.patheos.com/blogs/sermonsfromthemound/2014/05/polytheistic-monism-christopher-scott-thompson-part-2/

Thornton, Paul. "Some lady to some reporter: The Bible hates gays." *The Los Angeles Times* (Feb. 24, 2010). http://opinion.latimes.com/opinionla/2010/02/some-lady-to-some-reporter-the-bible-hates-gays.html

Toomey, Diane. "Exploring How and Why Trees 'Talk' to Each Other." *Yale Environment 360* (Sept. 1, 2016). https://e360.yale.edu/features/exploring_how_and_why_trees_talk_to_each_other

Toulmin, Stephen. *Cosmopolis: The Hidden Agenda of Modernity.* Chicago: University of Chicago Press, 1990.

ushistory.org. "The Southern Argument for Slavery." *U. S. History Online Textbook* (Dec. 17, 2018). http://www.ushistory.org/us/27f.asp

Van Biema, David and Jeff Chu. "Does God Want You To Be Rich? A growing number of Protestant evangelists raise a joyful Yes! But the idea is poison to other, more mainstream pastors." *Time* (Sept. 10, 2006).

van der Wal, Arianne J. and Hannah M. Schade, Lydia Krabbendam, and Mark van Vugt. "Do natural landscapes reduce future discounting in humans?" *Proceedings of the Royal Society B* (Oct. 2013). https://royalsocietypublishing.org/doi/pdf/10.1098/rspb.2013.2295

Wade, Nicholas. "The Woolly Mammoth's Last Stand." *New York Times* (March 2, 2017). https://www.nytimes.com/2017/03/02/science/woolly-mammoth-extinct-genetics.html

Wallace, Anthony F. C. *Religion: An Anthropological View*. New York: Random House, 1966.

Ware, Bishop Kallistos. *The Orthodox Way*. Crestwood, NY: St. Vladimir's Seminary Press, 1979.

Webster, Sam. *The History of Theurgy From Iamblichus to the Golden Dawn*. Bristol, UK: PhD Dissertation, Department of History, University of Bristol, 2014.

Wendt, Alexander. *Quantum Mind and Social Science: Unifying Physical and Social Ontology*. Cambridge: Cambridge University Press, 2015.

West, M. L. "Towards Monotheism." *Pagan Monotheism in Late Antiquity*. Oxford: Oxford University Press, 1999.

West, Thomas G. *Vindicating the Founders*. Lanham: Rowman and Littlefield, 1997.

Williams, Florence. *The Nature Fix: Why Nature Makes Us Happier, Healthier, and More Creative*. New York: W. W. Norton, 2017.

Wilson, E. O. *The Social Conquest of the Earth*. New York: W. W. Norton, 2012.

Wilson, E. O. and B. Hölldobler. "Eusociality: Origin and Consequences." Proceedings of the National Academy of Sciences of the United States of America (Sept. 20, 2005). http://www.pnas.org/content/102/38/13367

Wolchover, Natalie. "First Support for a Physics Theory of Life." *Quanta Magazine* (July 26, 2017). https://www.quantamagazine.org/first-support-for-a-physics-theory-of-life-20170726/

_____. "A New Physics Theory of Life." *Quanta Magazine* (Jan. 22, 2014). https://www.quantamagazine.org/a-new-thermodynamics-theory-of -the-origin-of-life-20140122/

Yale Law School, Article 11. "Treaty of Peace and Friendship, 1796." *The Barbary Treaties 1786–1816.* http://avalon.law.yale.edu/18th_century /bar1796t.asp

Yates, Frances. *Giordano Bruno and the Hermetic Tradition.* New York: Vintage Books, 1969.

_____. *The Rosicrucian Enlightenment*, London: Routledge & Kegan Paul, 1972.

Yellis, Ken. "Jews Mostly Supported Slavery—Or Kept Silent—During Civil War." *Forward: Jewish, Fearless Since 1897* (July 1, 2013). https:// forward.com/opinion/179441/jews-mostly-supported-slavery-or-kept -silent-d/?p=all&p=all#ixzz326OPEy5Q

Yevtushenko, Yevgeny. *People, Selected Poems.* Baltimore: Penguin, 1966.

Yong, D. "A Brainless Slime That Shares Memories by Fusing." *The Atlantic* (Dec. 21, 2016). https://www.theatlantic.com/science/archive/2016/12 /the-brainless-slime-that-can-learn-by-fusing/511295/M

YouTube. "The Philip Experiment." https://www.youtube.com/watch?v =TP9lmP1hxNk.

Zachos, Frank. *Species Concept in Biology.* Switzerland: Springer International Publishing, 2016.

Ziman, John. *Public Knowledge: The Social Dimension of Science.* Cambridge: Cambridge University Press, 1968.

_____. *Reliable Knowledge: An Exploration of the grounds for Belief in Science.* Cambridge: Cambridge University Press, 1978.

Zimmer, Carl. "DNA Doubletake." *New York Times* (Sept 16, 2013). http:// www.nytimes.com/2013/09/17/science/dna-double-take.html?page wanted=all&_r=0.

INDEX

To Write to the Author

If you wish to contact the author or would like more information about this book, please write to the author in care of Llewellyn Worldwide Ltd. and we will forward your request. Both the author and publisher appreciate hearing from you and learning of your enjoyment of this book and how it has helped you. Llewellyn Worldwide Ltd. cannot guarantee that every letter written to the author can be answered, but all will be forwarded. Please write to:

Gus diZerega
℅ Llewellyn Worldwide
2143 Wooddale Drive
Woodbury, MN 55125-2989
Please enclose a self-addressed stamped envelope for reply,
or $1.00 to cover costs. If outside the U.S.A., enclose
an international postal reply coupon.

Many of Llewellyn's authors have websites with additional
information and resources. For more information,
please visit our website at http://www.llewellyn.com.